MW00580626

SALES AUTOMATION

SALES AUTOMATION

Concepts, Justification, Planning, and Implementation

Todd C. Scofield and Donald R. Shaw

amacom
American Management Association
New York • Atlanta • Boston • Chicago • Kansas City • San Francisco • Washington, D.C.
Brussels • Toronto • Mexico City

This book is available at a special discount when ordered in bulk quantities. For information, contact Special Sales Department, AMACOM, a division of American Management Association, 135 West 50th Street, New York, NY 10020.

Library of Congress Cataloging-in-Publication Data

Scofield, Todd C.
Sales automation : concepts, justification, planning, and implementation / Todd C. Scofield and Donald R. Shaw.
p. cm.
Includes index.
ISBN 0-8144-5000-8
1. Selling—Data processing. 2. Marketing—Data processing. I. Shaw, Donald R. II. Title.
HF5438.25.S344 1992
658.8'1'00285—dc20 *92-14664*
CIP

Printing number

10 9 8 7 6 5 4 3 2 1

Contents

Introduction

In the 1990s it's unusual to find a vast area of corporate business that has not yet been penetrated by computerization; yet this is the case in the realm of sales. Why is this so? What are the potential benefits of automating sales, and how does a business go about gaining them while minimizing costs and risks? How can the natural resistance of the salespeople to computers be overcome and their willing cooperation enlisted?

This book, based on direct, hands-on experience with sales automation, endeavors to answer those questions and many others concerning the justification, planning, and implementation of such systems.

Sales automation is the use of computing to support the selling and marketing process, more or less *while it's happening*. This does not mean computers are used merely for gathering statistics and intelligence, although such information may be a useful by-product, nor does it mean using computers only for planning the process, although, again, planning may be an integral part of the application. Rather, sales automation is the tactical use of computers, databases, and data communications to enhance the business of identifying prospective customers; making them customers; serving them; keeping them as customers; and all the attendant and related planning, analytical, and administrative uses of information thrown off as a by-product of that tactical utilization.

Our concern in this book is enhancing sales performance in the field, however this is defined in your company. The term *field* might mean a field sales organization consisting of branch offices, each with local sales and customer support people. On the other hand, it might refer to a network of retailers, dealers, or distributors. *Field* might refer to a room full of telephone sales reps, or, as is often the case in aggressive and diversified businesses, it might mean all of the foregoing, plus, perhaps, the use of direct mail, electronic catalogs, and other as yet undreamed-of ways of contacting, motivating, and serving buyers of whatever your company has to sell.

The second concept essential to sales force automation is tying in field sales automation to other related functions that either direct it, support it, or benefit from it. For example, consider something as simple as lead generation, distribution, and tracking in a typical business-to-business industrial sales situation. In pre–sales automation days, a company's advertising department captured leads from ads, mailers, and trade shows, sorted them by location, and mailed them to the field. That was the last that home office advertising or marketing knew about the disposition of the leads except for occasional complaints from sales that not enough leads were being generated. Marketing sometimes retaliated for this criticism by conducting follow-up audits to show that sales was not responding properly or at all to the leads already in-house.

Today, at the forefront of sales automation, leads are entered into a computer system as they are received, prequalified by specialized contact, by mail or phone or both, and forwarded to the field electronically. The field then phones or calls on these semiqualified prospects, performs further qualifying and selling functions, turns some (a majority, it hopes) into customers, and feeds the results of each and every case back to marketing electronically. The base of knowledge gained becomes increasingly valuable for directing and targeting further advertising, promotion, and product management efforts. There is simply no substitute for knowing what works, what doesn't, and why. Tied-in (or closed loop) sales automation systems help the field improve the efficiency and effectiveness of its selling activities while building that all-important knowledge base so that marketers, planners, policy makers, and top managers can do their jobs more effectively.

Nobody objects to the achievement of such obviously beneficial results. But the costs and pitfalls encountered in pursuing them are many and varied. The history of sales automation, despite a few scattered early successes, more often resembled a stock car race, with many spectators unwilling to set foot on the track, some venturesome drivers out on the oval destroying their vehicles and themselves, and a few winners gaining the checkered flag while carefully picking their way through the wreckage left by their competitors.

This book is about whether and how to go down—or retrace, for those who have already tried it—the path to closed loop sales automation, what to expect from it, and how to justify it, plan it, implement it, and avoid the technical and human difficulties that have prevented or derailed so many previous attempts. Although this is very much a "how to" book, some time is spent on "what and whether," which, after all, are essential preliminaries.

The emphasis in this book is on tactical use of computing to enhance and support the selling process. However, we also consider the strategic advantage. In our view, strategic advantage means relating to the marketplace in new and unique ways that the competition is not yet prepared to match. Relating to the marketplace is more than a strategy; it comes down to actual selling and serving in the real world. Doing that in new and unique ways requires a dependable, lightning-fast, flexible, information-rich tool kit employed on a tactical basis day in and day out. As often as not, sales automation can be found at the heart of such tools; in many companies, it *is* the tool kit.

This book is meant for the people who will have a determining impact on the *what, whether,* and *how* decisions regarding sales automation—top management, sales management, marketing management, MIS executives, and any others concerned with fundamental sales and marketing strategy, tactics, and support. We also address those who will use the resulting systems: field sales reps and their managers, telesales and telemarketing reps, marketing people, and customer service people. Finally, we speak to those who have a role in implementing such systems, including analysts, planners, programmers, technicians, and trainers, to help them coordinate their efforts, focus on what's really needed, and avoid career- and company-killing mistakes.

We also believe that it wouldn't hurt consultants and vendors of sales automation systems to take a step back, gain some added perspective, and, perhaps, fine-tune their own selling and marketing a bit, perhaps setting the stage more accurately, toning down extravagant claims, and taking a more rigorous and thoughtful approach to implementation.

Consider the following statistics: Sales and marketing-related functions comprise from 15 to 35 percent or more of total corporate costs in large companies, according to Moriarity and Swartz in their seminal article on sales automation in the January-February 1989 *Harvard Business Review*. About a third of all workers in the United States and other advanced economies are engaged in selling, marketing, and customer service. Yet these functions are far and away the least automated of any in business today. Moriarity and Swartz estimate that less than 5 percent of the potential for such applications has been achieved, and our own experiences as active practitioners amply confirm the point. We believe that sales automation will be one of the great waves of the decade, perhaps dwarfing all other new applications of computing. If we're right, it behooves you to get in early, put the preliminary learning and experimentation behind you quickly, and bolster your competitive posture and cost-effectiveness against the untold but probably immense pressures that lie ahead.

Before we begin, here is a quick rundown of what we'll be covering. Chapter 1 describes the uses to which the systems are put, providing you with a kind of shopping list of useful applications.

Chapter 2 explains how sales automation can help track and propel prospects through the process of making them customers and follow customers through the repetitive buying cycle. It also describes how the system can build up by-product information at no added exertion or cost that can be extremely valuable to the sales rep, sales supervisors, and the business.

In Chapter 3 we zero in on how computers can build a better relationship with customers by providing more, and more readily accessible, information about that relationship, enabling everyone in the organization who has any contact with the customer to "do the right thing."

The vital core role in sales automation systems played by telecommunications and database management techniques are dealt with in Chapters 4, 5, and 6. Here we explain the voice, fax, and data networking capability that is required and how it all comes together in a structured repository of information. We also discuss how to achieve proper data security and interaction with other related corporate data processing systems.

In the second part of the book, Chapters 7 through 9, we walk you through the analytical side of sales automation—determining if you need it, and, if so, in what form, planning the program, determining its cost, and assessing the likely benefits.

Finally, in Part III, we focus on the practical implementation issues of sales automation—overcoming the human, organizational, and political problems involved, introducing the system, training the people, measuring results, and making necessary adjustments to ensure that the objectives are being achieved.

We also endeavor to forecast what you'll be doing in the field of sales automation in coming years—what new benefits in communications, computers, and software will be available to you and what you should do now to get ready to take advantage of them.

Part I

Application and Technology Overview

Chapter 1

Concepts and Principles of Sales Automation

In the sense of using data processing systems to keep track of sales volume by product and by customer, sales automation (SA) is as old as the hills. One of the very first uses for punched card automation back in the 1920s and 1930s was billing. In this procedure, the user pulled cards prepunched with product code, price, and description from a tub file that contained cards representing every item in inventory. The items ordered by a specific customer were lined up behind a customer "header," prepunched with static customer information, on which, perhaps, the current date was entered. A ship-to address card was then added, and the whole stack was processed through an accumulating printing tabulator. The original item cards were then "gang-punched" with the customer number and kept for later sorting and analysis. It was a simple but time-consuming and laborious matter to tabulate what items had been sold to whom. The cards remaining in the tub file, of course, represented remaining on-hand inventory.

It was possible and, as time went on, increasingly convenient to summarize and keep running totals by product, customer, and perhaps sales representative and territory. Still later, in the 1950s, statistical forecasting techniques (particularly one called exponential smoothing, which weighted recent sales more heavily than earlier ones) were used to forecast sales by item or item category in the interest of more efficient manufacturing, buying, and inventory control.

In contrast with earlier sales automation applications, which were concerned exclusively with past events and which only occasionally extrapolated from history into the future on an aggregate basis, this book is concerned with the application of computing to what is happening *now* in order to optimize current sales and marketing activities. Analyzing past events is but one facet of modern SA and a relatively minor one to all but product managers and strategists. Furthermore, the best, most accurate, and least expensive historical analysis comes about as a by-product of automating the process of selling and marketing. In other words, if the activity is automated more or less as it takes place, the requisite historical and analytical data can be captured with little or no further effort.

For example, if total sales of product or service X over a period of months is known as a by-product of customer billing and shipping, it is possible to plot the trend and get some idea, with appropriate seasonal and other adjustments, of whether business is getting better or worse. If, on the other hand, an automated order entry process can capture demand data ahead of actual shipment and billing, those data can serve as a kind of "early warning"—or, if things are going well, an early "warming" analysis—of what's happening in the marketplace.

The ability to go one step back in the process and capture *potential* demand, based on application of computers to such processes as capturing responses to magazine ads, tracking outstanding sales proposals, gathering "grass roots" likely-to-buy forecasts of individual customers' intentions from sales representatives, dealers, or retailers, provides the ultimate in early warning information, allowing the organization to do something that could affect the result. If activity levels are too low, the company can escalate its advertising and promotional effort, reduce prices, create special deals, "whip up" the sales force, extend warranties, or do whatever else is appropriate. If activity levels are high, it can up production or buying, raise prices, and reduce special incentives. The relative time scales of the three types of analysis are depicted in Figure 1-1.

Improving the analysis and decision support process is one of two extremely good reasons to move computing upstream into the selling and marketing process. The other rea-

Figure 1-1. Timing relevance of SA data derived by differing means for analysis and decision making.

	DATA AVAILABLE	
Derived from customer billing and shipping	Derived from customer orders, commitments	Derived from the selling and marketing process
	TIMING	
Weeks or months after the fact	Typically around the time things are happening	Weeks or months before the fact

son is to add value to the process itself. Think of the analogous manufacturing function. As recently as the early 1980s, computers applied to manufacturing were used mainly for engineering and accounting. Computers generated performance, cost, and other design data for analysis by engineers seeking to improve the design of the product or process; computers also provided company controllers with their all-important cost, inventory, and payroll data for posting the books, paying employees, and keeping tabs on the efficiency (profitability) of the various facets of the manufacturing process. But now, computer-integrated manufacturing has made its appearance, along with just-in-time inventory control, concurrent engineering, flexible scheduling, total quality control, design for manufacturability, and a host of other computerized improvements. All of these have had a powerful impact on the *way* manufacturing is done and on its inherent efficiency and profitability.

A similar phenomenon is occurring in sales, tied closely with marketing. The long-standing application of computing to order entry, billing, shipping, inventory control, and accounting continues to improve in comprehensiveness, speed, and responsiveness and to produce increasingly valuable analytical information. But now computer programs are being applied to the prospecting, selling, and customer servicing functions as they happen, producing dramatic improvements in the timeliness and quality of the analytical and management information available and, even more important, in the efficiency and effectiveness of the processes themselves. This has enabled companies to close more accounts, sell more to each customer, achieve a more optimal product mix, get better prices, achieve higher levels of customer satisfaction and account retention, protect markets, and offer faster, better sales training, all at the same or lower expense.

Without underestimating the importance of the more mundane computer applications such as automated order entry and inventory control, we still believe the newest, least explored, and potentially most rewarding frontier in sales and marketing to be supporting the process itself with computer hardware, software, and communications, often tying these newer applications to the old for still greater overall integration and cost-effectiveness. (This topic is discussed more fully in the next chapter.) It is this newest frontier to which we give our primary attention in this book.

Let's summarize the applicability and benefits of computing and data processing to the various sales and sales-related processes:

- *Order entry*. Capturing customer orders is the first step in fulfilling them. By-product information is helpful in discerning trends in customer, product, and other ordering patterns while there is still some time to do something about them. There is potential advantage in capturing the order as early and as far upstream in the process as possible, even encouraging customers to place their own orders directly into the supplier's system. Doing so makes information available just that much sooner, allows orders to be filled sooner, and, in many cases, yields a competitive advantage by locking in customers to the particular supplier's system. American Airlines, for example, achieved an early and significant competitive edge with its Sabre reservation system, the first to be extended for direct use by travel agents right from their desks. Today, no airline could survive without providing such access, either on its own or by subscribing to another's on-line reservation and ticketing system.

Those automated order entry systems that can be integrated with other sales-related activities by the representative in the field or that take place in the customer's office, warehouse, store, or other point of sale are particularly applicable in modern sales automation.

• *Order tracking*. Probably the question most often heard in business is "Where's my order?" In the case of service businesses, of course, it's "When are you coming to do my job?" Federal Express is one of a number of companies that have made a fetish of providing correct answers to those questions instantly, while the conversation with the customer is still taking place, rather than putting the customer off. The results have been very positive. Customers like to do business with people who know what's what and can give straight answers. In the case of a small business whose proprietor knows everything that's happening in both the front and back rooms, instantaneous order tracking is part and parcel of what the company does and a key to its continued survival.

As many businesses grow, however, there comes a time when information starts getting blurred or hard to find. If the business manages to bridge the gap and survive to the automation stage, all is potentially well because, once again, instant, accurate information can be obtained. Such is the value of an automated order tracking system looked at from the outside. Inside, of course, there are other benefits, including improved production and transportation planning, manufacturing and distribution scheduling and control, and document preparation.

From a sales point of view, there's nothing better than getting an order, so using technology to make that process easier or more attractive makes sense. The next best thing that can happen is to fulfill that order in the most satisfactory possible manner, keeping the customer informed and happy all the way. Thus, a really good order entry and order tracking system is indeed the salesperson's friend.

• *Proposing, quoting, and specifying applications.* When you are selling complex products and services, it's often necessary to do some research to determine a proper match between what the customer needs and what your company supplies. If configuring the product is complicated and if customization is required, then pricing and delivery may be equally complicated. Even describing your solution in detail can be complex. In the good old days, sales representatives took copious notes regarding customer requirements, got back to the office or laboratory with the data all in good time, often waited a very long time for appropriate departments to come up with specifications and prices, and then spent still more time dictating or handwriting long, complicated proposals or formal quotations detailing the offering, which then had to be typed, proofread, and corrected.

Today, in contrast, representatives, engineers, and customer service people are able to use the logical capabilities of the computer, together with its limitless ability to store and link words, phrases, paragraphs, diagrams, and whole documents and to insert appropriate variables, to produce a perfectly composed, perfectly printed custom proposal virtually instantaneously. Even in the simpler case of preparing a confirming letter to the prospect stating product and price, word processing has shaved days off the process.

The incentive for using technology in this way is obvious; if the competitors aren't doing it, it's a way to get the jump on them, responding more quickly and professionally to customer demands. If the competition is already using automation in sales, it's the way to keep from being left at the starting gate.

• *Activity and expense reporting systems.* It's tough to determine what a sales representative hates more—keyboarding call reports into a computer or filling them out by hand. Let's say keyboarding could allow the representative to avoid having to summarize them manually at period-end; to avoid manually preparing account-by-account sales forecasts; to gain automatic calendarized scheduling of future commitments, visits, and phone calls; to obtain all manner of computerized assistance in preparing correspondence, proposals, mailing labels, and automatic follow-up notices; and, perhaps, with a few extra keystrokes for mileage and lunches, to avoid having to fill out expense reports. Well, if keyboarding could do all that, the representative would be in sales heaven, right?

Right. In theory, and certainly in potential practice. But two things regularly seem to go wrong to prevent this happy outcome. First, the systems needed to handle this information are so poorly implemented that nobody wants to, or understands how to, use them; second, perfectly mature, otherwise grown-up, intelligent sales representatives are struck dumb with fear, hostility, or confusion by computers and simply cannot bring themselves to learn how to use these valuable tools.

Chapter 10 offers a number of time-tested methods for overcoming such deficiencies and neutralizing the almost inevitable resistance you'll encounter.

• *Territory management aids.* Computers have been used for a long time to assist management in allocating territories based on sales history and demographics. The latter is especially important in new territories or in novel situations, where one can infer the potential only by knowing how many potential buyers of what kind and size exist within a given area. If, as is the case with consumer packaged-goods companies that sell to and through retailers, the purchasing points in the territories are all well-known, the computer's role may be to help plan routing and scheduling for the representative or to identify which retailers are not doing an adequate job of moving particular brands.

In the 1990s, however, computers are being used more and more as tools to guide territory coverage and, as an adjunct, to keep the necessary records. For example, in food, beverage, health and beauty aids, and many other packaged-goods industries, representatives carry handheld or laptop computers to:

- Remind them whom to call on, when, and in what sequence.
- Take inventory and suggest rebuy quantities.

- Analyze shelf space and layout and make suggestions for improvement.
- Enter orders and transmit them to headquarters.
- Record and track virtually everything important about what the representative is observing and doing.

Even for business-to-business marketers, computers are used to help representatives plan coverage so that every customer and prospect gets the appropriate level of attention and nothing falls through the cracks.

When it comes time to reshuffle territories, sales managers can use computers to model the actual and potential revenue impact on representatives of each possible move. Similarly, exactly the right mix of large, medium, small, new, old, prospect, and suspect accounts can be combined to match the experience levels and, not inconsequentially, the income needs of each specific territory representative.

• *"Electronic daytimer" applications.* Many personal computer (PC) and portable PC sales applications today are replacing the functions traditionally performed by daytimers and pocket calendars, such as keeping track of the representative's schedule, recording appointments and follow-ups, and leaving room for occasional notes and comments as reminders of what is to be done or as records of what has already been accomplished. Think of it as a combination calendar, Rolodex file, and diary. The majority of these "electronic daytimer" programs include names, addresses, phone numbers, other needed data about each customer and prospect, and key dates, together with a kind of alarm clock function that reminds the representative of appointments and commitments when they come due and with modem and autodial features that can automatically phone individual contacts on command or at the preappointed hour.

Imagine the advantages of having an electronic appointment book that explains itself, prints itself out when needed, notifies its owner of upcoming events, provides reminders of missed commitments, dials the phone and makes a note of having done so, and encourages one to punch in new appointments, events, promises, and commentary, all of which become a part of the permanent, readily accessible, and eminently usable record of all activities—and that can, and usually does, go on to feed call reporting, expense reporting, forecasting, and other territory management and administrative functions automatically! Sounds ideal, and it is in many cases; but, like so much else in sales automation, it comes not without effort, the smallest part of which is the instrumentation. The real price is eternal vigilance—never letting future commitments or feedback on current activities get away from the system. A calendarization and follow-up system is an all-or-nothing proposition—either everything the user wants to do and has done is in the system or it's totally worthless. Imagine a telephone answering service that does or doesn't take messages depending on whim or work load. What good would it be to you? How would you know when and when not to depend on it?

• *Telemarketing support*. Many SA software packages provide, in effect, an autodialed electronic phone book and telephone follow-up diary. Full-time professional telemarketers demand systems that go much farther, typically including "branched scripting," which reminds the telemarketer what to say initially and then projects various possible paths (branches) in the dialog depending on what the respondent says, what questions are asked, and what objections are raised. These systems often include computer screens containing preformatted questions and blank or multiple-choice answer fields to facilitate on-the-spot recording of dialogs, results, or survey data. Such software packages usually provide statistics by time of day on number of dialings, number of calls completed, or recorded results for each individual telemarketer and for the department overall.

Some SA systems route outbound calls via the least expensive carrier, depending on specific area code and exchange. Others are set up specifically to field inbound "800" inquiries. Some can switch calls to customer service, technical support, or other departments as needed.

• *Administrative support*. Many sales-oriented computer

software packages include (usually simplified) word processors capable of producing straightforward letters, envelopes, and labels. Some provide subsystems to support literature fulfillment, that is, produce pick-lists, mailing labels, and inventory listings of various kinds of promotional literature.

Many packages also have in-built electronic mail (Email) or other communications features that promote transfer of information among representatives, between representatives and managers, and between the field and headquarters for the purpose of coordinating sales and customer service activities. Many SA systems include on-line customer order entry, and a few permit order tracking. Almost all facilitate standard activity reporting, both locally and up the line to various levels of management. Ideally, the creation of these activity reports should be an automatic by-product of the electronic daytimer functions described earlier in this chapter, thus providing another major reward for diligently keeping up the computerized calendar and diary.

Some SA complements support sophisticated graphics for use in creating proposals, slides, and other customized promotional material; some include spreadsheet packages for analysis, budgeting, and forecasting. Still others have in-built decision-making, guidance, and training features. The rule is, Give the troops whatever they need to get the job done.

• *Utilization of SA systems.* One overriding issue that needs to be faced right at the beginning of any consideration of SA is the human element. Somebody, somewhere—a representative, a dealer, a customer—has to initiate the processes we've been talking about and follow through with all the required informational and directional data. One of the keys to success in SA is making the needed effort:

- As easy to learn and do as possible
- As mistake-proof as possible
- As nonvoluminous as possible

In the days of on-line order entry to mainframe computers by clerks using attached terminals (days that may not yet have faded into history for many companies), the entry people made a career of doing one thing—entering orders. If the task was boring, repetitive, full of hard-to-remember codes and keyboard sequences, if it presented screens full of daunting jumbled symbols and abbreviations, people got used to it. That was their job. It took a long time to gain proficiency at it, and the clerks, once they had mastered the job, tended to stay at it for months or years.

Things are most emphatically different with people whose job it is to deal with customers. They have other priorities. They are, for the most part, unwilling to invest the time it takes to master such arcane computer arts; some are constitutionally unable to do it, and virtually all rebel at the prospect.

If, even after you've designed the world's friendliest, simplest, easiest-to-use SA system, you expect salespeople to take, and take kindly, to it, especially if they have to access it personally, you are probably in for a very rude awakening. Getting salespeople to use computers won't be easy. In fact, in a few situations it may prove to be impossible or at least ill-advised. There may be other paths to the same end, for example, using clerical intermediaries in personal or telephone contact with the primary users. This human factor surfaces frequently throughout this book and is dealt with in much detail in Chapter 10; it's SA's Achilles' heel, the single most prominent cause of virtually every failure that has occurred to date in attempts to implement SA.

Think of the closed loop system we spoke of in the Introduction. If there is one link in the loop that is open or erratic or undependable, then the entire loop is suspect, useless. Guess where that weak link is most likely to be? At risk of giving away the plot, let us hint that strengthening the loop's most vulnerable point is going to require the most exquisite, painstaking effort on your part to:

- Make the system easy, even fun, to use.
- Most important, sell the users on the benefits they will obtain personally from doing so.

Much more on this later. Now let's get on to some of the functional aspects of sales automation.

Chapter 2
Managing the Sales Cycle

Tracking the selling cycle by computer offers improved discipline in what has traditionally been at best a paper-and-pencil exercise and more often a completely undisciplined, intuitive process. Salespeople have learned that the conviction that eventually leads to placing an order develops in stages in the minds of prospective customers. It begins with a flicker of interest; then it passes through various stages—concern and questioning, objection raising, claims verification, relating claimed benefits to the buyer's personal objectives, gathering conviction, making the decision, and often, after-the-fact rekindling of doubt known as buyers' remorse.

There are various steps to take and actions to avoid at each stage in the buying cycle. For example, a sales rep might present testimonials from satisfied customers at the verification stage; at a certain point, a demonstration, a visit to another user, or a home office visit may be in order. Reps do not attempt to close the order while fielding objections. Further, certain kinds of sales result from collaborative, group decisions with different classes of influencers; typically, there is one final yea- or nay-sayer who will not act until all obstacles have been cleared with the other participants. Strategies exist for dealing with various classes of objections and reservations; for example, various kinds of proof statements and assurances can be applied to nullify obstacles.

If you were to sit down and analyze in writing a particular prospect or account, subjecting it to a detailed dissection in accordance with whatever selling cycle guidelines you've learned or are currently imposed by your company, you would undoubtedly be able to distill a set of next-step actions to be taken with the account. If you followed those steps, performed another analysis, and derived and followed more steps, and so on down the line, your chances of getting the business would undoubtedly be enhanced. The problem is, most people don't have (or take) the time to do that kind of painstaking analysis on even one account, much less a whole portfolio of customers and prospects.

But suppose you have a little electronic helpmate that simply cries out for classification and action data in a predetermined structure that corresponds exactly to whatever schema you or your company has determined is a logical representation of the stages of your selling cycle and the activities appropriate to each.

The "I'll get back to you on that" items traditionally end up scribbled in a pocket calendar or on the back of an envelope or lodged in your head somewhere. A proper computer system wants to know, "To whom did you make the commitment? What did you commit to do? When did you say you'd respond? How is the customer expecting to hear from you? What else do you have to do to make good on this promise?" As often as not, this dialog can be a series of single key depressions selecting options from a table or menu, rather than drawn-out data entry narratives (see Figures 2-1 through 2-11). Furthermore, once the data are in the system, the computer will not let you forget what you said, no matter how many things you committed to do for no matter how many different prospects and customers. This is the essence of sales cycle tracking, or contact management, by computer. Let's illustrate and discuss such a system.

Setting Up a Basic Account Record—An Example

At the heart of every sales automation system is an account record containing information about the customer—the individual if it's a consumer account or the company and one or more individual contacts if it's a business account. This entry can be very simple or quite complex and voluminous, depending on the size of the account and the type of business you do (or intend to do) with it.

Just to get the feel of a representative SA approach, let's step through an account record for a mythical company with a single buying influence using a typical personal computer–based sales automation software package, one of literally hundreds of good ones available. This one is called The Maximizer, published by Richmond Technologies & Software, Inc.

Recording a Typical Account Record

Figure 2-1 You are setting up Worldbeaters, Ltd., as a key account. All the vital information is entered in the first screen. To the right of the word *comments* in the left column, you have entered the descriptive term *key*

Figure 2-1. Setting up an account record—step 1.

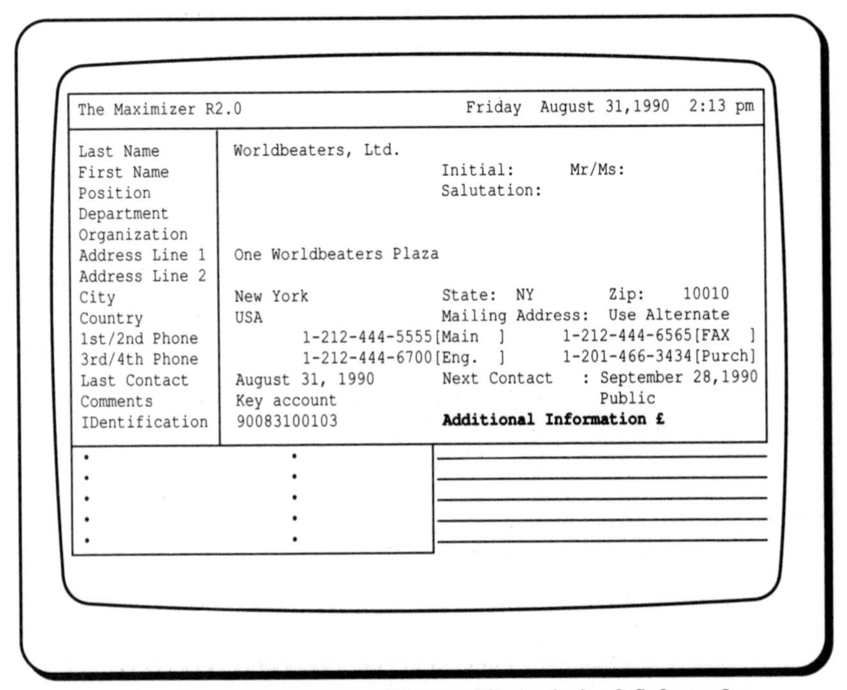

Used by permission of Richmond Technologies & Software Inc.

account as a reminder of the importance of this client. The comment could be anything else or nothing, depending on what you feel is appropriate. The cursor (the little flashing indicator that indicates where you are on a computer screen) now rests on the last field, "Additional Information," at the bottom right of the screen.

Figure 2-2 If you press Enter, a menu pops up in the upper right corner, giving the option of entering four different kinds of additional information about this account. Choose "Contacts."

Figure 2-3 A panel opens in the middle of the screen, into which you can enter important information about this particular contact individual.

Figure 2-4 Information about the purchasing agent,

Figure 2-2. Setting up an account record—step 2.

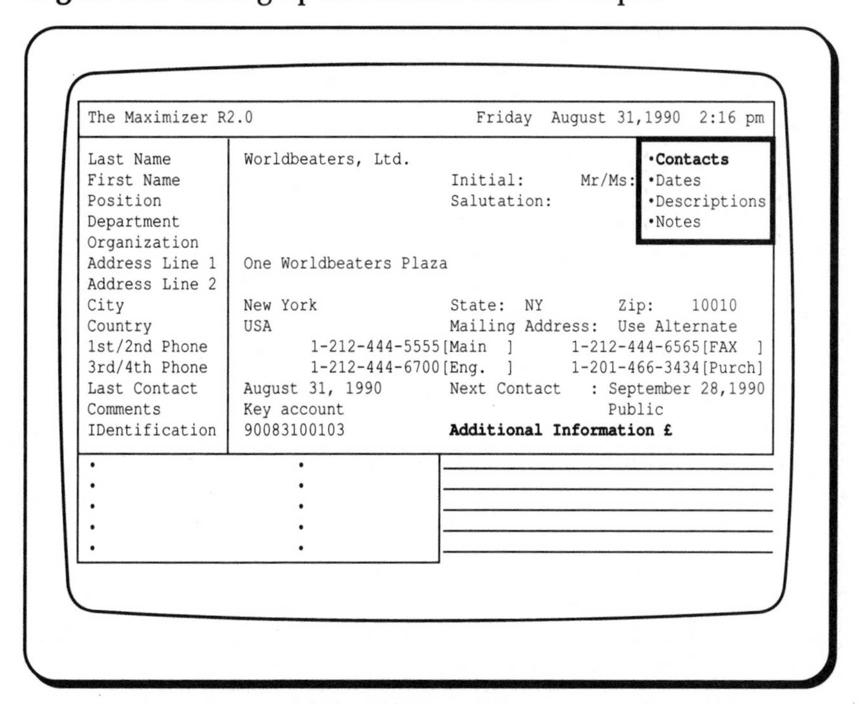

Used by permission of Richmond Technologies & Software Inc.

Figure 2-3. Setting up an account record—step 3.

```
The Maximizer R2.0                    Friday  August 31,1990  2:18 pm

Last Name     Worldbeaters, Ltd.                        • Contacts
First Name                       Initial:  Mr/Ms:       • Dates
Position                         Salutation:            • Descriptions
                                                        • Notes
Last Name
First Name                        Initial:   Mr/Ms:
Position                          Salutation:
1st/2nd Phone                    [    ]                  [    ]
3rd/4th Phone                    [    ]                  [    ]
Last Contact                      Next Contact   :
Comments
Letter Type                            Receives Letters: No
Address       Use Main                 Notes/Dates     : Notes
```

Used by permission of Richmond Technologies & Software Inc.

Mr. Arnold Toughnut, is entered. The software provides a simple visual means of selecting key dates, such as those shown here for last contact and next contact, via a calendar on the screen on which you can move around by using the arrow keys on your keyboard. You select a particular date by pressing the Enter key when the cursor is posed on that day in the past, present, or future. The cursor now rests on the last field, "Notes/Dates." Select "Notes." Another window opens immediately at the bottom of the screen into which you can enter relevant remarks about Mr. Toughnut. In this case, you note that he will indeed be a tough nut to crack.

Figure 2-5 As you continue to enter data, the system gives you more room—as much as you need. In this

Figure 2-4. Setting up an account record—step 4.

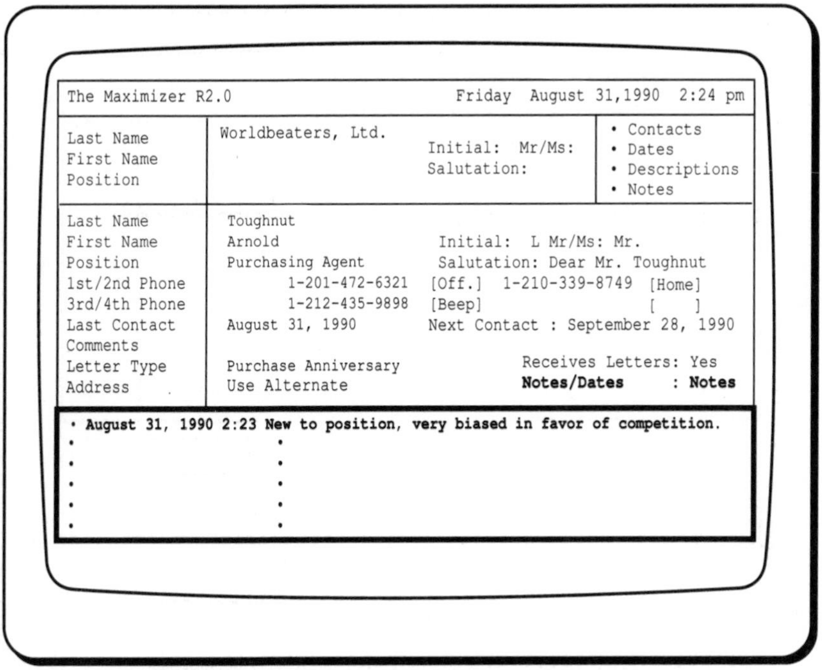

```
The Maximizer R2.0                    Friday  August 31,1990  2:24 pm

Last Name        Worldbeaters, Ltd.                      • Contacts
First Name                          Initial:  Mr/Ms:     • Dates
Position                            Salutation:          • Descriptions
                                                         • Notes

Last Name        Toughnut
First Name       Arnold                Initial:  L Mr/Ms: Mr.
Position         Purchasing Agent      Salutation: Dear Mr. Toughnut
1st/2nd Phone         1-201-472-6321  [Off.]  1-210-339-8749  [Home]
3rd/4th Phone         1-212-435-9898  [Beep]                  [    ]
Last Contact     August 31, 1990      Next Contact : September 28, 1990
Comments
Letter Type      Purchase Anniversary          Receives Letters: Yes
Address          Use Alternate                 Notes/Dates     : Notes

• August 31, 1990 2:23 New to position, very biased in favor of competition.
•                       •
•                       •
•                       •
•                       •
•                       •
```

Used by permission of Richmond Technologies & Software Inc.

example, you conclude that a visit to one of your better accounts, Zepher Industries, might be helpful in bringing Mr. Toughnut around and making a believer out of him.

Figure 2-6 Next go back to "Additional Information" on the main screen, and this time select "Descriptions," which automatically triggers another pop-up selection screen that allows you to select the category of description. By moving the cursor down, pick "Record Type," and then press Return.

Figure 2-7 Immediately, another subsidiary list representing what you have defined as relevant categories pops up. From this list, select the first one, "Client."

Figure 2-8 Look back at Figure 2-6. You could have selected the category "Next Objective." Add that to

Figure 2-5. Setting up an account record—step 5.

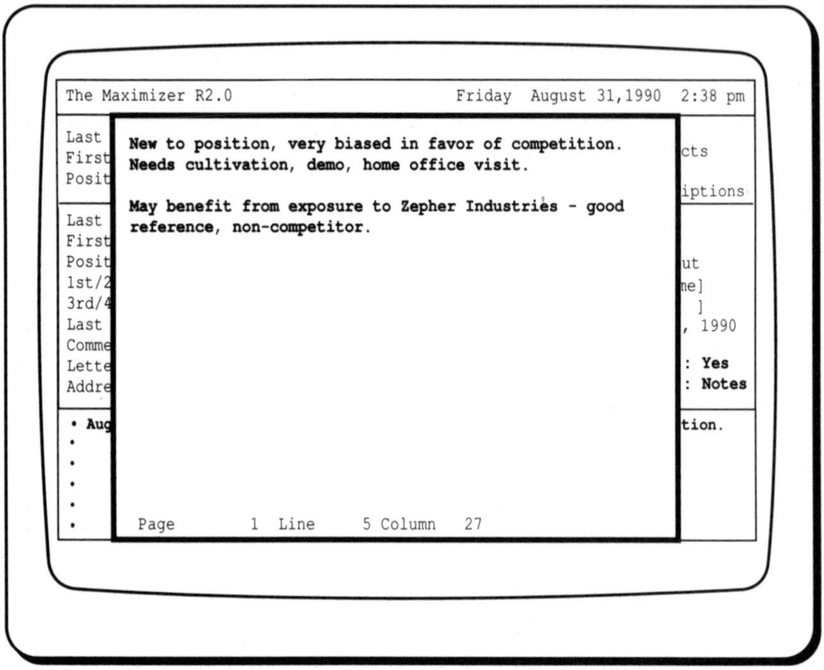

```
The Maximizer R2.0                    Friday  August 31,1990  2:38 pm
Last   New to position, very biased in favor of competition.   cts
First  Needs cultivation, demo, home office visit.
Posit                                                          iptions
       May benefit from exposure to Zepher Industries - good
Last   reference, non-competitor.
First
Posit                                                          ut
1st/2                                                          ne]
3rd/4                                                            ]
Last                                                           , 1990
Comme
Lette                                                          : Yes
Addre                                                          : Notes
• Aug                                                          tion.
•
•
•
•
•        Page        1  Line      5 Column   27
```

Used by permission of Richmond Technologies & Software Inc.

what you've already done by moving the cursor there and pressing Enter. Now a different list of options shows up in the window on the left. This time select "Show/Demonstrate," which is one of six relevant stages in the sales process in your particular business.

Figure 2-9 Now let's go all the way back to the "Additional Information" options and this time select "Dates." This automatically brings up a list at the lower left of important categories of dates. In this instance, move the cursor to "Purchase Anniversary," and, using the date selection system, pick June 22, 1987, with only a couple of keystrokes, as the appropriate date. Later, perhaps, you'll instruct the system to remind you of the purchase anniversaries of all of your clients as they occur and perhaps automatically

Figure 2-6. Setting up an account record—step 6.

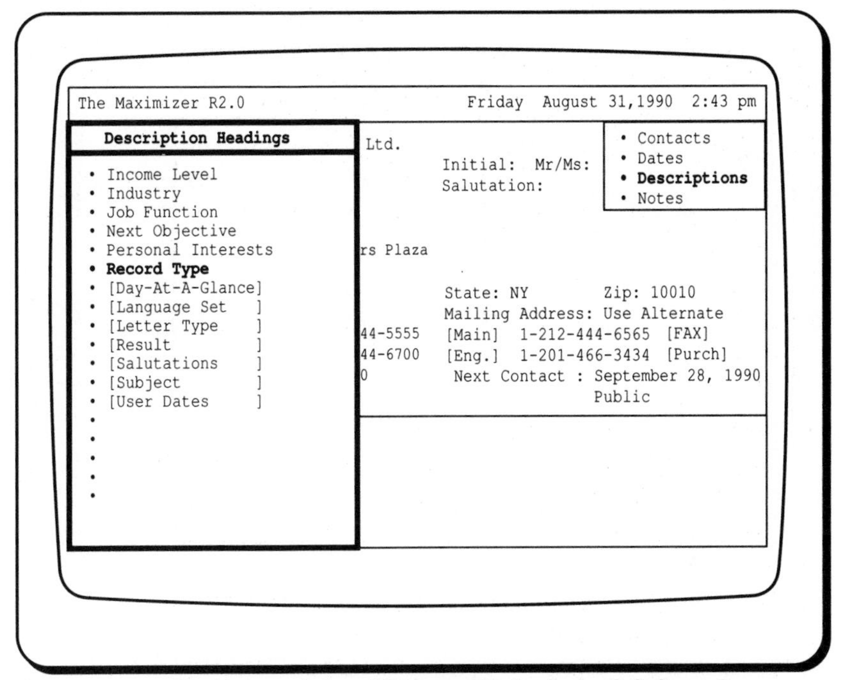

Used by permission of Richmond Technologies & Software Inc.

initiate commemorative cards or letters to key contacts as these dates come up.

Figure 2-10 Like many other sales automation packages, this one supports correspondence with the account. If you touch a particular function key, a pop-up menu on the upper right provides the opportunity to select, among other things, "Mail-Out." A little menu at the bottom asks whether you wish to create a letter, label, or envelope or to merge the account information with an external word processing package. In this case, suppose you want to send a letter; you make your selection accordingly.

Figure 2-11 Most of the screen is given over to a writing space, which is already headed, dated, and addressed and contains a salutation to Mr. Toughnut. You can

Figure 2-7. Setting up an account record—step 7.

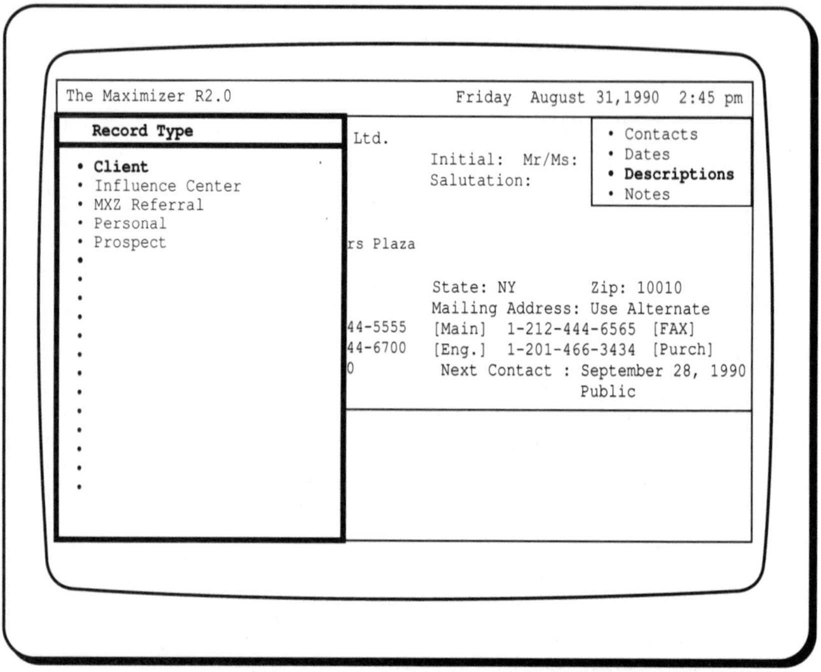

```
The Maximizer R2.0                        Friday  August 31,1990  2:45 pm
 Record Type            Ltd.                          • Contacts
                                     Initial:  Mr/Ms:  • Dates
 • Client                            Salutation:       • Descriptions
 • Influence Center                                    • Notes
 • MXZ Referral
 • Personal
 • Prospect             rs Plaza
 •
 •                                   State: NY        Zip: 10010
 •                                   Mailing Address: Use Alternate
 •                      44-5555      [Main]  1-212-444-6565  [FAX]
 •                      44-6700      [Eng.]  1-201-466-3434  [Purch]
 •                      0             Next Contact : September 28, 1990
 •                                                   Public
 •
 •
 •
 •
 •
```

Used by permission of Richmond Technologies & Software Inc.

now go on to create a letter and have the PC print it out, along with an envelope. You could have selected from a library of prestored letters and had the system integrate it with Mr. Toughnut's name, address, and salutation; in that case you wouldn't have had to write anything, but Mr. Toughnut would have received a "personal" letter, anyway. Based on the various descriptive categories, textual notes, and other data and selections you've entered into the record, you can make all sorts of things happen automatically or on command in the future with respect to Mr. Toughnut or to Worldbeaters, Ltd., as a whole.

This example demonstrates how a growing body of organized knowledge about a specific account, be it suspect, pros-

Figure 2-8. Setting up an account record—step 8.

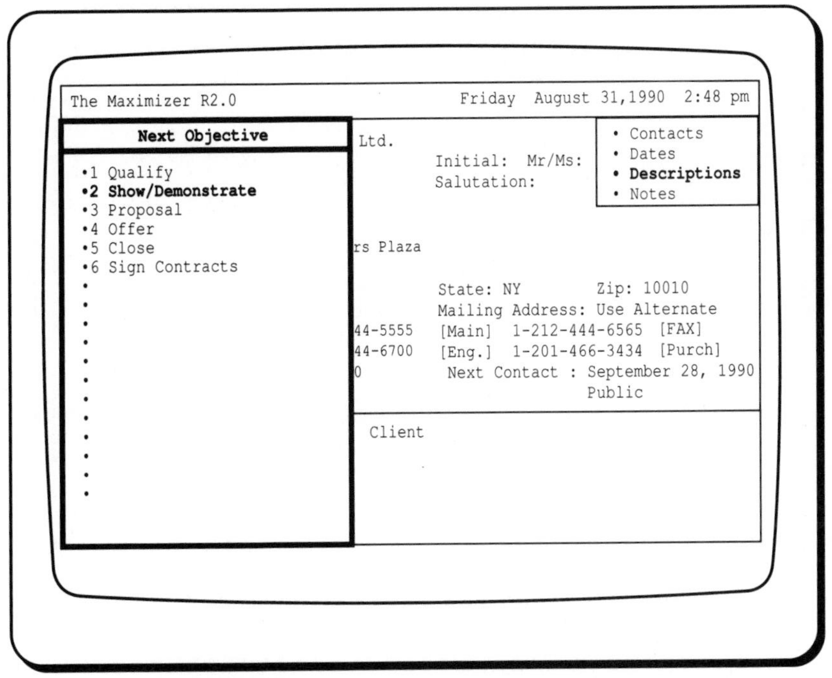

Used by permission of Richmond Technologies & Software Inc.

pect, or customer, can be built up and how, in a properly organized system, that information can be used to trigger and support various important activities, such as sending an acknowledgment, remembering to call back, mailing literature, scheduling a visit or a demonstration, or what have you.

Starting Out as Lead

Most new entries into an existing system begin at the beginning—when the prospect first appears, commonly in the form of a lead. Leads may come as a response to an advertisement, as a drop-in at a trade show booth, or as a name on a computerized list of suspects purchased from a trade magazine. In any case, at this stage little is known about the prospect, but you do know something, even if it's only a name and telephone number.

Figure 2-9. Setting up an account record—step 9.

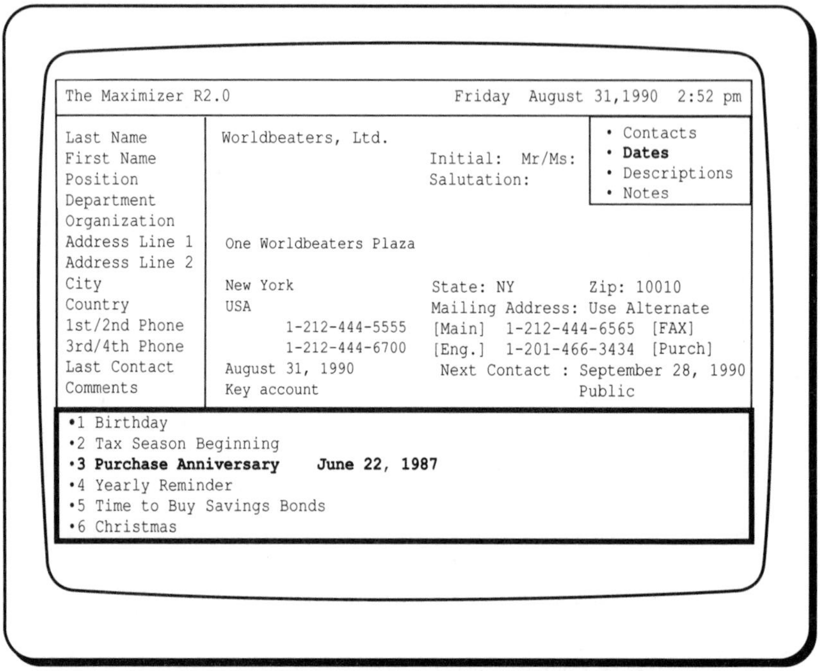

```
The Maximizer R2.0                              Friday  August 31,1990  2:52 pm

Last Name        Worldbeaters, Ltd.                          • Contacts
First Name                              Initial:  Mr/Ms:     • Dates
Position                                Salutation:          • Descriptions
Department                                                   • Notes
Organization
Address Line 1   One Worldbeaters Plaza
Address Line 2
City             New York               State: NY        Zip: 10010
Country          USA                    Mailing Address: Use Alternate
1st/2nd Phone          1-212-444-5555   [Main]  1-212-444-6565  [FAX]
3rd/4th Phone          1-212-444-6700   [Eng.]  1-201-466-3434  [Purch]
Last Contact     August 31, 1990         Next Contact : September 28, 1990
Comments         Key account                           Public

•1 Birthday
•2 Tax Season Beginning
•3 Purchase Anniversary    June 22, 1987
•4 Yearly Reminder
•5 Time to Buy Savings Bonds
•6 Christmas
```

Used by permission of Richmond Technologies & Software Inc.

If you decide to follow up on this lead, it makes sense to enter what essential information you have into an account record for three important reasons:

1. You probably want the system to help perform the subsequent steps you plan to take to develop this lead into a customer. These steps may include letter writing, telephoning, and personal calling. How the system can help you in these steps is discussed in this chapter.

2. Because this is not your only sales lead—let's hope you have hundreds or thousands to deal with at a time—the system should be able to help keep track of them and to follow up relentlessly in accordance with your policy. No good to say that, twenty-one days after mailing sales literature piece YZX, if you haven't heard from a prospect, you make it a practice to

Figure 2-10. Setting up an account record—step 10.

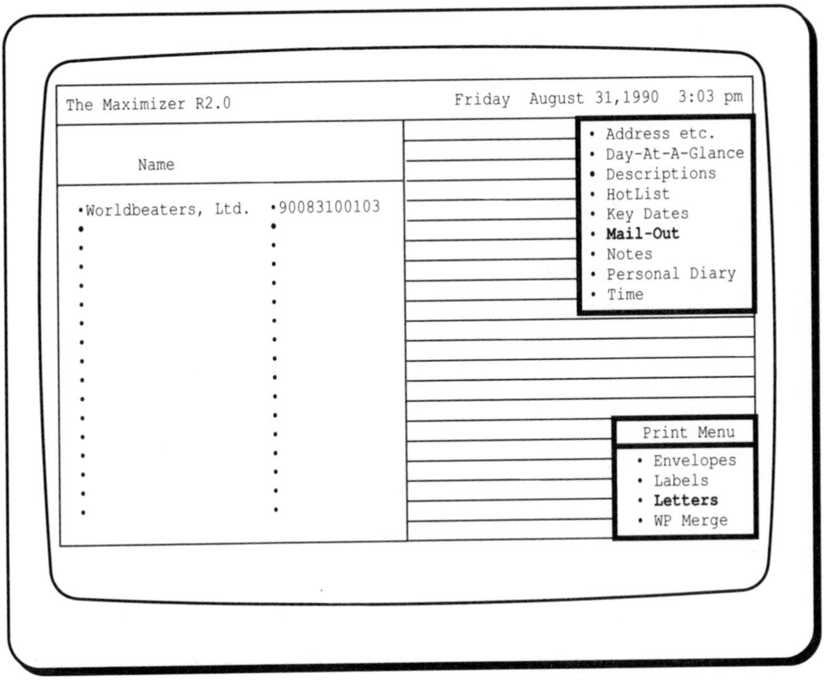

The Maximizer R2.0
Friday August 31,1990 3:03 pm
Name
•Worldbeaters, Ltd. •90083100103
• Address etc.
• Day-At-A-Glance
• Descriptions
• HotList
• Key Dates
• **Mail-Out**
• Notes
• Personal Diary
• Time
Print Menu
• Envelopes
• Labels
• **Letters**
• WP Merge

Used by permission of Richmond Technologies & Software Inc.

mail piece CBA . . . and then forget about doing it. If you've set up a computer system to do exactly that, it will get done. Period!

3. Finally, if all goes well, this prospect will be with you for a very long time. If so, it makes sense to carry over all or most of the information you've painstakingly gathered in the qualifying process directly into your customer information system without having to reenter it. Names, addresses, phone numbers, and classification data should simply slide forward effortlessly into your order entry, billing, and sales analysis systems when the time comes.

Starting Out as Existing Customer

Few if any businesses are born with a sales automation system. Automation usually comes later, after there are some sales to

Figure 2-11. Setting up an account record—step 11.

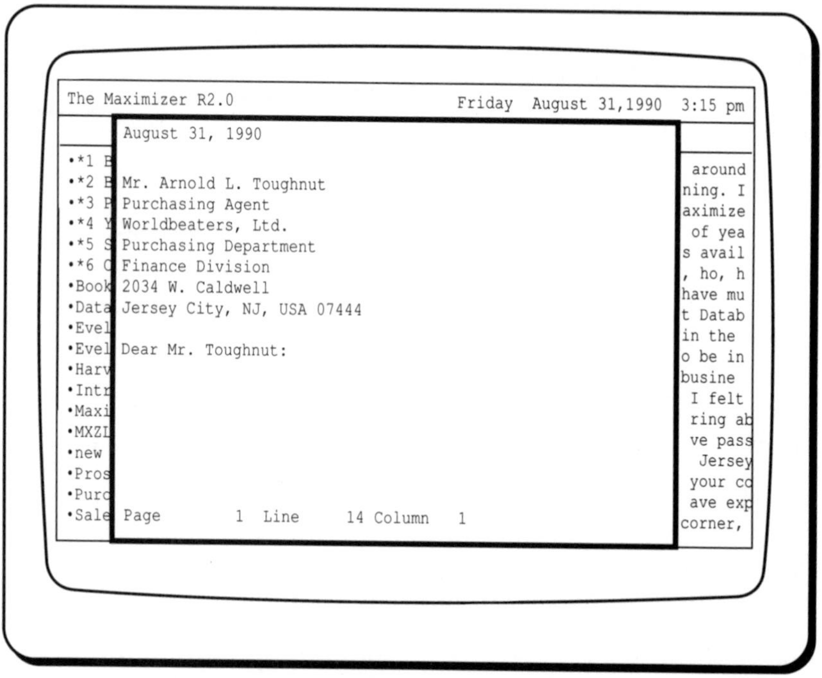

```
The Maximizer R2.0                          Friday  August 31,1990  3:15 pm
      August 31, 1990
•*1 B                                                               around
•*2 B Mr. Arnold L. Toughnut                                       ning. I
•*3 P Purchasing Agent                                             aximize
•*4 Y Worldbeaters, Ltd.                                           of yea
•*5 S Purchasing Department                                        s avail
•*6 C Finance Division                                             , ho, h
•Book 2034 W. Caldwell                                             have mu
•Data Jersey City, NJ, USA 07444                                   t Datab
•Evel                                                              in the
•Evel Dear Mr. Toughnut:                                           o be in
•Harv                                                              busine
•Intr                                                              I felt
•Maxi                                                              ring ab
•MXZI                                                              ve pass
•new                                                               Jersey
•Pros                                                              your co
•Purc                                                              ave exp
•Sale Page        1  Line     14 Column    1                       corner,
```

Used by permission of Richmond Technologies & Software Inc.

automate. Consequently, you'll probably have to convert data from the existing system into the new one. If the sources of data on existing accounts are all manual, then the task is pretty straightforward: Somebody has to enter the relevant information into the appropriate blanks in the SA system, as was illustrated in Figure 2-1.

If, on the other hand, there is an existing computerized customer information system, such as automated billing and accounts receivable, then part—but not all—of the job may already be done. You can simply transfer the information over more or less mechanically. Can't you?

Well, no, not exactly. In all probability the accounting department's definition of a customer may differ from the sales department's. Accounting may consider the client's accounts payable department as "customer" and plant and warehouse locations as "customer name and address," for example. Sales, on the other hand, may view a certain administrative or technical headquarters as the customer location and individuals at those locations as the key contacts. Furthermore, responsibility may be spread among a number of different sales offices or representatives or distributors. So, the problem of mapping existing data over into the new system is not as simple as it appears and may require a lot of planning and analysis before you can actually "push the button."

Customer numbering is an important issue in the case of industrial and commercial accounts, especially if there are multiple subsidiaries, divisions, branches, and other buying and influencing points. It would be nice to adopt a system that enables you to bring some or all of that information together in order to formulate pricing, plan better coverage, use success in one area to promote sales in another, and coordinate sales and customer service activities throughout the target company, no matter how diverse and dispersed it might be. Perhaps you already have a comprehensive account numbering scheme that allows you to link different members of corporate "families" to one another. If not, perhaps you should think of adopting a commercially available one, such as Duns Numbers from Dun & Bradstreet.

Accounting records and sales department records can be quite different. Certainly, they share some universals: the name of the customer, the type of account, the line of business if it's more than a consumer account, the type and volume of business done with the account, and certain names, addresses, and telephone numbers (if they're the same for selling and billing purposes). However, sales wants to know all about decision, influencing, and coordinating points; it needs a running account of selling and servicing activities for each of these, as well as information on coverage, problems, complaints, satisfaction, competitive threats, and future plans.

That's where the accumulated account and contact records illustrated in Figures 2-1 through 2-11 come in.

The Contact Record—Its Relation to the Account Record

A contact is someone within an account who is involved with the sale of your goods or services to that account. It could be the decision maker, whether CEO or purchasing agent, or anybody else who has something to say about whether or what the company buys from you and whether it will continue to do so. In most business accounts for most suppliers there is more than a single relevant contact. Therefore, by definition, multiple contact records are needed for each account. Matters are further complicated, as stated earlier, by the fact that there are very often multiple accounts within a single corporate family—and you may need to relate them all at times.

Most SA users have found that the most practical solution to the necessary record keeping and active tracking of this multiplicity is to assign a single account record to each "customer," or major final decision/buying point, and allow multiple contact records to attach to each account record. Multiple customers within a single corporate family are linked usually in one of two ways—through a hierarchically structured account numbering scheme, such as Duns Numbers, or via a master account record, perhaps maintained at headquarters under the care of the major accounts group or a similar department.

The point here is not to overcomplicate things. A representative who is going to be working with a computerized tracking system should be able to access information within it by any of three simple, directly relevant means:

1. *Company (account) name.* No matter that the L. P. Jones Company is a subsidiary of Worldbeaters, Ltd. The representative handling the L. P. Jones account should be able to access it as Jones or LPJ or something else relevant and familiar.

2. *Contact name.* A rep who wants to contact Patricia Smith—even if she's momentarily forgotten that Smith works for the L. P. Jones Company, much less that the company is a subsidiary of Worldbeaters—should be able to get right to her information by last name, part of last name, or first name and part of last.

3. *Location.* A rep who is planning a trip to Ohio, or Cleveland, or even a particular section of Cleveland should be able to call up all his accounts and contacts in that area to

Figure 2-12. A contact record format—example 1.

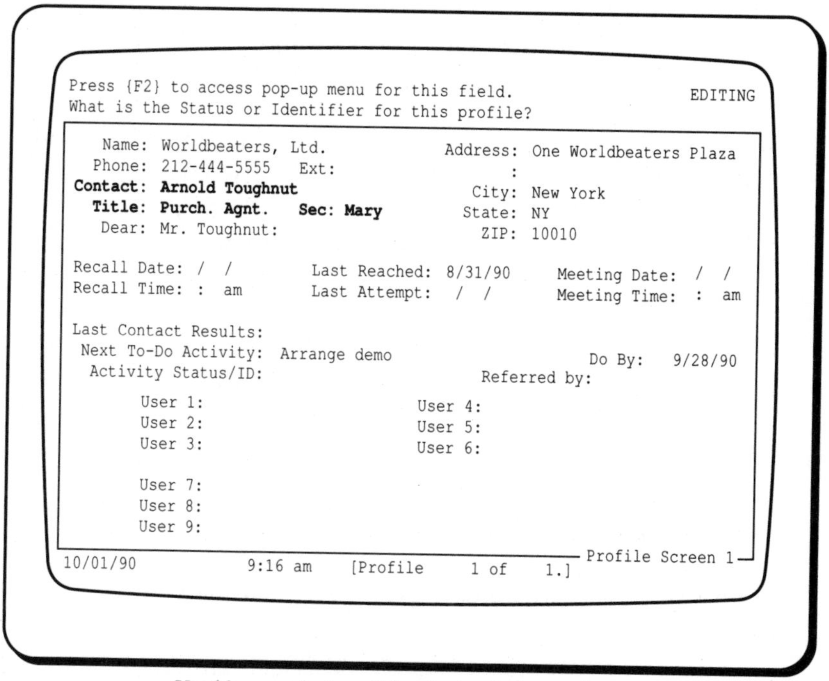

```
Press {F2} to access pop-up menu for this field.                EDITING
What is the Status or Identifier for this profile?

   Name: Worldbeaters, Ltd.              Address: One Worldbeaters Plaza
  Phone: 212-444-5555   Ext:                     :
Contact: Arnold Toughnut                    City: New York
  Title: Purch. Agnt.   Sec: Mary          State: NY
   Dear: Mr. Toughnut:                       ZIP: 10010

Recall Date:  /  /       Last Reached: 8/31/90     Meeting Date:  /  /
Recall Time:  :  am      Last Attempt:  /  /       Meeting Time:  :  am

Last Contact Results:
 Next To-Do Activity: Arrange demo                  Do By:   9/28/90
  Activity Status/ID:                     Referred by:
       User 1:                     User 4:
       User 2:                     User 5:
       User 3:                     User 6:

       User 7:
       User 8:
       User 9:
10/01/90          9:16 am    [Profile    1 of    1.]  Profile Screen 1
```

Used by permission of Conductor Software, Inc.

review them or perhaps to formulate a printed or on-screen report of all future plans and forward commitments to accounts and contacts in the targeted area.

Figures 2-12 and 2-13 illustrate account and contact record formats from a currently popular SA software package called ACT! from Conductor Software, Inc. You'll note that there is a space for designating one key contact within an account on the first screen (Figure 2-12); on the second screen for each account (Figure 2-13), there is space for more information on the key contact and an opportunity to designate the names and phone numbers of two alternate contacts.

A number of other SA packages, such as the one illustrated in Figures 2-1 through 2-11, allow an unlimited number of contacts to be appended to each account. Note also that ACT!

Figure 2-13. A contact record format—example 2.

```
Press {F2} to access pop-up menu for this field.                    EDITING
What is this Alternate Contact's Phone Number?  (Area Code First)

      Contact: Arnold Toughnut
       Phone2: 201-472-6321    Ext:          City: Jersey City
     Address2: Purch. Dept./Fin. Div.       State: NJ
             : 2034 W. Caldwell               ZIP: 07444

  Alternate 1: Jane Lane                Alternate 2: Paul Timothy
        Title: Asst. Purch. Agnt.             Title: Asst. to Jane Lane
        Phone:    -   -      Ext:             Phone:    -   -        Ext:
 Last Reached:   /  /                  Last Reached:   /  /

   User 10:                           User 13:
   User 11:                           User 14:
   User 12:                           User 15:

        Total Phoned:                   Last Meeting:   /  /
      Total Reached:                  Total Meetings:

 No. of Letters sent:                  Profile Owner:
 Date of Last Letter:   /  /         Profile Manager:
 Name of Last Letter:                Profile Created:   /  /
                                                        Profile Screen 2
10/01/90            9:20 am    [Profile      1 of     1.]
```

Used by permission of Conductor Software, Inc.

allows up to fifteen "User" data fields that can be named and used for any purpose desired; some packages allow fewer, some more, and some are completely open-ended. Brokers Ally, from Scherrer Resources, Inc., in contrast to both ACT! and The Maximizer, has no contact record apart from the specific customer, because in the business for which it is designed, retail stock brokerage, the contact is the account. On the other side of the ledger, several functions are found in Brokers Ally that are not common in industrial packages, for example, an appended portfolio record for each account that details such data as what securities the customer owns, when purchased, the price, and current gain or loss. Similarly, EZ Data, an SA package designed for insurance sales representatives, maintains records of insurance policies, trust accounts, equity holdings, and pension funds and tracks the underwriting of an insurance policy, something totally foreign to other types of packages.

ASIS, an industrial-style SA package from Computer Technology Consultants, Inc. (illustrated in Figures 2-14 and 2-15) leaves room for precisely four contacts per account (Figure 2-15). On the other hand, screen 1 (Figure 2-14) has space for an entirely separate "Remit" name and address for billing purposes.

No two SA packages are exactly alike—exactly as easy to use, as flexible, as applicable to a specific line of business, and as appropriate for communications or for independent use. That's part of what makes the field so fascinating and what keeps consultants and systems integrators so busily and gainfully employed.

Figure 2-14. Sample contact screen (customer information).

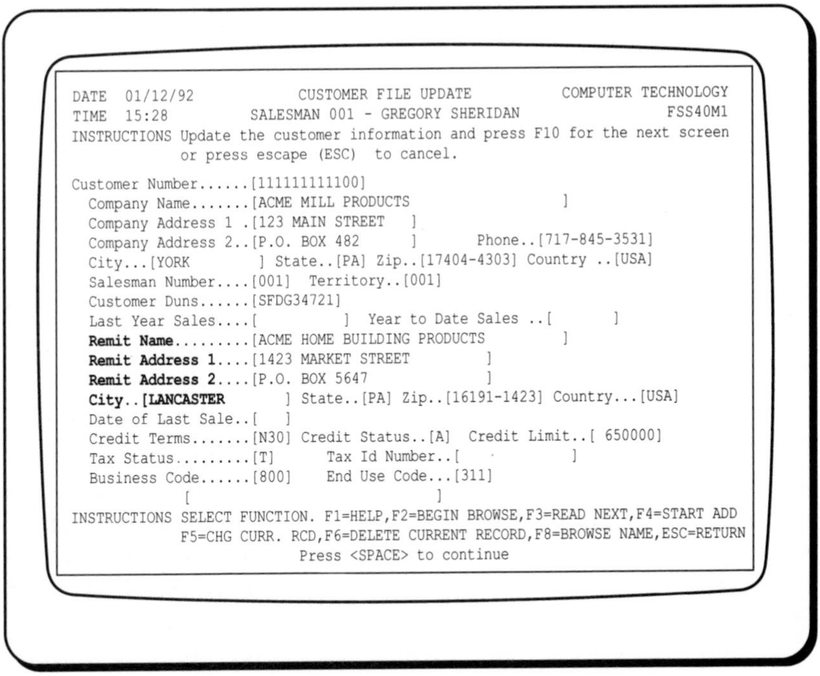

```
DATE  01/12/92              CUSTOMER FILE UPDATE           COMPUTER TECHNOLOGY
TIME  15:28            SALESMAN 001 - GREGORY SHERIDAN                FSS40M1
INSTRUCTIONS Update the customer information and press F10 for the next screen
             or press escape (ESC)  to cancel.

Customer Number......[111111111100]
  Company Name.......[ACME MILL PRODUCTS                  ]
  Company Address 1 .[123 MAIN STREET   ]
  Company Address 2..[P.O. BOX 482      ]        Phone..[717-845-3531]
  City...[YORK          ] State..[PA] Zip..[17404-4303] Country ..[USA]
  Salesman Number....[001]  Territory..[001]
  Customer Duns......[SFDG34721]
  Last Year Sales....[           ]  Year to Date Sales ..[          ]
  Remit Name.........[ACME HOME BUILDING PRODUCTS         ]
  Remit Address 1....[1423 MARKET STREET          ]
  Remit Address 2....[P.O. BOX 5647               ]
  City..[LANCASTER        ] State..[PA] Zip..[16191-1423] Country...[USA]
  Date of Last Sale..[  ]
  Credit Terms.......[N30] Credit Status..[A]  Credit Limit..[ 650000]
  Tax Status.........[T]      Tax Id Number..[              ]
  Business Code......[800]    End Use Code...[311]
             [                              ]
INSTRUCTIONS SELECT FUNCTION. F1=HELP,F2=BEGIN BROWSE,F3=READ NEXT,F4=START ADD
             F5=CHG CURR. RCD,F6=DELETE CURRENT RECORD,F8=BROWSE NAME,ESC=RETURN
                          Press <SPACE> to continue
```

Used by permission of Computer Technology Consultants, Inc.

How Does the Information Get Into the System?

Downloaded Customer Data

Having very carefully specified which kind of information in exactly what kind of identification scheme you want from the existing MIS system (e.g., existing computerized shipping and accounting files), you can "download" or "import" the data automatically, probably with some help from the MIS people. Having accomplished that, there still remain serious issues regarding maintenance of the two files, how new accounts find their way into each, and how changes and deletions are coordinated between the two. Appropriate systems and procedures have to be devised and put in place (more on this in our discussion of implementation in Chapter 12).

Figure 2-15. Sample prospect file screen.

```
DATE  01/12/92            PROSPECT FILE UPDATE             COMPUTER TECHNOLOGY
TIME  16:28          SALESMAN 001 - GREGORY SHERIDAN                   FSS40M2

Contacts
1 Name..[ERIC SCHENK            ]      Salutation..[Mr. Eric Schenk            ]
  Title.[V.P. SALES        ]           Phone.......[717-843-5487] Ext. [3345]
  Addr1.[123 MAIN STREET           ]   Addr2..[P.O. BOX 482                    ]
  City..[YORK              ] St....[PA] Zip....[17404     ]      Country..[USA]
2 Name..[DAVE WELLS             ]      Salutation..[Mr. Dave Wells             ]
  Title.[REGIONAL MANAGER  ]           Phone.......[215-453-4820] Ext. [1100]
  Addr1.[2031 RITTENHOUSE SQUARE   ]   Addr2..[                                ]
  City..[PHILADELPHIA      ] St....[PA] Zip....[19103-5858]      Country..[USA]
3 Name..[KARL RICE              ]      Salutation..[Mr. Karl Rice              ]
  Title.[DISTRICT MANAGER  ]           Phone.......[309-682-5737] Ext. [1029]
  Addr1.[1701 NORTH 17TH STREET    ]   Addr2..[P.O. BOX 1315                   ]
  City..[BALTIMORE         ] St....[MD] Zip....[45626-1315]      Country..[USA]
4 Name..[                       ]      Salutation..[                           ]
  Title.[                  ]           Phone.......[            ] Ext. [    ]
  Addr1.[                          ]   Addr2..[                                ]
  City..[                  ] St....[  ] Zip....[    CONTACTS      ]     [     ]

                    [                                  ]
INSTRUCTIONS SELECT FUNCTION. F1=HELP,F2=BEGIN BROWSE,F3=READ NEXT,F4=START ADD
             F5=CHG CURR. RCD,F6=DELETE CURRENT RECORD,F8=BROWSE NAME,ESC=RETURN
                           Press <SPACE> to continue
```

Used by permission of Computer Technology Consultants, Inc.

Data Downloaded as a Lead

In many systems, a customer first appears as a suspect, or lead record, downloaded to the field from somebody in the home office who handles lead "bingo cards," "800" number inquiries, trade show contact cards, or similar sources. As further qualifying and selling steps are taken, the record is updated until that happy day when the first sale is recorded—or the less happy one when the customer is put into mothballs as a lost cause. Even then, however, the account should stay alive in the sense that it can be resurrected by some appropriate promotional means in the future.

Data Downloaded From an Exogenous Source

In some cases the leads you begin with are purchased names and associated data from some outside source, such as a list house. In some (rare) cases these are downloaded directly to sales representatives and constitute a kind of territory reservoir from which the rep can draw for prospecting purposes. Some companies move through an orchestrated series of steps for further qualifying prospects before delivery of such lists to representatives. In either case, the representative begins telephoning or calling with a computerized record already resident in the system. As the qualifying and selling drama unfolds, the record is kept up to date as both a current pointer and a historical indicator of what should happen, what is happening, and what has happened.

Data Entered Locally

However the account record begins, it soon takes on a life of its own in the hands of the skilled sales or telesales representative handling the account. The representative—either directly by keyboard or through a clerical intermediary—signifies each action step planned, each step taken, the results, and, of course, what's next and when.

What keeps the file current? In the case of outside "feeds" (from such sources as the corporate billing file), appropriate updating procedures have to be put in place. If you're dealing with a major national or international account that is handled from several locations, then a framework for exchange of information has to be set up. (Chapter 5 discusses the issue of communications.)

By and large, the accuracy and consistency of SA data in the hands of sales representatives depends entirely on the representatives themselves. If they use it to their own benefit, and if that benefit depends on having correct information, then the representative will see to it that the corrections are made and, in fact, will make the changes herself most of the time. Telephone numbers will be correct if the representative uses them to dial contacts; addresses will be accurate if the representative uses the system for correspondence and literature fulfillment. Call records will be accurate and complete if the representative uses the system to generate call reports automatically for management review. Business potential, likelihood, and timing estimates will be up to date to the extent the representative uses them as the basis for local grass-roots sales forecasting.

Still and all, some trash will accumulate in the system and will need to be reviewed and hauled away periodically. Some of this review may be accomplished by matching against corporate data, some by simply purging records that have not been used for a given period, say a year, and most by a systematic manual review to see what's out of kilter or no longer relevant.

Other Types of Data and Functions

Comments and Notes

Virtually every SA system invites the recording of notes and comments directly into the account and contact record. This constitutes one of the most valuable features of SA. Data—commitments, observations, events, plans, ideas—recorded into an SA system are there for good, or for as long as you need them to be. They constitute a running account of everything relevant to selling, servicing, and keeping the customer.

Dates

SA systems are big on dates. Most of them automatically record the date, often the time, that events occur in which they have a role—for example, phone calls, letters, and mailing labels they initiate or that are processed through them. When a person enters an action item into the system, it demands to know when, or by when, the designated action is to take place. Any future commitment in the form of next visit, next phone contact, send proposal, or send brochure requires a date. And most systems are set up to pour those dates and events directly into the representative's computerized personal calendar.

Diary/Calendar/Scheduling

Time is every sales representative's most valuable and most limited commodity; therefore SA tackles the issue of representative scheduling in a very vigorous fashion. As we have noted, almost all SA systems have action- and commitment-recording facilities. It is a simple matter to flow this data into a matrix organized like a monthly, weekly, or daily calendar. All such systems allow manual entry into the calendar and are designed to cover future activities that are not directly related to a particular account, such as personal time, staff meetings, or time needed to prepare a mass mailing or a seminar.

Most SA systems have alarms and "hot list" features to alert users to important upcoming events and to nag them after the fact if no new data have been entered.

Automatic Follow-Up

Not only can alarms and reminders be triggered, but the system can actually be instructed to take action on its own. For example, in the case of telemarketing-oriented systems, the next number to be called may come up and be dialed automatically without the user having to initiate anything. Some systems can be set up to mail follow-ups after a given number of days to contacts who have not responded to a previous calling or mailing. They can be set up to mail anniversary or birthday cards to clients a predetermined number of working days prior to the event without the representative having to do anything but turn on the daily mailing routine.

Telephone Support

Professional telesales and telemarketing applications are discussed in Chapter 4, but it is important to note here the very significant telephone support features available as well to the up-and-down-the-street sales representative. Most representatives spend as much time on the telephone with customers and prospects as they do in front of them—some much more. A combination of directory, dialing, logging, and follow-up features can be a powerful boost to the effectiveness of that telephone time. Figure 2-16 illustrates the basic account screen

Figure 2-16. A typical call report system—step 1.

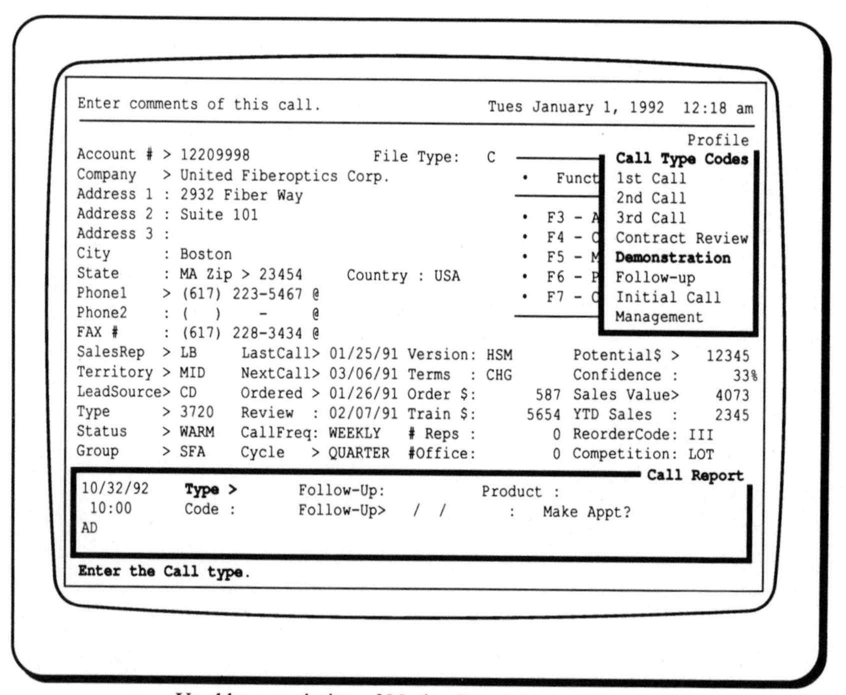

Used by permission of Market Power, Inc.

for a hypothetical company called United Fiberoptics, using an SA package called Matrix from Market Power, Inc. Suppose you have just completed a demonstration of product 21 to United Fiberoptics. Notice at the bottom of the screen a "Call Report" section, which you called up with a single key and are now in the process of filling in. The cursor is on the call "Type" field near the bottom left. Notice that in the upper right corner of the screen a menu of selections for "Call Type Codes" has popped up. The pointer has been moved to "Demonstration" by using the arrow keys, and you are about to push Return, which will deliver the right code for this call report.

Note that this is exactly what has happened, not only to the type field but to all the others as well, in Figure 2-17. The only thing you have typed is the optional last line, noting that the demo went well and that the prospect is awaiting a proposal.

Figure 2-17. A typical call report system—step 2.

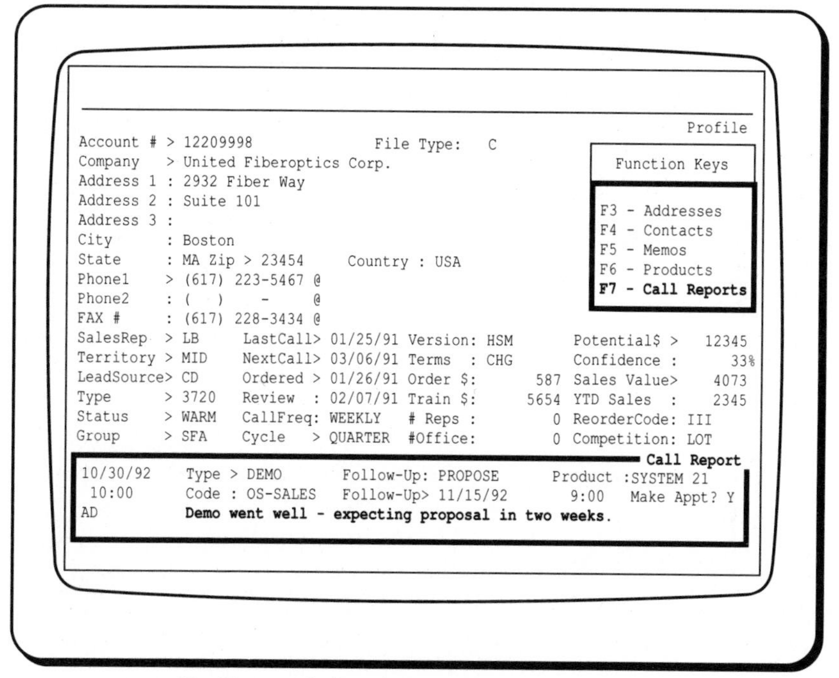

Used by permission of Market Power, Inc.

Automating Reports via SA Systems

Standard Reports

Virtually every SA system has a repertoire of standard reports that can be reviewed on screen, printed out locally, transmitted to headquarters, filed, or mailed. Typical features include:

- "To do" lists
- Overdue action lists
- Weekly and monthly call reports
- New account closes
- Expense reports
- Travel reports
- Monthly activity (statistical) reports
- Periodic account or territory sales forecasts
- Account lists
- Suspense items in need of action by others
- Leads opened, closed, and abandoned
- References received, opened, closed, and abandoned

Figures 2-18 and 2-19 are fragments of two reports generated from the Matrix package with three key depressions each, using sample data.

Ad Hoc Reports

Most systems also support ad hoc reporting, which allows representatives to view their own data and also permits others to view the data, perhaps aggregated with those of other representatives.

For example, suppose a startlingly new application for your industrial fasteners in the manufacture of certain types of wooden but nonupholstered furniture is discovered. You ask all representatives to dip into their territory account records and, using the ad hoc reporting capability, pull out a report of all customers and prospects containing a primary or secondary SIC (Standard Industrial Classification) code of 2511 and call on them immediately or send them a special product bulletin on

Figure 2-18. Sample report fragment created by an SA program.

LEAD SOURCE REPORT
New Accounts

01/01/92 to 01/07/92

ACCOUNT NAME	LEAD SOURCE
Future Systems, Inc. DATE:01/06/92	ATA
Grid Systems DATE:01/19/92	ATA
Managers Software Distributors, Inc. DATE:01/24/92	ATA
Jerrod And Associates DATE:01/06/92	BMR
The Wish-4-Company DATE:01/18/92	BSO
Lanes' Software Store DATE:12/31/91	BYTE
Multi-Scanning Technology Corp. DATE:01/24/92	CAD
United Fiberoptics Corp. DATE:01/24/92	CD
IFS Systems, Inc. DATE:01/24/92	DAT
Imperial Bank of England DATE:01/02/92	PC-WORLD
Andrew Williams, Inc. DATE:01/07/92	QUE
On Line Systems, Inc. DATE:01/04/92	RADIO#17
Canadian Imperial Bank Of Commerce DATE:01/06/92	REF

the new technique, to be followed by a phone call, or some other appropriate strategy.

Alternatively, if you maintain some kind of consolidated or summary account file in the home office, you could pull the list of casual furniture manufacturers yourself, do a mailing, break them out by territory, and request that representatives follow through and report back on level of interest.

Figure 2-19. Sample report produced by an SA program.

```
                    ACCOUNTS SCHEDULED FOR CALLBACK
                DATE OF REPORT: Tuesday October 2, 1992

COMPANY NAME/PHONE
_________________________________________________________________
United Fiberoptics Corp. (617) 223-5467 @
CONTACT:Lori Peterson
MEMO:Will be in the area on 10-24-92 to meet with Tom Carr. Would like
     to meet Lori in the a.m. to demo THE SALES MANAGER.
_________________________________________________________________
Future Systems, Inc. (415) 356-4545 @64
CONTACT:Jim Smith
MEMO:Spoke with Mr. Smith re: setting up training with software install.
     Will have all sales reps there with laptops. Will have overhead
     projector to facilitate MP Trainer. Check on availability of rooms.
_________________________________________________________________
The Wish-4-Company (212) 555-1212 @12
CONTACT:Thomas Halverson
MEMO:Tom likes country music.

_________________________________________________________________
Managers Software Distributors, Inc. (612) 694-2305 @
CONTACT:James Conners
MEMO:Jim plays a good game of tennis and golf.

_________________________________________________________________
Multi-Scanning Technology Corp. (213) 345-5655 @
CONTACT:Simon Chouldjian
MEMO:The last memo entered will appear on the main Profile until another
     memo is entered.
_________________________________________________________________
Jerrod And Associates (618) 582-2429 @
CONTACT:Arthur Schalick
MEMO:The last memo entered will appear on the main Profile until another
     memo is entered.
_________________________________________________________________
IFS Systems, Inc. (212) 213-4444 @234
CONTACT:James Thompson
MEMO:The last memo entered will appear on the main Profile until another
     memo is entered.
_________________________________________________________________
Imperial Bank of England (501) 444-2000 @
CONTACT:Sam Wilson
MEMO:Meeting set for 3-8-93 for VP of Marketing.

_________________________________________________________________
Andrew Williams, Inc. (213) 444-5000 @
CONTACT:Andrew Williams
MEMO:Meeting set for 3-8-93 for VP of Marketing.

_________________________________________________________________
Canadian Imperial Bank Of Commerce (416) 555-1212 @
CONTACT:Wendy Turner
MEMO:
```

Used by permission of Market Power, Inc.

Facilitating Linkages With SA

If representatives are totally isolated and independent and do not communicate extensively with each other or with headquarters, linkage between individual SA systems may not be required. Such a situation is rare, however, because there is generally much to be gained by keeping representatives in the increasingly competitive and complex marketplace informed and in touch with each other. Even if the fundamental account data are never shared, as is the case in some businesses, if headquarters needs to pass down guidance, policy, news, competitive data, and other useful information, and if representatives and offices need to exchange leads and worthwhile selling ideas and submit reports and memos to headquarters, then why not accomplish it through the SA system?

Many companies already have data communications networks installed in support of order processing, billing, accounting, production, and other applications. PCs and laptop machines can be connected to a wide area network (WAN) by making them "look like" other terminals already on the network. If that connection is full-time, then the PC or laptop in effect becomes a terminal on the network, although it may also be able to perform other related or unrelated functions at the same time.

By far the most common communication mode for SA systems is dial-up connection, initiated either by the representative or by a central "polling" system, using ordinary modems and voice-grade telephone lines or mobile cellular services. The resulting transmission takes place flawlessly, can flow one way or both ways, and is relatively fast by individual standards; a lengthy memo, half a dozen call reports, and an expense report can be transmitted to headquarters in two or three minutes. Such transmissions go faster than fax, as a matter of fact, because no "white space" is transmitted.

Another common hookup for SA systems is the local area network, or LAN, by which PCs are linked locally, usually in a single office or work group, in a device and data-sharing arrangement. This topic is discussed more fully in Chapter 5, but for the moment, let us say that SA computers thus interconnected can communicate with each other, and through a "gateway" connecting the LAN to other networks, in a seamless and unobtrusive manner.

Such linkages allow for the exchange of useful information among representatives, the exchange of data with field sales management and headquarters, and the completion of routine administrative work in an automatic fashion instead of through the traditional piles of paperwork. In the special case of major accounts spread across several sales territories, it's hard to imagine how an SA system could be very useful without such linkages. Some other special cases discussed in this book are on-line order entry (see Chapter 5), order tracking (see Chapter 1), and electronic data interchange (EDI) (see Chapter 12).

Related Applications of SA Systems

Proposal and Quote Preparation

Every business is different; some require formal quotations, some do business on a handshake or over the telephone. To the extent that your representatives do engage in formal document preparation for customer proposals and quotations, you are probably already employing some kind of computerized word processing to speed the procedure, improve accuracy, and produce better-looking documents.

Many field representatives do their own illustrations and proposals using a combination of company-supplied boilerplate together with their own customizing. This is relatively easy for them to do, and it gets the job done exactly how and when the representative wants it, without being subject to the vagaries of an administrative or secretarial pool that may be overloaded and located far from the scene of the action.

The same thing goes for presentation support, up to and including a complete computer-based "theater." For example, we are often called upon to make selling or consulting presentations to prospects and clients. Both of us make our own overhead transparencies, 35-mm. slides, and flip charts, using commonly available PC-based tools. Why? Because it's faster, it's cheaper, and it gets the presentation done exactly the way we want it. And we can change it easily, at the last minute if need be, only moments before going on stage. Possibly the same capability would be advantageous to your representatives.

Thanks to ever-improving graphics and animation techniques and larger and larger magnetic disk and compact disk storage capabilities, computers—even portables—are acquiring the capacity to produce sophisticated presentations for both selling and training. Once again, businesses vary in their needs; some never resort to canned presentations, some have no need for them. But to the extent that the presentation can be made to vary interactively, with the representative or the customer at the controls, adjusting the dialog to the whims, interests, and needs of the viewer, perhaps a new meaning of the word *canned* will evolve. It is not out of line to assert that right now, today, using existing artificial intelligence techniques, an interactive presentation can be created that is the equal of the best that an experienced trainer could do. This suggests the possibility that a rep's best efforts could be enhanced by the use of such techniques and that the performance of the average salesperson could approach that of the "stars" in the organization.

Computer-based interactive presentation material can be effective as a training tool for customers and for sales representatives, communicating how to use the product or service in the first case and how to sell it in the latter. Although not the subject of this book—perhaps of a future one—such capabilities can be made an important adjunct to SA systems, thereby greatly extending their value to the representative.

Benefits of Sales Automation

Benefits for the Representative

Having access to a miraculous little box full of information on suspects, prospects, and customers—a box that issues reminders of what to do when, that grinds out first-rate proposals and presentation materials as needed with very little human assistance, and that handles most of the corresponding, telephoning, and administrative headaches that plague salespeople—sounds like sales nirvana. Actually it can be, and is being, achieved in a growing number of companies. It is still early in the game, though, and a lot is still unknown, particularly about making these tools acceptable and easy to use for the representatives involved. Much of what follows in this book deals with the practical concerns and with making these benefits readily accessible to salespeople.

Benefits for the Sales Manager

Certainly, a modern automation tool that improves the productivity, performance, and predictability of sales representatives benefits a sales manager. But this is only part of the story. The manager gets to use the same tool kit for his own purposes: receiving, compiling, and reviewing call reports; combining grass-roots sales forecasts into area-, office-, and companywide projections; tracking the activities of each representative and the status of accounts in each territory; allocating territories based on business potential; coaching specific representatives on specific sales situations or on problems or weaknesses in matters of coverage, activity levels, tactics, and follow-through.

The manager can have as much information and awareness of what's happening in the field as she wants through a sales automation system. Practical limits, however, dictate how far a manager should go in using the system as a tool for keeping tabs on reps and for assessing field performance (see Chapter 10 for a discussion of human factors in SA).

Benefits for Other Management and Staff

A properly designed and implemented SA system can pay huge dividends to decision makers throughout the organization by virtue of the nature of information it collects, that is, a complete and up-to-date picture of what is happening in each prospect and customer account. Most current information systems don't have even a fraction of this data at hand, and most collect what information they do on a monthly, quarterly, or even annual basis. And information delayed is no information at all.

The potential for so-called decision support applications is great for an SA system networked in a way that brings details together quickly and makes them available in convenient and digestible formats to decision makers and strategists. Nowhere is this clearer than in the marketing and product development realms. Information on what's selling to what kind of customer, what isn't, and why is priceless for a marketer, product manager, or product planner. Accurate forecasting, derived on an account-by-account basis, is equally valuable. Knowing what deals are lost to which competitors and why is similarly of great importance. There is a caveat, however: The window into what's happening in the field has to be a painless by-product of what the field reps need to do for themselves; otherwise some grave difficulties may arise in motivating them to use the system.

Benefits for Your Customers

No discussion of the benefits of sales automation would be complete without mentioning what it can do for the customer. We talk more about how it can enhance cooperation between buyer and seller, to the benefit of each, in Chapter 3. By and large, SA offers a more informed, accurate, and dependable basis upon which your representatives and your company can interact with the marketplace, which translates into better-informed decisions by the customer and better, more responsive service by your company before, during, and after the sale.

In addition, the SA system can provide a conduit through which customers can obtain not just information—although that alone justifies many such systems—but the tangible support of technical and logistical resources. Representatives and in some cases customers themselves can pass requests for special action on up the line to customer service, production, engineering, R&D, and other specialists, with a high degree of assurance that the request will reach its destination at the speed of light and in a sufficiently regularized format that it cannot easily be ignored or set aside.

Some Real and Imagined Drawbacks of Sales Automation

It's probably not fair to close this lengthy and glowing paean to sales automation without at least mentioning some downside aspects. We wrestle with each of them in subsequent chapters and suggest ways to prevent or overcome them, but there are some serious problems and pitfalls connected with implementing SA that should be stated at the start. These include:

- *Playing "computer jockey" instead of selling.* Is it possible your representatives will become so taken with the technology that computer wizardry will become the major preoccupation? It has happened. There are ways to guard against it.
- *Loss of the personal touch.* Does computer regimentation cause representatives to become automatons, out of touch with the personalities involved and relying too much on computation instead of that all-important selling instinct? We think not. If anything, a good SA system should free up more of the representative's time and thoughts for the person-to-person aspects of selling, but it is well to be sure in the planning process that this will, indeed, be the case. We deal with this issue in several chapters covering planning, implementation, human factors, and training.
- *Cost, technical, and obsolescence issues.* A fully implemented, companywide sales automation system is expensive, costing as much as $15,000 per representative, depending on who does the calculating and how and, of course, on the extent of the system. Yet we've often found evidence of ample benefits supporting such expenditures. (The topic of feasibility, cost, and justification is dealt with at length in Chapter 9).

After the SA system is installed, won't it obsolesce quickly? Yes. Whatever you can plan or even conceive now is already obsolete as compared to what will come off the drawing boards in the near future. The trick is to keep the system flexible, open-ended, and modular, so that each important advance can be added and the system can grow with the technology and with your changing needs.

This is not an idle dream or unattainable goal. Many SA systems are under constant evolutionary development yet produce solid benefits right now, day in and day out. American Express, Frito-Lay, and Hewlett-Packard have had their SA systems under development for several years and have derived major benefits at each stage along the way. The chairman of Frito-Lay has been quoted as saying his system is saving the company $20 million a year; and Hewlett Packard has documented increases of 27 percent in face-to-face selling time and 10 to 15 percent in sales productivity, along with a major improvement in customer satisfaction levels, as a direct result of its SA system. Yet this system, which is in the hands of all its representatives, has only about half of its intended applications and features fully implemented.

Go thou and do likewise.

Chapter 3

Managing the Customer Relationship

To dramatize the importance of successfully managing relationships with existing customers, imagine what your business would be like if you had to achieve all your revenue each year from new accounts, with no carryover, no repeat business, and no reorders. For most companies the results would be catastrophic; revenue targets would be unachievable and marketing costs as a percentage of revenue would simply go through the roof.

To take another tack, calculate what it costs to attract and develop new accounts—including advertising, promotion, public relations, and a healthy piece of total sales department expense—divided by the number of new accounts closed in a year's time. Compare the result to the out-of-pocket costs of maintaining an existing account. There is no comparison!

Not only is the process of attracting attention in the marketplace and leading "suspects" through the long, arduous, and costly ritual of becoming first prospects and then buyers extremely expensive, it is a sometimes hit and mostly miss process. That is, a majority of the effort is spent on targets who do not buy; most companies sell only a fraction of the suspects who flit across the horizon.

Keeping Customers Satisfied

Once an account becomes a customer, it makes sense to go all out to keep it that way. Surprisingly, many companies do not.

Sold accounts are turned over to the second team, the junior varsity. Nonsales-oriented customer service representatives are given responsibility for managing the account but are not given the necessary tools and training to go along with those responsibilities. These undertrained, undersupported people are then frequently measured on performance criteria that have little to do with satisfying and keeping customers, such as the total number of calls received or the number of "trouble reports" initiated, instead of overall account retention rate, average level of reported account satisfaction, number of problems resolved without referral to others, or number and value of suggested new ideas for improving customer satisfaction.

Even if the top sales professionals in your organization retain their sold-account responsibilities or a top-quality, well-trained and well-motivated service representative takes over, it's a sure bet that lots of other people in your organization come in contact with the customer or are called upon to perform business duties directly concerned with delivering results and fulfilling obligations to the account. How well-trained, motivated, and informed are these people? How much do they know about the account? How much do they need to know or could they benefit from knowing? How much really useful information about the account, its needs, its concerns, and its problems gets back to those who can do something about it? How well-protected are you from the problems that can be created by a single cranky, lazy, or uninformed employee who mishandles an encounter with someone from the customer's shop?

The issue comes down to the fact that to a customer dealing with a member of your organization, that member *is* your company. It doesn't matter what your policy is, or your official credo, or how high the degree of professionalism and skill exhibited by your official account manager—if the customer gets bad treatment, bad service, or bad information, your company will be perceived negatively. That's why so many companies implementing so-called total quality programs don't stop with the product: They insist on a sweeping alteration of the company's culture that makes every encounter, phone call, document, and transaction the occasion for a "quality" experience. This attitude reaches far beyond achieving "zero defects" in the plant; it extends to cleaning up cigarette butts and soda cans in the parking lot, eliminating smudges on bills of lading, answering the telephone with a verbal smile and a helpful attitude, and, we think, providing employees with the best possible tools to assist them in responding to and solving customer problems and needs.

Let's bring it down to cases. Suppose we are advising you on the design and selection of a sales automation system. After painstaking analysis, with all kinds of practical considerations at hand, we have recommended a particular approach, namely that instead of having your field sales representatives carry laptop or handheld computers, you have them interact with the system verbally over cellular telephones in dialog with sales secretaries back in the office.

Suppose now that one of our service people, while having coffee with one of your key players, relates her personal observations on how well another of her accounts, which happens to be a competitor of yours, is doing, having equipped its sales force with portable computers. "Also, the representatives are doing a lot of their work after hours and on weekends," she goes on to say. Your man is impressed.

However, we did not come to our conclusion lightly. There are good, solid tactical and strategic reasons for it in this case. We built our brief carefully. It took quite a while to develop a consensus. Furthermore, unknown to our coffee-klatch strategist, we have given thought to the after-hours question and have concluded arrangements for nationwide coverage using inbound "800" numbers through a third party.

Now suddenly confusion reigns, and our credibility is seriously weakened. Fanciful example? Many companies try to speak with a single voice by imposing strong discipline and rigid structure throughout their organizations, and big organizations get especially good at policing utterances to the outside world and making sure that no heterodoxy escapes from under the iron blanket. But how much better it is to let employees understand what the company is up to and encourage them to help communicate it in a cooperative, spirited, and unified way.

In our example, the harm done was psychological; but it could have been worse. A technical support representative could have misunderstood how a customer was using a particular piece of machinery and given wrong advice, causing a catastrophic failure. For example, a customer who had not had a basic course could have been mistakenly enrolled in an advanced course, wasting much of his, the instructor's, and other students' time. Or a customer could have mistakenly been told that a particular shipment was on the way, when in reality a supplier labor stoppage would prevent it from reaching its destination until long after the customer's critical need had passed.

There is a way to get everyone "singing from the same hymnal" while arming them with more information and facilitating better coordination than they've ever experienced. These results can be achieved through the use of a relationship management system, which is nothing more than sales automation with a few expanded features and significantly wider accessibility.

Figure 3-1 shows the schematic structure of a typical SA system in which the sales representative, sales managers, and home office decision makers and analysts play a role and enjoy the benefits. The representative puts in lots of information about what he's doing and receives help in prioritizing and managing those activities and reporting on them. Sales management gives and gets guidance in the fulfillment of its responsibilities, and many of its routine administrative chores are done automatically. Marketing puts in solid product, market, and competitive data and gets back accurate measurement of field results and fresh marketplace intelligence. Management promulgates guidelines and policies through the system and gains clear insight into what's really happening in the sales and marketing arena.

Now, let's add some additional features to help serve the account after it's been sold (see Figure 3-2). Here we've incorporated an "interface," as the technicians call it, with components of corporate MIS (management information systems) concerned with order entry and order processing. Not every business requires this information, but most companies en-

Figure 3-1. Sales/marketing database.

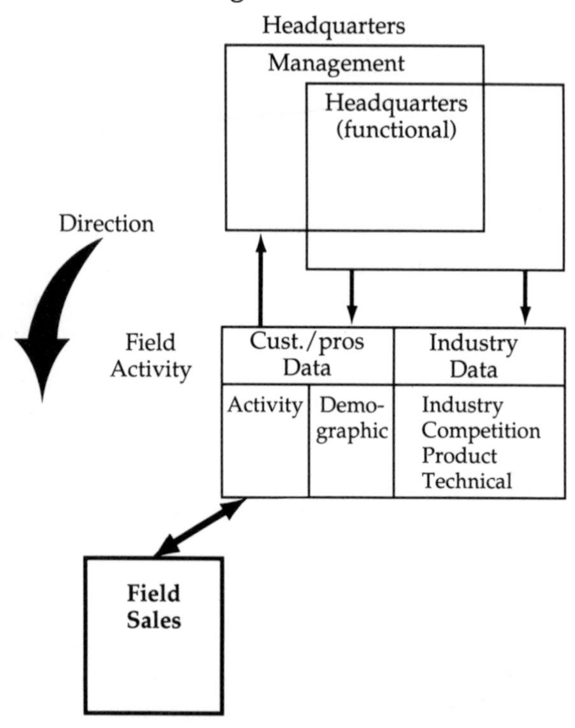

gaged in manufacturing and/or distribution benefit from the ability to enter orders immediately, electronically, and directly from the field, perhaps with immediate confirmation and notification of stockouts or possible delays, together with recommended alternatives. The field representative can use this interface to obtain up-to-the-minute manufacturing or shipping status information for customers while the order is in process; also, the representative and her managers may find it useful to be able to dissect and analyze past and present purchasing patterns of this and other accounts. Adding this information to the database doesn't change the basic product or service you sell, yet you've succeeded in adding value to it. Value added may be your only edge, your competitive differentiator, as more and more sophisticated competitors appear; it may also be the only means of maintaining a decent profit margin.

Figure 3-2. Sales/marketing database interfaced with MIS.

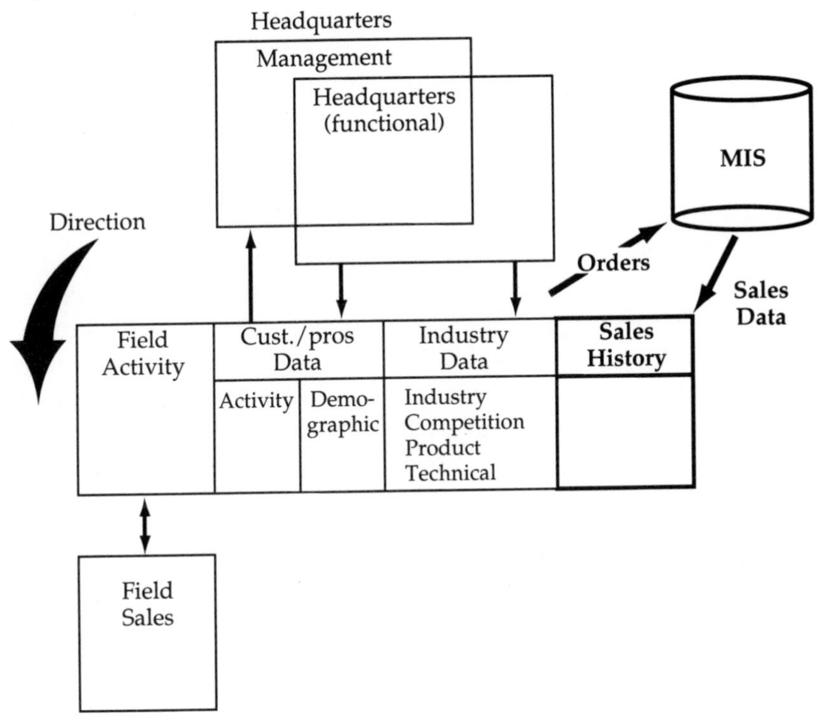

What, you say? This is so elementary it hardly bears stating! Of course we're dedicated to the value added concept! Of course we want such things as competitive differentiation and strategic advantage!

Our question to you is, How are you going to create and maintain it? If you depend on the better mousetrap principle, what prevents somebody else, sooner or later, from introducing a still better one? If you depend on megascale, low-cost production, what prevents another company from doing likewise, perhaps even going one better? If you depend on "presence," financial heft, geographic coverage, or some other physical, monetary, or organizational advantage, you must admit that mergers, restructuring, or foreign competition may alter that comfortable picture unexpectedly. However, there is one durable advantage that, once achieved, is very resistant to erosion, and that is your relationship with customers. If it's outstandingly good, it will survive all the perils we've listed and then some and will imbue your company with added value that competitive price, product, and promotional heft can't touch. That's why we believe technical tools that serve to enhance and perpetuate a solid sales relationship can be of paramount importance.

Frank Popoff, the CEO of Dow Chemical Company, after having doubled the company's sales and quadrupled its profits in only two years, was quoted in a *Marketing News* article as saying, "Today we are developing more synergistic customer and technological partnerships." The article describes various independent marketing organizations operating harmoniously across product lines and describes company teams comprising representatives from marketing, R&D, manufacturing, treasury, foreign exchange, legal, and information systems as responsible for success in joint ventures. But the following statement may be the most telling:

> We achieved marketing growth by focusing on customer success, not customer satisfaction. Sales representatives are constantly analyzing all the customers' quality and productivity concerns, plus offering improved, more timely delivery, accurate orders, and correct packaging.
>
> We're concerned with where our customers want to be five years from now, something we didn't focus on five years back.

If your people are working with customers on solving problems and adding value to their future products and services, it is unlikely that the customers will give up this relationship for some short-run advantage such as quick delivery or a lower price on a few current orders. We believe the real reason many foreign companies find doing business in Japan so difficult is the importance of such relationships. Call it Kieretsu, call it conspiracy—we see it as relationships; Japanese companies work together so closely, trust and depend on each other so completely, that they find it difficult to consider dealing with newcomers, even those with overwhelming immediate product and price advantages. To them, keeping long-term productive relationships intact is more important.

In the interest of promoting relationship selling and the teamwork that goes along with it, you can open up the system for input and output to and from other workers in your company who are involved in responding to customers. They might include technical support, customer service, maintenance, installation, accounting, engineering, research, shipping, top management—anyone who comes in contact with the customer base, however tangentially. The cast varies in each company and every kind of business. But at the very least, if you have any kind of external field service and/or an inside customer service, inquiry, order handling, or troubleshooting kind of function, then they ought to be included in the system, as illustrated in Figure 3-3.

In Figure 3-3, not only is the whole choir singing from the same hymnal, members are writing notes to one another in the margins. If Worldbeaters, Ltd., is having trouble with one of your products, shouldn't field service let everyone concerned with supporting the account know about it and, further, know exactly what remedial action is being taken? Your sales or customer service representative will appear much stronger and more professional when confronted with the problem out of the blue if she is able to respond, "Yes, we're aware of that problem at your Cincinnati office, and engineering is on top of it. Here's what they plan to do." Furthermore, if the matter requires further research or action, shouldn't the individual involved have the same kind of assistance in logging commitments and the same kind of prodding to make sure those commitments are fulfilled as a sales representative pursuing his responsibilities?

It's simply good sense to extend the same recording, tracking, reminding, calendarizing, telephone-dialing, and reporting facilities to everyone concerned with the account and to use the account record as the master switchboard for information and messages that need to reach all employees involved with the account. Does this mean that everything has to be shared? Certainly not. Some parts of the database must be private to the originator or a small circle of authorized partici-

Figure 3-3. A full-scale relationship management system with a sales/marketing database.

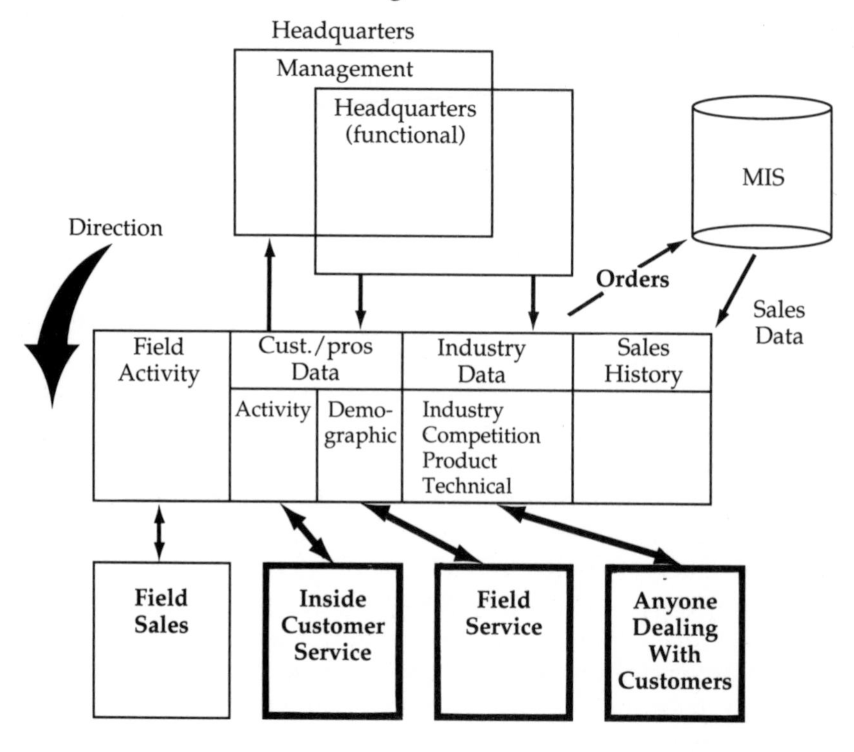

pants. Other parts may reflect masses of local detail of absolutely no interest or relevance to other departments. But certainly there are some key elements that should be made generally visible to all or most of the participants:

- The names, titles, addresses, phone numbers, and responsibilities of key players on both sides, yours and the customer's.
- Current account activity—how important the account is and its sensitivities and priorities, how much business it generates, and whether the level of activity is growing, static, or declining and why.

• Future plans and possibilities with this account—what's coming, and what your organization should begin to get ready for.

• The current status and history of problems with this account—the sore spots and what can be and is being done about them.

• Special projects—custom design or consultations, joint developments, cooperative R&D, joint marketing—anything that sets this account apart and demands special attention or handling by anyone anywhere in your organization.

• A portfolio of observations, insights, news clips, or rumors that might have some bearing on problems, opportunities, and future potential in this account. IBM sales representatives used to say that their best source of information on what was really going on in their accounts was customer engineering, the folks who repaired the machines and kept them running; customers often "let their hair down" with the CEs.

Account records need to be tailored to each functional department—sales, customer service, operations—but certain types of shared data should be held in common, with ample opportunity for all concerned to exchange useful intelligence. The specific information and communications architectures necessary for doing this are the subject of Chapter 5. Conceptually, however, you want a system that provides access to common information and that, in most cases, permits the participants to "converse" with one another electronically when need be.

Improving In-House Coordination and Communication

One of the key characteristics of a relationship management system is that it keep your team marching, if not in lockstep, at least in roughly the same direction. Funneling important communications with the customer through one or a handful of individuals simply will not achieve the same level of service.

For one thing, even a small handful of people can't keep current with one another on a number of different matters, or even one complex one, if they don't work in the same area and see each other constantly. Researcher Tom Allen at the Massachusetts Institute of Technology found in a broad sampling of U.S. companies that people who work more than thirty feet (ten meters) apart have a less than 10 percent chance of communicating with one another as often as once a week. Intracompany communications are the most difficult, most fragile, most easily distorted and disrupted characteristic of any business.

Second, the marketplace conditions faced by most companies today and in the future are so competitive, so diverse, and so complex that a team approach may be the only way to meet them. One department, much less one individual, may well not have the time, the variety of skills, the imagination, or the command over diverse company resources necessary to fulfill the customer's needs.

For example, suppose you sell containers, mainly of glass, and you sit and wait for the customer to design his next generation of product packaging, hoping to bid on it. Where will you be if a resourceful competitor gets into the product and packaging design departments and comes up with a unique and uniquely cost-effective paper package that mates perfectly with the customer's products—for which, in truth, the new packaging has been designed? Even if you're given a chance to bid, in all likelihood you'll be coming from behind against a stacked deck.

Making a sale isn't just a matter of business as usual. It may take a collaborative, creative effort that may span months or years and involve dozens of specialists on both sides. Keeping these specialists current and informed, and coordinating the whole process, will place demands on the sales department that have seldom if ever been faced.

Early involvement may be only one of several new complications facing sales as it works to add value to your products and services in the eyes of your customers. Forward deployment of inventory may be required to meet the customer's new just-in-time production methods. Perhaps fast turnaround, custom design, a twenty-four-hour "hot line" consultation, or any of a myriad of other creative and complex factors needs to be introduced. Keeping up with, much less in command of, all of these elements applied to a whole portfolio of accounts is simply not going to be feasible using 1980s techniques and 1980s technology. The sales department needs help. Fortunately help is at hand.

The Relationship Management System of the 1990s

Architecture aside—that is, who's touching what keyboard and where the data are physically housed—the modern relationship management system has four common characteristics:

1. *It is simple, friendly, and easy to use.* The communications linkage between users is transparent, so that information gets to and from the appropriate parties without their having to master complex communications protocols. Ideally, communicating should be as simple as using the telephone.

2. *It makes commonly needed information commonly available to each and every participant.* If three departments and seven individuals have occasion to telephone Ms. Jones at Worldbeaters, Ltd., concerning purchase orders at one time or another, they should all have access to a common repository (or, at worst, a faithful copy of the common repository) of vital information about Ms. Jones—who she is, what her duties are, what her addresses and telephone numbers are, how to reach her after hours, whom she reports to, what matters need to be directed to her attention and what matters exceed her authority, what special problems or sensitivities exist in dealing with her, who else in your own organization you should confer with before contacting her, and—don't snicker, this isn't meant to be humorous—her interests, her hobbies, the names of her children, or her favorite sports team. Almost all business conversations are leavened with small talk. Since this is the case, why not help make the small talk relevant?

3. *There is some means of adding to the store of knowledge about*

the account for others to see. This is probably done in at least two different ways: (1) notes reflecting what has happened or what has been observed, appended to the basic record for all to see, and (2) an electronic message facility, usually called Email, that allows specific telememos, if you will, to be directed to one or several individuals concerned with serving or managing the account.

The electronic mail feature may be embedded in the relationship management system itself, or it can be available companywide for purposes beyond sales and customer service. What is important is that it be used to keep others, particularly those in other departments or at different locations, informed about what's going on in this and all other accounts in which they play a role.

Incidentally, some people strongly prefer voice mail to Email for this purpose. Certainly, that's a way out for the keyboard-averse or for people on the move. However, we are postulating the existence of a sales automation or relationship management system, one that for the immediate future is going to depend mainly on PCs and terminals with keyboards for access. As long as this is true, a keyboard-oriented Email system imposes no additional threat to or burden on the users. Perhaps in the next century things will be different. (We take a heroic stab at foretelling the future in Chapter 14.) Meanwhile, we stand by the foregoing.

4. *Finally, there has to be local application support particularized for the individual functional user.* For example, the product support group, if you have one, is going to need, in addition to everything else we've described, a trouble-report recording, tracking, and reporting facility, as well as access to technical reference data and, perhaps, a running history of solutions to past problems. To what extent this is or is not integrated into the relationship management system is unimportant so long as the fundamental precepts of intraorganizational, multifunctional information exchange are observed. The systems could be more or less independent, if that turns out to be the optimum way of building them, but they need to be able to exchange data when and where it counts.

For example, Southern New England Telephone Company (SNET) sales and customer service representatives need to access selective data from eight different, incompatible large-scale mainframe computer applications. To relieve the nightmare of requiring field representatives to master the complex on-line protocols of each of these massive applications, the company designed a ninth system, which brings together abstracts of selected data from the other eight needed to answer inquiries and conduct business with subscribers. Now, those in contact with customers can get to everything they need in a more or less instantaneous manner. And it's easy to do. SNET paid particular attention to the "front end" of this sales information system, making it easy to get to any customer's records instantly if the representative knows the subscriber's name, the address of any location occupied by this subscriber, or the number of any telephone assigned to this subscriber anywhere. For SNET, this turned out to be the eminently practical way of bringing together customer relationship information from otherwise disconnected sources.

Have we outlined a fairy tale or sketched the impossible dream? Certainly not. The technology exists today to do everything we've described in almost every business of almost any size. Scale is not a problem. Both Digital Equipment Corporation and General Motors (through its EDS subsidiary) maintain networks of 100,000 or more PCs and terminals. Texas Instruments boasts a network nearly that size.

Scale is not a problem on the low end, either. A PC or a few of them tied together via a local area network (LAN) can be programmed to do everything we've described. Better still, at this end of the spectrum, one is quite likely to find inexpensive, off-the-shelf software, avoiding custom development altogether.

Furthermore, many companies and, in some cases, whole industries (such as financial services) are well down the road toward implementing relationship management systems such as we've described. Chances are when you call your banker, broker, or insurance agent, after a minute or so she is looking at a complete electronic dossier of all the various services, business arrangements, portfolios, and policies that define your dealings with each other. Unsettled claims, overdue balances, idle cash, renewals coming up—the system knows about all these things and forcibly reminds whoever is talking to you about them.

On the other hand, we don't want to mislead you into thinking that such systems are easy to put together and universally accepted. Neither is true. Except for pockets of progress in the financial services sector and in some companies' handling of major accounts, true relationship management systems are few and far between. Yet the enabling technology is growing so rapidly and becoming so inexpensive compared to former costs, and the economic and competitive forces demanding improved methods of dealing with customers are becoming so strong, that few businesses will be able to hold out much longer. The process has already extended itself even to the supermarket checkout line, where in some stores a regular customer proffering a magnetically encoded "frequent shopper card" is automatically granted special, selected discounts and earns points toward further awards and emoluments. In return, of course, the store earns consumer loyalty and a treasure trove of valuable information about individual buying habits, some of which can be sold back to manufacturers for pinpoint measurement of the effectiveness of their promotional efforts.

Probably the greatest single danger faced by designers contemplating such systems is what we call the "5-million-pound marshmallow" syndrome, that is, overcomplexity resulting from trying to do everything for everybody in one system. There are ways, as we discuss in Chapter 5, for keeping smaller, relatively independent, and relatively simple systems in concert with one another without getting them overly enmeshed. This modular, distributed approach is our recommended one.

Chapter 4

Coordination With Marketing, Direct Mail, Telemarketing, and Other Promotional Activities

It's axiomatic that companies have only so much money to spend on sales and marketing. Advertising, in particular, is often looked upon as a discretionary expense, largely because results are hard to pin down directly and the effectiveness of any one campaign, level of spending, or type of appeal is very difficult to determine. The use of sophisticated market research techniques such as audience measurement, consumer response measurement, polling, and focus groups is growing as marketers attempt to overcome this difficulty, and several prestigious business schools are readying graduate degree programs leading to the degree of MMR, or master of market research, intended to match the master of business administration in quality and intensity.

One very simple, effective, and relatively inexpensive way of improving marketing efficiency in most companies—linking marketing campaigns and the frontline selling effort—is regularly overlooked. Such a linkage enables the two aspects of sales to support each other and also enables the latter to feed back results to the former. Evidence that this technique is ignored is the frequency with which companies spend big budgets to generate sales leads, send them to sales offices, and then watch them disappear into a black hole. Other evidence includes product designs that have nothing to do with what customers want, pricing and other policies that are out of step with competition and the marketplace, promotional themes that fail to reflect what the sales department can sell, and, ghastly as it may seem, marketing and home office–based quasi-sales organizations that are set up to promote sales but that end up crossing swords with their own sales departments in the marketplace.

In the rest of this chapter, we explain and promote the kind of sales-marketing communications that companies are finding helpful in promoting understanding, coordination, and mutual support between these two functional areas, which are intimately related in theory but so often isolated and at odds with one another in practice.

Using SA Systems to Target Marketing Activities and Coordinate Sales Programs

A key to successful coordination of sales and marketing is feedback from the field. This can be accomplished through a database incorporating information on demographics, psychographics, activity levels, proposals, competitive data, and notes and comments from the representative, customers, and prospects. What better ammunition can a marketer ask for in fashioning product promotion and development programs than that kind of direct feedback from the trenches? While market research can often reveal similar information and lead to similar conclusions, companies can avoid the expense and delay by simply harvesting the information from a sales automation system already bought and paid for by the sales department! Although the SA system does not deal with the entire population of prospective buyers and the sample of buyers is not scientifically stratified, random, and unbiased, the sample does have one overwhelming virtue: It's real, it's active, and it is responding to real offers of products and services by the company.

Let's look now at the sources of information for marketing and how the information is incrementally enhanced and used.

Static and Dynamic Analysis

Creating a comprehensive picture of all prospects being contacted by the field (and remember that *field* here means everyone soliciting business, even those sitting at telephones in the home office), as well as a demographic study of everyone already sold, is the first step toward understanding where the company's attention is currently focused and where its current business is coming from. In Figure 4-1, we present data on a hypothetical company's prospects "in the mill" worldwide. On the basis of each prospect's position in the sales cycle and the representative's estimate of the potential value of each sale if and when it is closed, the report projects likely sales from this particular portfolio of prospects by time period. This sort of useful picture can be obtained easily by polling a sales automation system.

But this information presents a static picture; useful as it is, it doesn't lend itself very well to experimentation and learning. For that, you need dynamic feedback that conveys the results of advertising, lead-generation, and promotional campaigns. The same kind of linkages that make possible the static analysis can provide a dynamic one as well.

So-called direct marketers, or database marketers, have this process down to a science. They build or acquire a mailing list and then contact (by mail or telephone) a carefully selected sample drawn from different classes of entries on the list. In the case of consumers, this means using respondents who vary by location, socioeconomic class, income level, past shopping habits, or whatever other classifications are available and potentially relevant. In the case of businesses, the classification process typically involves size, line of business, headquarters or branch designation, public or private ownership, and geographic location. In either case, the direct marketer measures the response from the various classifications in order to focus further sales efforts on the high-response categories and eliminate those respondents with little or no interest.

Figure 4-1. An example of a static analysis.

Census of Marketing Activity: Period Ending 8/23

					*Factored Likely Closing Value**		
Domestic	*No. of Prospects*	*No. Commercial*	*No. Industrial*	*Total Forecast Value*	*This Quarter*	*Next Quarter*	*By Year-End*
Eastern Region	404	300	104	1,438,000	570,000	755,160	112,840
Southern Region	212	200	12	763,000	346,000	362,790	54,210
Midwest Region	392	300	92	1,244,000	683,000	488,070	72,930
Pacific Region	275	214	61	816,000	392,000	368,880	55,120
Independent Reps	40	19	21	236,000	160,000	66,120	9,880
U. S. Total	1,323	1,033	290	4,497,000	2,151,000	2,041,020	304,980
Foreign							
Canada & Mexico	598	287	311	2,200,000			
Central America	460	200	260	1,790,800			
South America	300	143	157				
Pacific Rim							
U.K.							
Western Europe							

**Note:* Factored value = est. rev. × % likely to close (derived from sales cycle progress code). Timing per rep estimate, adjusted for cycle code.

The "Greening" of a Lead

Once a lead comes to the attention of sales, it becomes part of the SA database, although it may yet be withheld from field sales until it is further qualified.

To assess the viability of a lead, someone must respond to it, perhaps by mailing a "fulfillment" package consisting of brochures, press releases, or copies of laudatory trade journal articles. The prospect may also be "telequalified." (Sometimes telequalifying happens in the field, but, for illustrative purposes, we are positing a specialized telemarketing function that calls the prospect and inquires whether the response fulfillment information has arrived and is sufficient and whether there is any further interest.) Depending on the response to the telemarketing inquiry, the representative might dispatch further promotional or technical materials, make further follow-up telephone calls, or set up a definite appointment for a field representative to visit. Results of such contacts are carefully entered into the lead record in the database.

If the lead is ready for the field, it is transmitted electronically to the representative handling the particular territory in which the prospect resides. If further material is to be sent, a mailing label and a picking slip are produced as part of a batch printing for the literature fulfillment unit that will pick and ship the desired documents. Alternatively, the prospect's record may turn up on the telemarketer's screen in two weeks at the same time the system is automatically dialing the prospect's telephone number for a follow-up call.

Even if the prospect says no to the telemarketing representative, a properly designed system will have extracted a wealth of information about this presumably dead prospect. First, it knows his demographics, which can tell the company a lot about where not to target its marketing efforts in the future. Second, if the sales department is smart, it will have captured some reasons for the apparent lack of interest—price, a satisfactory alternative, or inappropriateness of the product, for example. (It's always possible that the dead prospect with a price objection will come to life later when the company launches a two-for-the-price-of-one sale.)

Thus, the SA system has provided a great deal of valuable information. The company now knows which classes of suspects are prospects and which are not, why not, and which individual leads are potentially worthy of further pursuit. The qualified or semiqualified leads go out to the field, where individual sales representatives are encouraged to follow them. These reps should be required, if at all possible, to provide further tracking data. Which of these leads have been called on, with what results? Which are in what further stage of the selling cycle? Which ones actually bought? What? How much? Who turned out to be a dud? Specifically why?

These data provide more, and more important, grist for the marketing and planning mill. If certain categories of prospects and promotional methods are more productive than others, then the company can do more of what works and less of what doesn't. Or it can fix what doesn't work so it does. In Figure 4-2 we present an example of a report containing information on how various campaigns and promotional methods are doing currently and cumulatively; this information can be used to adjust advertising and promotional expenditures as necessary.

Obviously, judgment is required to evaluate the intangibles in the marketing process. However, if a company is interested in what is generating leads at what cost, and how much actual business those leads are yielding over time, there is no better source than an SA system set up to track leads from inception to final resolution. And, best of all, the cost of gathering this by-product information can be, if not zero, at least trivial in comparison to its value.

Stratified Selling

Sales automation can also support the creation of extra dimensions to the selling effort itself. It can accomplish this by two means: by keeping the various segments of the sales effort apart and by facilitating passage of an account from one sales function to the next. That seems like a contradiction, but it isn't.

Suppose you decide, on the basis of the fundamental

Figure 4-2. Sales data used for evaluating promotional efforts.

Campaign Effectiveness Report: Period Ending 8/23

	This Period		*Attributable $*			
Campaign	*Number of Inquiries*	*Number Closed*	*Revenue This Period*	*Revenue to Date*	*Number of New Accts.*	*New Acct. Revenues*
General Media	112	42	56,000	987,000	12	14,000
Trade Blitz	85	30	76,700	1,234,890	23	37,000
Tool Show	*	12	18,000	849,150	14	72,000

From Inception to Date

Campaign	*Total Costs ($)*	*Costs per Inquiry*	*Revenue per Inquiry*	*Cost as % of (New) Revenue*
General Media	1,240,000	2,400	6,500	36.9
Trade Blitz	877,000	766	2,800	27.4
Tool Show	167,800	900	4,590	19.6

**Note*: June show produced total of 185 inquiries.

economics of marketing and the differences in cost among the various means (see Figure 4-3), that direct sales, the most expensive strategy, will be reserved for accounts capable of generating at least $5,000 per year in revenue and that accounts with a potential of between $500 and $5,000 per year can be effectively and profitably handled over the phone by a telesales unit. Accounts falling below the $500 mark will be pursued by catalog and mail only. How are you going to refrain from mailing catalogs to field and telephone accounts? How are you going to be sure the field doesn't stumble into a telesales account? How are you going to avoid the confusion and embarrassment of having telesales solicit a customer already being handled by field sales?

One sure way of orchestrating this kind of three-way stratified sales effort is to have all three work from the same

Figure 4-3. The logic of marketing integration: cost-effectiveness.

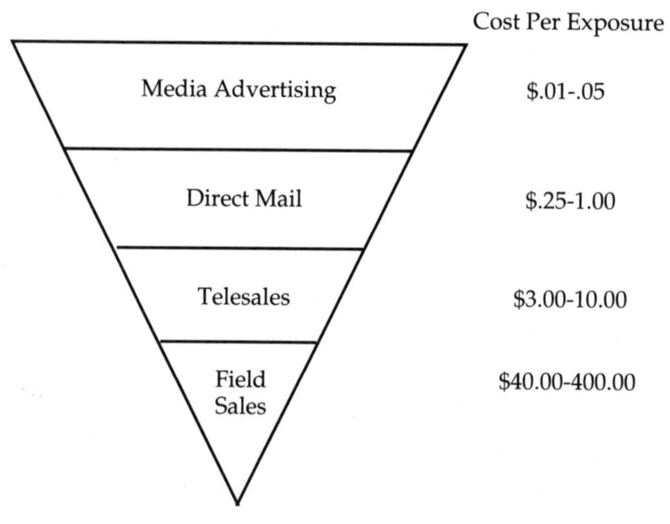

Used by permission of Victor L. Hunter, Hunter Business Direct, Inc.

fundamental database so that leads are channeled appropriately and solicitation attempts by one group on another's territory are automatically deflected. As an account "graduates" from the $500 level to a higher one, it can be automatically delivered to a teleseller in whose territory it falls; as a telesales account passes the $5,000 mark, it can be passed along to the appropriate field representative.

Sales veterans immediately raise objections to such a mechanistic-sounding procedure. Granted, a human intervention point between stages is often needed so that judgment can be made as to when and whether to transfer a client, but once the decision is made, the transfer of vital information can be seamless and automatic. Another obvious problem in passing accounts back and forth between departments and individuals involves the impact on commission incomes. Some thought clearly must go into providing incentives, softening adverse impacts, and allowing a graceful transfer for the client. But such steps are being taken successfully in many companies today.

The trade press recently reported that Rank-Xerox in the United Kingdom was finding it impossible to sell low-end copying machines profitably through its direct sales force. The company instituted a process much like that discussed here, in which whole suspect populations are solicited by a specialized telemarketing unit whose job it is to verify addresses and telephone numbers, get the names of decision makers, determine the potential copy volume levels in the company, find out what copying equipment, if any, is currently installed and its age, and under what kind of contract it is installed and the contract's expiration date.

Qualified leads, that is, those companies with sufficient copy volume and whose equipment is nearing replacement age, are passed along to sales. According to the company, sales representative productivity has increased 200 percent as a direct result of the new system, and Rank-Xerox has been able to stay in a market that it would otherwise have had to abandon. Further, unqualified leads, as the right amount of time passes, are automatically reentered into the process and requalified; often as not, they provide genuine new prospects for the sales department. This result supports the wisdom of keeping leads perpetually somewhere in the system, for ongoing analysis and for eventual resurrection.

A customer profile record can be established, without having turned the field representative into a keypunch operator, simply by capturing a lead early in its gestation as a suspect and adding information systematically to the file during the follow-through, qualification, and selling processes.

Creating a Multifaceted, Structured Sales Effort

A properly designed and shared SA system provides the basis for a multifaceted, structured, layered sales effort in which the effort and cost expended are in direct proportion to purchasing potential:

- Direct mail and catalog solicitation and, perhaps, electronic shopping play an early role for all and a continuing role for the smaller purchasers.
- Telemarketing captures and prequalifies certain types of leads.
- Telesales pursues smaller or geographically inaccessible accounts.
- Sales goes after the big ones.

All the while everyone is working from a computer database within which records glide effortlessly from category to category and from one level of qualification to the next.

Does this work? You bet it does. Think back for a moment how often you've sent back a reader inquiry card seeking material on an interesting ad or story in a trade journal, received a telephone call a few days after the brochure arrived, and then ended up seeing a sales representative shortly thereafter. Or, conversely, having given the whole proposition a closer and more informed look, you waved off the telemarketer and avoided having to endure a sales call at all.

The kind of "closed loop" sales and marketing system we've been describing is a marketer's dream because, at last, advertising and promotional campaigns can be measured on the basis of real results; overall effectiveness, lead quality, cost per unit, cost as a percentage of actual sales generated are all factors that can be assessed from having captured and tracked leads through the whole process. Other benefits include:

- *Possibility of midcourse correction, retargeting, and changing sales or market focus while the campaign is still in progress.* If data are feeding back in real time, then steps can be taken to alter and reprioritize campaigns while they're still in motion.
- *Longer-range decision support for themes, targets, budgets, media, and tactics.* Knowing exactly what has worked, how well, and what has not and why is the sine qua non of good future planning. This is the sort of material that can take next year's plan off the Ouija board and put it on the quota board instead.
- *Possible influence on overall corporate strategy, product management, and R&D.* In navigating the big corporate ship, there is no substitute for radar. Aggregated data at the base of the closed loop we've been talking about are exactly that—marketing radar.

Let's not overstate the case for SA. Some of the vitally needed data may not come from sales at all; nothing prevents marketing from doing its own tests and surveys—in fact, logic demands it. There are many aspects of future market requirements—global economics and social, political, and technological trends—that are untouched by the mechanics of SA systems. But, in the short run, nothing beats knowing what's going on with prospects and customers in the field here and now.

Preventing Sales Rivalries

Sales representatives are notoriously jealous of their prerogatives in "their" accounts. They are suspicious of any intervention in accounts from the outside—and with good reason. A representative's biggest nightmare is losing an account that has been painstakingly developed and labored on to another representative; the second biggest is having someone from elsewhere in the company suggest a product or solution to the account different from the one the representative has been so laboriously cultivating.

Therefore, it is of vital importance that each sales unit stay on its side of the border, that the rules against poaching be crystal clear, and that when an account does pass from one jurisdiction to the next, the representatives involved work together in smoothing the transition. One company we know pays double commissions for a year in such cases. Others pay referral bonuses. Some get by on corporate patriotism or by promoting the philosophy "Win some, lose some, it all balances out in the end." In any case, this fear is a problem that must be dealt with.

At the very least, a proper SA system identifies the ownership of prospects and customers and, when appropriate, alerts each player to the fact that someone else is already active in the account. As accounts move smoothly from one sales arm to the next, salespeople should view each other as facets of the same entity instead of as adversaries, as may have been true in the past.

Using SA Data Throughout the Company

Making data from SA systems available throughout the company yields dramatic benefits, particularly for operational and service functions of the company that come in contact with the client. Many of these functions can have a profound impact on whether the company gets and keeps the customer.

To the extent that each member of the team involved with the account has a window into what's happening and can record his or her actions and observations, coordination, responsiveness, and the ability to "speak with a common voice" are greatly facilitated. (This subject is discussed more fully in Chapters 3 and 5.)

Think of it this way. Suppose an engineer from the transformer division of Worldbeaters, Ltd., in Westchester responds to an ad by inquiring through your "800" number about your Wooly Widget Wonder. Wouldn't it be something if you could respond instantly with the information that Worldbeaters' Wire and Cable Division in Wilmington has already tested Wooly Widget Wonders and is about to place an order? Isn't that a more powerful response than sending a brochure? Is that really hard to do? No—not with a properly designed system.

Chapter 5
Communications

Almost every sales automation system includes data communications; the ability for different parts of the company to share information is critical if each part is to perform optimally. Information from the frontline representative is vital to the company's reporting, managing, and strategic "tuning" process; information to and from other representatives handling different parts of the customer's corporate family may be vital to coordination of major account selling. Exchange of applicational, technical, and competitive information among various players may enhance sales productivity. Last, creating and maintaining a strong relationship with the customer may demand intercommunication among the team members who work with the client. Almost without exception, no complex business problem is solved by a single individual in today's intensely competitive global economy, and no important customer's relationship with a supplier consists solely of contact with a single individual. Like it or not, we live in a team-playing environment. And teamwork demands communication.

According to a number of market researchers, about half of all the personal computers currently in use are equipped with some form of communications facilities, and it is not hard to imagine that proportion rising to near 100 percent by early in the twenty-first century, given the impetus toward interconnected work-group computing, telecommuting, and, of course, sales automation and relationship management systems. For example, Dataquest, Inc., a computer market research firm, estimates that 11 percent of the personal computers sold in a recent year in the United States were of the laptop/notebook type. Lest you think that's a small number, total PC sales that year were about 6 million units, so the portable share was nearly 700,000 machines. Dataquest, based on current trends and surveys, projects that the portable share will rise to 48 percent by 1994, or 2.5 million units. The vast majority of the machines are going to be used in sales and customer service applications, and the vast majority of them will be communications-equipped.

A study of sales automation entitled "Computer-Based Sales Force Support," published in 1990 by the Conference Board, reported on interviews with more than 200 companies that have implemented, or are in the process of implementing, SA. Slightly more than 40 percent of the machines used, both portable and desktop, are equipped with modems (telephone line attachment devices). Our experience is that virtually everyone involved in SA is planning communications hookups of one form or another.

These hookups generally conform to one of three types of systems architecture—the way in which the systems, specifically the communications linkages, are put together. These three options are described and evaluated in the following sections.

The Freestanding Approach

Figure 5-1 presents PCs—desktop, laptop, notebook, handheld, or other machines—that have the capacity to function independently but that can be connected with another unit over the telephone network via "dial-up" facilities. This setup does require that each unit include a modem, but that is a relatively inexpensive add-on that "interfaces" to the telephone network and usually fits unobtrusively inside the computer; the only visible evidence is a standard modular telephone jack in the back of the machine. This jack is plugged into either the normal voice telephone line on the desk or a nearby wall outlet. The protocol or procedure for dialing another computer and

Figure 5-1. System architecture—the freestanding approach.

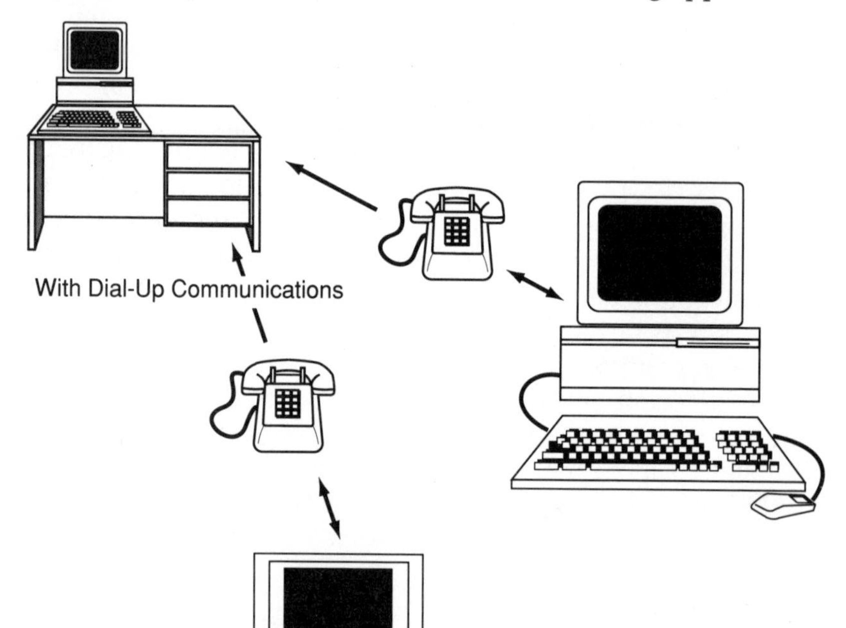

establishing contact is handled by software designed for that purpose.

Many SA packages have either built-in communications software or a relatively smooth and simple way of working with independent communications software. Let's examine two possible setups.

First we examine a simple import/export file transfer system. Suppose the representative wishes to transmit the week's calls, expenses, or sales forecast to the regional office. She goes through a simple menu selection procedure, which creates a file on floppy or hard disk containing the desired information. The file is given a name, such as "expense.rpt," either by the software or by the representative at the keyboard. The representative then makes another selection or two from a menu that causes the communications software in the machine to dial the number of the regional computer's modem, establish connection, and await further instruction. The representative is then asked to specify the file to be transmitted. She either types the name or, more likely, highlights "expense.rpt" from a list. The transmission then proceeds, taking a minute or a few minutes, at which point the system asks the representative whether there is more to transmit. If there is, the representative names another file; if not, she may lapse into receive mode and take a ration of information from headquarters in reverse. That return transmission could have been entirely automatic, or it might have been triggered by a message on the representative's screen notifying her that traffic for her is waiting in her "mailbox" and inquiring whether she wishes to receive it at that particular moment. The details vary, but the principles are the same; there is an orderly procedure for exchanging files between machines, and those files can then be read, processed, and acted upon at either end, as appropriate.

In order to avoid unauthorized transmissions and to prevent data from being available to those who should not have access to them, all modern data communications systems have user identification coding and password protection. Callers must come up with the right ID code and must input the correct secret password in order to exchange data. Although these precautions sound good, systems of this nature are only as good as the discipline that is imposed over codes and passwords. In other words, if the codes aren't changed often, if access codes aren't immediately cancelled for employees who leave, or if it's the habit to stick such hard-to-remember information to the sides of machines with Post-It notes or in top right drawers, then no amount of coding will protect you.

Another, higher level of protection is the call-back method in which the initiator, in this case the field representative, requests access by identifying himself, after which the headquarters machine breaks off the call and then dials back the representative's preestablished, preauthorized phone number and proceeds with the contact. The benefit is that no one who isn't physically in that representative's home or office can get into the system. The drawback is that it's almost impossible to establish the connection through an outside switchboard when traveling, and permitting the use of public telephones as a way around this limitation defeats its purpose.

Our second example, the so-called polled system, is more elaborate technically, but not much more difficult to operate from the representative's point of view. As was the case with call-back security, the transmissions are pretty well confined to established locations such as the representative's branch office or home, because the central computer initiates the call. In this type of system the representative does his work during the day using a computer and then, just before leaving the office or, if at home, retiring for the night, plugs in the telephone line and puts the computer into a preestablished "twilight" sleep mode.

Then, during the night, the central system dials each remote computer in sequence, "wakes it up," and exchanges transmissions with it before going on to the next one. In the morning, the representative finds messages and other responses waiting for him, together with acknowledgment that the outbound transmission has been accomplished. The content of these transmissions to and from remote and headquarters machines is explored more fully in Chapter 6 on data and database management; transmissions can vary from a very simple exchange of telememos to very sophisticated searching and synchronization of databases.

One risk in this system is the vulnerability of the telephone network. It is possible for someone to tap a public or even a dedicated private telephone line and capture a copy of data being transmitted on it. Doing so is very complicated and leaves the tapper liable to federal prosecution if apprehended, but some companies may choose to take precautions against tapping, nevertheless. The most common precaution is data encryption, similar to that used by the military and the diplomatic corps to encode transmissions into gibberish that can be translated back into useful information at the receiving end only through the use of the proper decoding technique. Data encryption software and hardware are not terribly expensive and are readily available for those who need it. (In our experience, a far greater threat to security in most offices is the open files and the memos and reports scattered around on desks and tabletops. With no technology and very little risk, an enterprising industrial spy can find out most of what he wants to know while posing as a job applicant, building inspector, or repair or cleaning person, or while working as an employee "mole" planted for the purpose.)

Despite the risk of espionage, the freestanding approach with dial-up facilities affords simplicity and mobility to sales automation and similar systems while retaining necessary linkage with other systems on an as-needed basis.

The LAN Approach

In some companies, there is only one world as far as the SA system is concerned, and that is at the office, whether a branch, a district, or a region. Office-based inside sales and telemarketing departments and organizations in which representatives either don't travel or don't carry computers with them when they do or where interaction with the system is accomplished through clerical intermediaries are examples.

Many companies organized in this way prefer to connect a number of office-based PCs via a local area network, or LAN, usually over a cable spanning the particular work group (see Figure 5-2). This is relatively easy to do, although there are a number of technical choices involved, and relatively inexpensive, costing at most a few hundred dollars per machine. The transmission is generally very fast—on the order of ten thousand times the speed of dial-up communications over the telephone network. The whole LAN becomes a single "computer" for the purposes of accessing each computer's database as well as a central database and peripheral devices, such as large disk files and laser printers. Data retrieval, for example, can be accomplished for all practical purposes as fast from the central store on a PC designated as the LAN's file server as it

Figure 5-2. System architecture—the LAN (local area network).

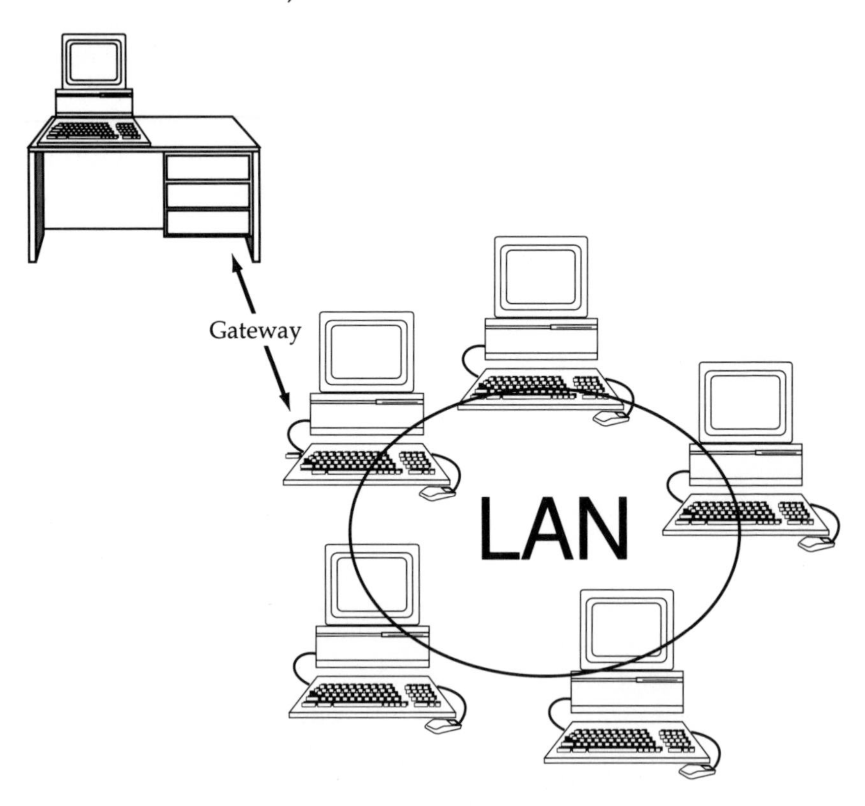

is from one's own internal disk drive. LANs offer economy, since each and every machine need not contain the same data or sport the same devices, and they permit a very high degree of communication and coordination among users, who can literally work different parts of the same problem simultaneously, update the same records (although not at the exact same instant), and exchange notes with one another freely. Certainly there are security issues here, too, and, once again, access to certain categories of information can be restricted by user. Representatives, for instance, may be able to access their own prospect and customer contact records but not those of their fellow representatives, whereas sales managers may have access to all such records within their particular domains but not those of other sales managers.

Like any shared facility, LANs need administration. Somebody has to be responsible for issuing ID codes and passwords and backing up the data, as well as troubleshooting problems and summoning help when necessary. On the other hand, a LAN with, say, five PC work stations, a file server, and a printer is not a whole MIS department and doesn't require a full-time administrator, just someone properly trained to watch over it as a part-time duty.

In Figure 5-2, one of the work stations is shown communicating with another, higher-level system through something called a gateway. Analogous to the file server's role with respect to data, one PC, often the file server itself, is designated to do all the communication for the LAN. When any particular system on the LAN needs to transmit or receive data from outside, then the communications server or gateway takes over, passing along requests, messages, or files. The gateway solves a big problem for sales departments in large companies, most of which cannot deal effectively with traditional MIS data processing networks and terminal protocols. In most companies that have developed computer-based networks over the years, the human interface with the system dates back to the days before "user-friendly" PCs became predominant. The gateway interacts appropriately with the older central computer networks, while transliterating back to PC protocol for nonexpert users on the remote end. The casual or nonprofessional user may never see (or care) how the data get back and forth.

Remote dial-up (see Figure 5-3) is another important facility that can be added to the LAN through the communications server or gateway. Such a system allows individuals who are away from the central facility to gain access to local facilities and data in the now-accustomed way. The gateway can insulate the user from the complexities of the headquarters system, translating information formats and protocols into familiar terms.

There is nothing "plug and play" about a communications

Figure 5-3. System architecture—the LAN (local area network) with added features.

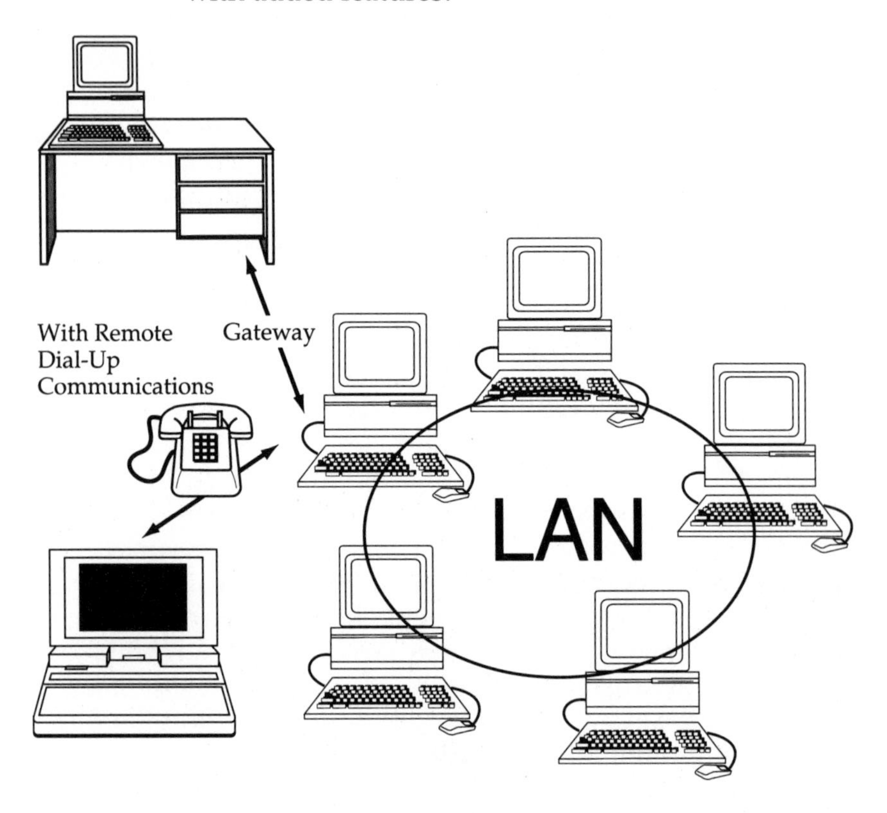

gateway, with or without local dial-up facilities. If this turns out to be the SA system you choose, your MIS department, perhaps with outside help, will probably have to be heavily involved in design and implementation. There are a number of consulting and systems integration firms that specialize in networking and that do a competent job of evaluating the trade-offs, planning the system, procuring and testing the components, and training users. Designed and done right, LANs are a troublefree, economical way of getting the work done and of tying users together into a team or work group.

Customer service and sales on the same LAN or on two

interconnected ones, for example, can easily trade information on what's happening in each account. A sales representative about to make a call on Worldbeaters, Ltd., could first call up the account record and review a running record of recent comments, requests, complaints, and other service activity in order to be better prepared for what is likely to come up in the conversation with the customer. Service, on the other hand, could be set up to see the account record virtually the instant a customer call comes in, not only for its own recording and reporting purposes but to add to its perspective on what's going on elsewhere in the account. On a LAN, this kind of interaction among departments is as simple as entering the necessary IDs, passwords, and access permission codes by means of a few keystrokes.

Centralized Systems

Early in the sales automation game, there were advocates of using central mainframe computers as the repository for sales force applications and data, and a handful of such systems were created. The best argument at the time was that the corporate mainframe represented the single nerve center for all information derived from or of use to the sales force. As compelling as this logic might have been, it was overwhelmed by three important practical considerations:

1. Mainframe systems and databases are extremely complex and are almost always overloaded with traffic, and new software development for the mainframes is almost always heavily backlogged. Project delays measured in years are not uncommon.

2. Response time—the time it takes to process a transaction, transmit a record, or fill the screen with data—for most on-line mainframe systems is long. It seems like an eternity compared to the snappy response of a PC, laptop, or handheld computer. The delay is perfectly understandable given the fact that the mainframe and its network are handling hundreds or

thousands of users simultaneously, while the little PC is dedicated to only one.

This point does raise an interesting concern about LANs. When the traffic on a LAN approaches or reaches the saturation point, the LAN begins to act like an overloaded mainframe; things get very slow indeed. There are practical limits to the number of stations and transaction loads that can be accommodated on all systems, LANs included. However, the remedies vary in cost and complexity, with the advantage almost always in favor of the LAN or other "distributed," as opposed to centralized, approaches.

3. Finally, there is the matter of flexibility. One of the hallmarks of sales and marketing is an ever-changing orientation to a perpetually churning marketplace. Large-scale systems don't adjust rapidly to changes in needs or changes of minds. No matter how hard mainframe software makers have tried to create easy, friendly, flexible facades in front of their applications and databases, the results have fallen far short of what has been accomplished on personal computers. For adaptability, PCs have no peer; they were designed for flexibility from their very inception.

Architectural Trade-Offs

It must be clear from the foregoing that we do not think much of the idea of building an SA system on the corporate mainframe. However, it is an alternative and ought to be considered. Chances are the development costs and timing alone will rule it out, but there are circumstances that favor it. For example, if the predominant application is order entry, not contact management, as might be the case with a consumer packaged-goods company dealing with a stable set of distributors and/or retailers, then most of the "action" could very well occur at the mainframe where production schedules and warehouse inventories are kept. That is certainly the case with companies like Frito-Lay, General Foods, and Nabisco, which deploy laptop and handheld computers to representatives who now capture ordering information right in their customer's store and transmit it to mainframes at headquarters for rapid fulfillment. These companies achieve an immediate benefit in faster turnaround on orders and fewer transcription errors. They are finding ways of exploiting the vastness and immediacy of the detailed sales information made available as a by-product of such systems. And some companies are even moving forward into predictive and diagnostic applications that enable representatives to do a better job of on-the-spot consultation with the retailer, suggesting ordering, promotion, and display patterns that will improve sales in the store, based on its specific size, layout, traffic, and competitive product allocations.

For most companies, the three likely choices of SA systems are:

1. A completely disconnected set of independent PCs or portables that representatives use for their own purposes, communicating with a higher headquarters-based system on an as-needed basis. This kind of system, pictured in Figure 5-1, is best for itinerant representatives who carry computers and mainly do their own work.

2. A LAN-based system, like that shown in Figure 5-2, in which a number of computers or work stations remain in constant contact, typically in the same building, sharing data, data storage, peripheral devices, and, often, communications facilities. This approach is best for the office-based system where the representatives themselves are office-bound or where they depend on office-based clerks and administrators to carry on dialog with the system on their behalf.

3. A centralized system, which may on the surface resemble one of the two just described—that is, the terminals on-line to the central system may be office-bound or portable. If portable, obviously, they would be in contact only when dialed into the central network; while in contact, the central system, not the terminal, would be doing the processing and data accessing.

Radio modems, to which portable terminals can be attached, look very promising. However, until we know what the economics of such systems will be and what if any other limitations might apply, we cannot adequately judge the trade-offs between them and the "distributed" approach. Portable PCs aren't standing still either. The size, weight, and price of a given level of processing power and data storage are all sinking rapidly. The practicability of equipping portables with CD storage drives containing billions of characters of data on digital compact disks is not far away, once again sharpening the battle lines between the centralized and decentralized approach.

Apart from the potential for on-line radio connectivity, networking in general is continuing to move forward. Hooking PCs into corporatewide communications networks, whether centralized or distributed, is not difficult. Special interface boards, like the famous "Irma Board" that makes a PC look to the network like the old standby IBM 3270 terminal, are abundant and abundantly useful in retrofitting into the existing corporate framework. Public value added networks, such as BT-Tymnet, Telenet, and GEIS, offer efficient, simple data communications connections to other subscribers, private dedicated networks, and special bulletin board, information bank, and electronic mail services like Compuserve, Dow Jones, and Nexis.

The eventual arrival of Integrated Services Digital Network (ISDN) from the telephone companies will make the connection even easier, eliminating modems altogether, multiplying transmission speeds in most cases by a factor of ten or more, and making it possible to direct-dial computers and terminals anywhere in the world.

Having some good options from among which to choose the underpinnings of a sales automation system is not the problem. Making the choices—the topic of Chapter 11—is far tougher.

Chapter 6
The Sales/Marketing Database

The sales/marketing database, like any other database, is a structured collection of computerized information, in this case specifically related to the sales and marketing arena. A collection of files full of orders, notes, lead sheets, and old call reports is not a sales/marketing database; it may contain the data needed for one, but it is unstructured and uncomputerized, hence useless for the purposes of sales automation. SA requires information that can be accessed (and shared) quickly and conveniently.

Before going on, the reader is advised to review the diagrams presented earlier in Figures 4-1 through 4-3. Here, the content of a typical sales and marketing database is specified in concept. Beyond this, however, a very significant determinant of the success of your SA system is going to be the specific "architecture" employed to structure and house the data. This architecture will be at the heart of field sales operations and reporting, customer service, management analysis and direction, and all manner of communication, information sharing, and coordination among all elements of the organization concerned with selling and satisfying customers. It will also be an invaluable pool of analytical and research information from which to derive and test various sales, marketing, and product development strategies that may be crucial in keeping your company competitive and profitable.

Two important considerations in designing the database

are accuracy and security. It's hard to imagine what value the database would have if it contained wrong names, addresses, and telephone numbers, omitted some key prospects and customers, or failed to reflect recent significant account activity. Nor would managers feel comfortable having all that vital information in the database, going to a good deal of trouble to ensure that it is kept accurate, up-to-date, and complete, if they strongly suspected that their chief competitors could get at it and use it to their disadvantage or that it might disappear completely due to a computer malfunction.

There are some clear requirements concerning the S&M database:

- It must be structured, that is, capable of containing all the necessary categories of information about prospects, customers, and sales-related activities in some semblance of order so that such data can be retrieved again when needed.
- It must be complete and accurate.
- It must be protected against loss and misuse.

Those are the musts. But there are plenty of needed and nice-to-have features as well. First and foremost among these is ease of getting data into and out of the system. As we repeat throughout this book, the data-capture function should be mostly a by-product of something the sales representative is doing to help him do a better, more effective, and/or easier job of selling customers and managing the territory. To the extent that the SA system is used as a prospecting, prioritizing, planning, and production tool in the representative's day-to-day work, the data are maintained for a specific purpose; if they aren't, the representative's personal performance will suffer, his work will be harder to do, and his income will likely be reduced and, perhaps, his livelihood threatened.

Another important and desirable feature of the S&M database is ease of retrieval and reporting. The user needs to have a very simple and instantaneous way of getting at a specific record. Similarly, the user needs a simple mechanism for generating a collation of like information about all the accounts in the database, such as the names, addresses, and telephone numbers of all prospects and customers who have received a special XYZ offer in the last two weeks but have not yet responded to it.

Almost all SA software packages contain a database and features to access it and report from it. The question is, Does the database have all the information you need and are the updating, retrieval, and reporting simple and sufficient for your needs? That is not an easy question to answer; it usually requires not only careful analysis but actual field experience in using the system on a pilot basis. More on that in Part III.

Another major issue is how to tie together related district, regional, subsidiary, and corporate databases. You and the MIS staff will have to decide as you plan your SA system just how the local SA databases will play together and tie into other company data and systems. Let us state again that the systems should communicate with one another where necessary but without becoming so intertwined that nothing can be changed in any one of them without massive redevelopment efforts touching all of them. If you believe and act on the foregoing, then you will probably save your company thousands of times the cost of this book and the cost of your time spent reading it. This precept alone militates highly in favor of the so-called distributed approach, which can range from completely disconnected, independent, freestanding databases on the one hand to related, coordinated databases in constant communication with one another on the other.

In the first extreme, each organizational element, perhaps right down to the representative level, has a private, unconnected database. If some other element of the organization needs information from this disconnected system, it can be supplied via printed or electronic media or specific data transmission. For example, suppose you're a sales manager who needs a listing of all accounts in the territory with a 3000-series SIC code that have more than fifty employees. You make a request to the representatives, who in turn print an appropriate report or put it out on a diskette or initiate a so-called batch file transfer via dial-up data transmission from their machines to yours over the phone line. The mode of transmission doesn't matter as long as you can get the information you need in usable form.

The other extreme is one in which the system is interconnected like a string of Christmas tree lights, each of different color. Someone sitting at the "green" terminal who wants "blue" receives the blue information "transparently," without having a sense of, or concern for, where it was physically derived from. This is typical of local area network systems and hierarchically interconnected wide area network systems, usually consisting of microcomputers in the field connected to minicomputers at intermediate headquarters connected to bigger minis or mainframes at higher headquarters. In either case, the information is not duplicated; whoever needs and is entitled to the information comes through the network either to the appropriate database to get it (in the distributed case) or to the central database.

As is so typical of the information systems world, it isn't always quite so simple. Mixtures of these schemas will probably persist. Some parts of the individual databases will never be shared or communicated, and other parts will be exchanged on an occasional batch file transfer or reporting basis. Other parts may come from faraway places as needed through elaborate network interplay, and still other aspects may be duplicated in order to promote quicker access for all concerned. The architecture of the system and its supporting databases will vary according to need and according to what is already in place prior to the establishment or extension of the sales and marketing database. The three figures that follow provide a schematic rendering of the most fundamental forms of database organization that might be employed in the sales and marketing arena. In Figure 6-1a, the classical centralized approach is depicted. This is the one traditionally honored in large companies with central mainframe computers containing all important data (and very often the applications themselves). The main difficulty with this approach is its inertia. To get anything designed, programmed, or altered, you must wait in the queue, generally a long one shared with all the other departments of the company. Likewise, when accessing the system, you may be confronted with delays stemming partly

Figure 6-1a. Centralized approach to database organization.

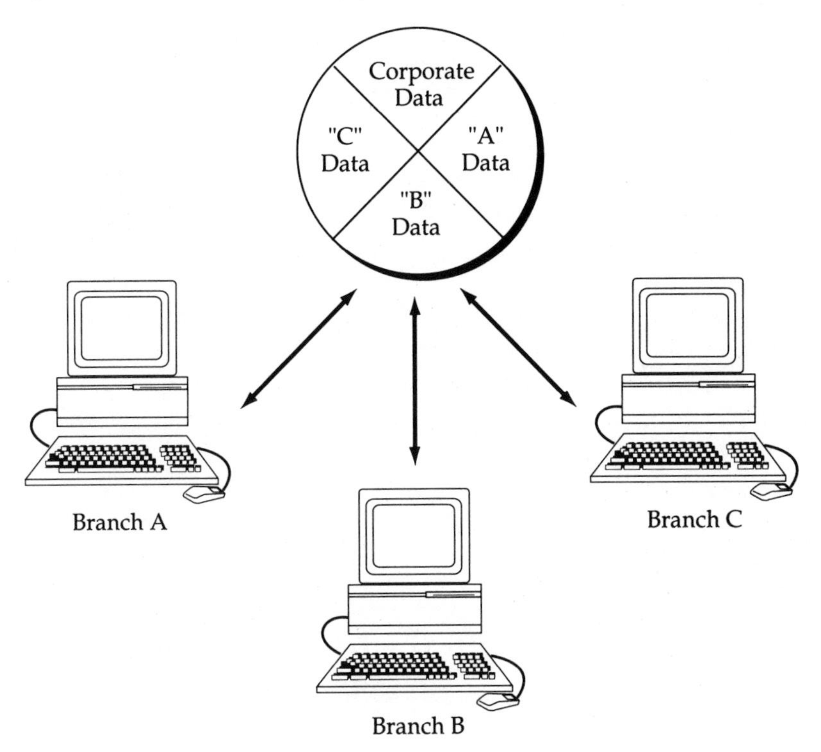

from conflicts with other departments and partly from a very bulky, complex protocol that is arcane, difficult to learn, and very slow.

In the second diagram, Figure 6-1b, we present a distributed approach in which the data that belong to various organizational elements, such as sales offices, stay with those elements. Access to companywide data is accomplished through a higher-level system, and communications and information transfer can take place in a number of different formats. For example, all such interchange can occur through the mainframe, or it can take place through LANs and other subsidiary networks, which, in turn, can be interconnected through the mainframe.

Figure 6-1b. Distributed approach to database organization.

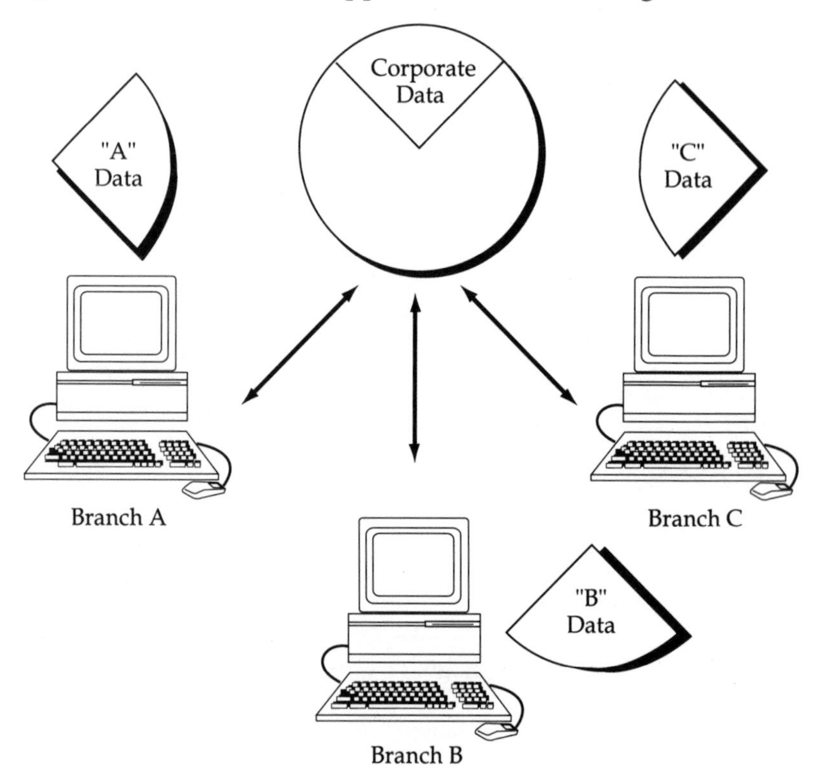

Making such a system work, however, often necessitates some compromises, such as duplicating some of the data to facilitate quick and convenient access. That situation is pictured in Figure 6-1c. Here, copies of all or selected portions of the data also reside centrally for at least two purposes: availability for higher-level needs, such as management analysis and central accounting, and access by other local units through the intermediation of the central system. A good example of the latter might be a logistical system in which regions keep their own stock but, when they run out of stock, can access the inventories of other regions through the computer at headquarters. Some of the most frequently needed "other" regional and

Figure 6-1c. Duplication of the data centrally and locally.

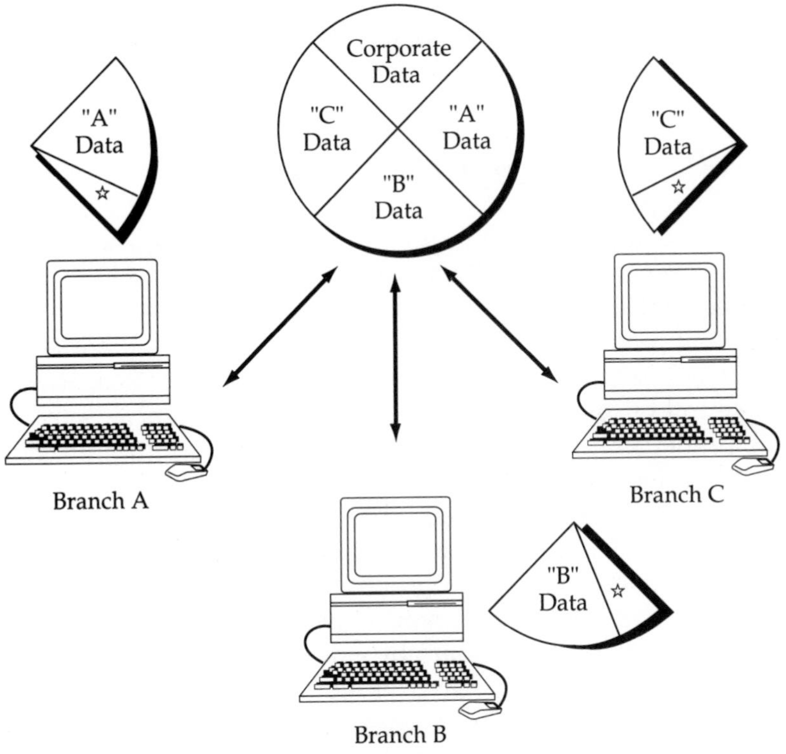

"A"
Data
☆

Corporate
Data
"C"
Data
"A"
Data
"B"
Data

"C"
Data
☆

Branch A

Branch C

"B"
Data
☆

Branch B

☆ Plus, undoubtedly, selected, abstracted data from corporate and other offices

headquarters data may already be downloaded into each of the distributed databases on the local level. Clearly this is redundant and complicates file maintenance, because not one but several copies of the data must be updated and kept intact. The good news is that simultaneous updating is both possible and not very expensive in this era of multimegahertz, multimegabyte powerhouse desktop systems. The issue of synchronizing the copies is usually handled simply by periodically downloading a fresh new copy to the distributed sites.

The final choice is up to you and IS, perhaps interacting with committee or task force members, vendors, consultants, and other interested parties.

General Features of SA Databases

What follows are some general concepts that may help you in designing or selecting databases and database management tools for an SA system.

Relational vs. Hierarchical Databases

The first concept to clear up is the biggest buzzword in databases—*relational*. To understand the significance of this term, it's necessary to review what relational databases are not. All computer databases began as "flat files." As illustrated in Figure 6-2, a flat file is simply a collection of like records, one after another, usually organized and stored around a "key," in this particular case a customer number. In the flat file, each record is self-contained and says all it has to say about itself. In the example, each customer record, identified by customer number and stored in customer number sequence, contains specific details on previous purchases. If you wanted to know who sold those products, you could match this file against another flat file of customers by sales representative, creating still another flat file, perhaps keyed by sales representative name or code, with each record containing accumulated dollar volume by product or, if desired, all the sales detail by product and customer now rearranged in sales representative records in sales representative sequence.

Now suppose somebody asks for either details or totals by branch office. You now have to introduce another flat file of branches containing the IDs of the sales representatives attached to each and do another merge and sort. And so on, ad infinitum.

Figure 6-2. Flat file.

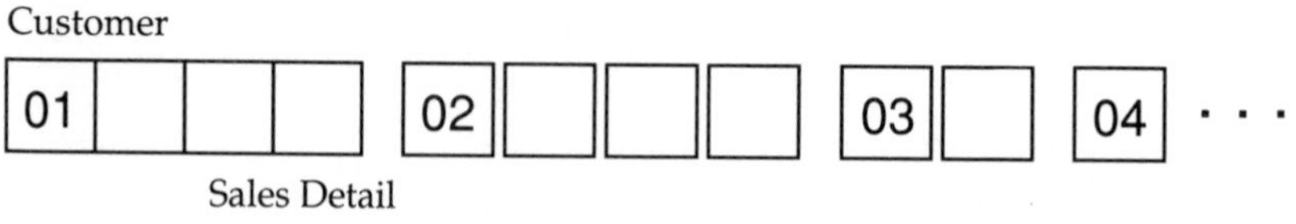

Customer

01				02				03		04	. . .

Sales Detail

It might be better, perhaps, to organize the sales analysis files into a database to begin with and make it a hierarchical one that reflects the order of "belongingness" of the various data elements, as depicted in Figure 6-3, since that's the way you have decided you want to view the information. So, in Figure 6-3, everything is organized in a single multilevel storage structure that maps the ownership feature that you have defined as your main interest. This may be the optimal way to organize the data for sales reporting in your company because

Figure 6-3. Files in a hierarchical system.

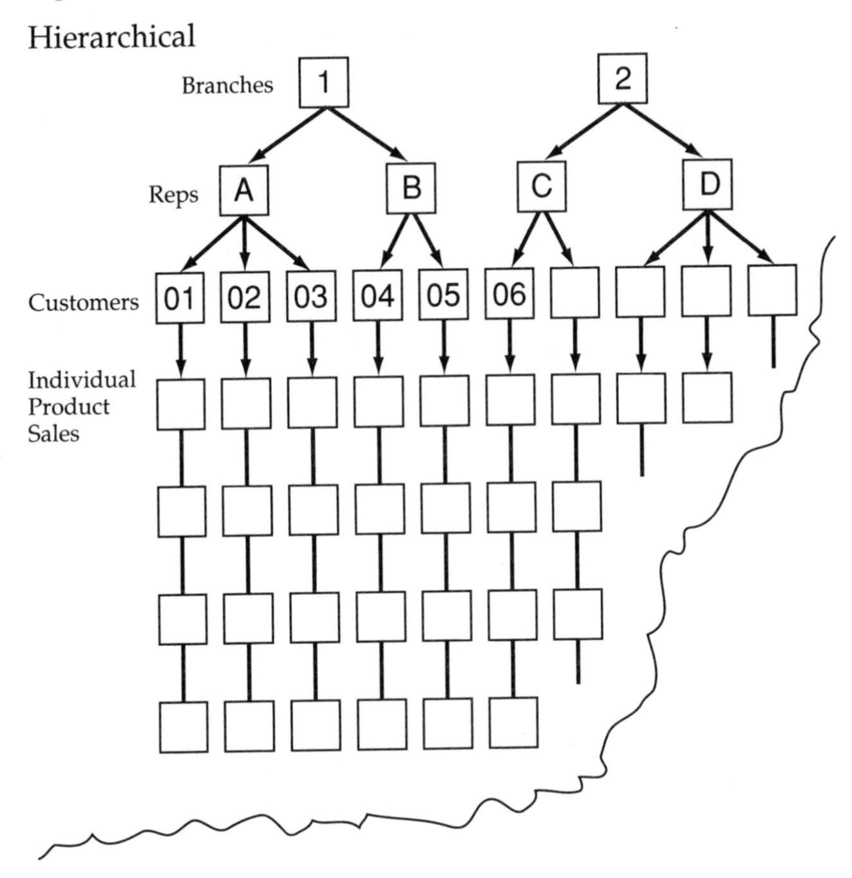

your reports customarily reflect sales within customer within representative within branch. On the other hand, if you want to know how much of product X customer 05 bought, you must first know (or find out) that customer 05 belongs to sales representative B in Branch 1 and then follow that thread through the database to the information sought.

Perish the thought, now, that someone wants to know how much of product X was bought by all customers or, worse, by all customers with an SIC code in the 2200 range, particularly if customer SIC code resides in a different file in another database that serves, perhaps, the market research department. The point here is that flat files and hierarchical databases are excellent repositories for data used in specific, predefined, and limited ways, but they may be extremely cumbersome or promote endless duplication of information if they are to be used for a wide variety of different "cuts," combinations, and cross sections. In the example just given, it would be tedious to cross-reference to the market research database every time you want to run a sales analysis report involving SIC codes, so you would probably take the easier road of incorporating SIC code into the customer portion of the hierarchical sales database. No big deal, except that every time a new customer is added, an SIC code changes, or a new secondary SIC code is added, you have to make the change in two places. Now, multiply that by the number of customer and SIC code–related databases around the company. Now multiply this situation by the number of different categorizations of customer, representative, product, and branch data that sales management is ever going to want to look at, and you have quite a potpourri on your hands.

That's why relational databases have become so popular. In the perfect relational scheme, a single piece of data would never appear more than once, but a multitude of relationships between it and other data elements would be available. Figure 6-4 presents a highly simplified example. Each data element about product sales is related to specific customer data elements through cross-referencing pointers contained in dictionaries or directories, which are in turn related to data elements about sales representatives and branches. The whole database

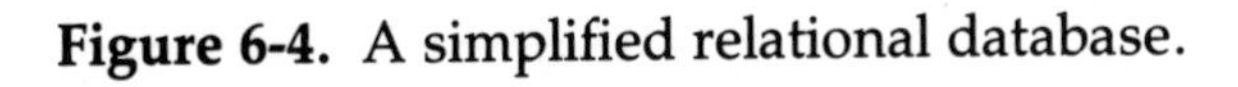

Figure 6-4. A simplified relational database.

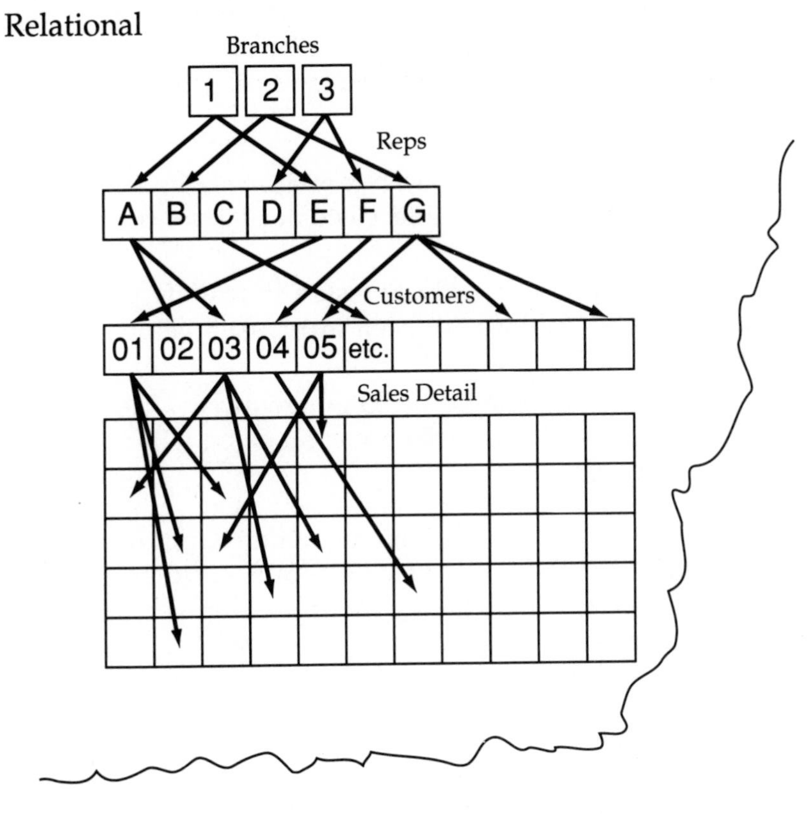

consists of everything that is known, recorded precisely once, and thrown together in an apparent jumble but cross-referenced to each other endlessly and exquisitely like the threads of a spider web. The cost and complexities of such "inverted" database structures used to be prohibitive, but recent strides in hardware speeds and program architecture have made relational databases not only practical but preferred for all but certain super-high-volume transaction-processing applications, such as airline reservation systems.

There is a sacrifice in speed and directness in constructing records "on the fly," so to speak, using the relational approach for routine, predetermined applications, such as order entry or sales forecasting. But that sacrifice is generally slight in comparison with the ease of connecting in unique and novel ways at will and with the efficiency of entering each data item only once regardless of the range of applications it may have.

Three important points should govern database and related systems design:

1. It should not be carried out exclusively by technicians or systems architects. User and customer influences must be strongly felt.
2. It should be exhaustively tested in real-life pilot situations to see what might have been overlooked before it is put to full use.
3. The structure should be so inherently flexible that unexpected changes can be easily accommodated without upsetting the apple cart.

Other things equal, sales and marketing applications work best on relational database systems because of their inherent need for flexibility. There are excellent, well-proven, packaged relational database management systems available for computers of all sizes, from mainframes to vest-pocket machines.

Ease of Backup

Another important feature of any database system is backup. Every currently available operating system supplied with every currently available type of computer in the world contains backup facilities whereby data can be copied from the system and preserved externally. If that externalized copy of the database is stored somewhere away from the computer site, then the data are protected not only from computer failure and other forms of electronic destruction but from fire, flood, and other physical catastrophes as well.

The problem with backup procedures is not availability; it's, of course, use (see Chapter 10). Let's grant that periodic backup is a pain. It's usually quite slow and clumsy; it's not unusual to have to sit still for a half hour or more feeding diskette after diskette into the computer while executing the standard backup procedure. Two remedies for this headache are: (1) uploading all or the most important and/or dynamic portions of the data to a higher-level system where they may be needed anyway and where they will be professionally cared for and preserved, and (2) using a faster, more convenient backup utility program that compacts the needed data into a much smaller amount of space and can be evoked more easily, even automatically, as needed. There are a number of operating system "shell" and disk file management software packages available commercially, and at least some of the popular sales automation packages have condensed data backup built right in.

Reconstructing lost data from backup media is often slower and trickier than creating the media in the first place, but reconstruction is necessary only when there has actually been a catastrophe, which, by definition, is not very often.

Security

Security is another important aspect of database management systems. It's important to be protected against wrongful access, theft, and tampering. Industrial espionage, grudge tampering, and computer "hacking" are three hypothetical risks to which your system might be subject.

The three most common barriers to improper access and use are user codes, passwords, and encryption. The first two are almost ubiquitous; virtually every software package limits access only to users who provide a valid user ID code, together with an associated secret password. A determined industrial spy can probably penetrate this defense using a combination of intuition and repetitive-trial computer code generation techniques. In such cases, the interloper won't make it in on the first, the third, or perhaps even the thirtieth try, so many security systems have a feature to notify the user or, better, the system administrator when a given number of failed attempts to gain access have occurred in a short period of time.

Much more practical means of penetrating the system are either enlisting the cooperation of an insider, perhaps someone who recently left the company, or simply walking around the office after hours, picking up slips of paper stuck to the sides of terminals, on desks, and in top drawers containing all the codes and passwords needed to roam merrily through the database. The latter is by far the method of choice for spies of all stripes. It is foolproof, is difficult to detect, and, at worst, costs only a few days of employment on the office cleanup crew.

As for encryption of data transmitted and stored, it is a case of getting what you pay for. Inexpensive packaged encryption software systems are relatively easy for a determined professional cryptologist to crack. A military-style system, on the other hand, presents a real challenge to the would-be spy, but the cost of acquiring, tailoring, and supporting it may exceed the potential cost of penetration if it were to occur. Very few companies find it feasible and cost-effective to use such airtight systems.

Finally, the risks that your computer systems will be penetrated must be evaluated in light of the security of your entire company environment. Unless you already employ distribution control, logging, shredding, and locked files for sales and marketing data both at headquarters and in the field, it's hard to see how putting the computer database under heavy guard is going to help.

Whatever means you choose should be undertaken in view of your companywide security plan and must be rigidly administered and enforced. That means that passwords and encryption keys must be under responsible control and must be changed frequently; when employees leave, their codes and passwords must be invalidated immediately.

Compatibility With Other Databases

Handing data between systems implies some degree of database compatibility. Such compatibility can range from a rigorous commonality of database and communications systems to an eclectic collection of systems that exchange messages and files using some common standard format. Virtually every commercially available SA software package sports one or more standard file communication protocols that can be used at the very least in a manually initiated file transfer to another system. In Chapter 7 we suggest means by which you can gather the facts and choose the best approach for your needs.

Custody and Corruption of Data

In most companies, the issues of computer security, integrity, communications, and backup can be—and are—left to the professionals in the information systems department. IS may even have complete custody of the sales and marketing database. Does this mean that the using department has no responsibility for its contents? Emphatically not! Think of it as renting a safe deposit box in a bank. The bank provides the physical structure and protective features and the bank controls access, but you, the user, determine what goes in the box, how and when it's used, and its worth.

It's another manifestation of the old "garbage in, garbage out" principle. A major responsibility falls squarely on using organizations to screen data going into the system, to detect and correct mistakes that have crept in despite the screening, and to do everything possible to ensure that data stay up to date and accurate. The biggest worry is not about the portion of the database that is used day in and day out to make calls, run the territory, place orders, and initiate correspondence; that portion has a tendency to police itself. The real problem is with infrequently used historical, classification, and reference information that either doesn't get into the system in the first place, usually because of user procrastination, or that is incorrect at inception or over time. As an example, think of codes, such as Duns Numbers, that link a particular business to its corporate parent and cousins before and after a merger, acquisition, or reorganization. How are organizational changes going to be recognized and reflected in the system with any assurance or regularity? All you can do is the best you can do. Much will slip through the cracks. The only way to compensate is to do periodic "sweeps" of the database, printing out segments, for example, and asking representatives or their telemarketing surrogates to contact the target entities to verify selected information or backfill the blanks, making sure, of course, that someone then follows through by inputting the corrections and additions into the system.

Maintaining accurate prospect lists is a never-ending chore. People and businesses have an incurable habit of changing addresses, telephone numbers, and even names. Executive lists incorporating names and titles are notoriously volatile. Classifiers such as family income, number of employees, line of business, names of children living at home, and similar groupings are equally volatile. So-called database marketing, which uses an orchestrated approach to targeting, qualifying, or selling by mail and/or telephone, fights the list maintenance battle continuously, merging, purging, and "laundering" lists endlessly.

Purging and Archiving

Although this is not an immediate threat, there will come a time perhaps when the sales and marketing database is overaged with ancient history. Contact management systems, for example, log phone calls, visits, and notes. These data will be very valuable for a few weeks or months while the company is in active pursuit of a project, program, or piece of business. However, with the passage of time, they will become meaningless. Therefore, in addition to all the other needed disciplines applied to the database, you are probably going to want to consider either in-built or manually initiated elimination of inactive information that, if it has historical value, could be offloaded to some inactive storage medium and placed in the company archives against the possibility that it may be needed some day.

The choice of architecture and disciplines surrounding the SA database is of paramount importance in determining its success. Ease of use, reliability, security, and, perhaps above all, flexibility are hallmarks of the good choice. Deciding which system fulfills these criteria and your specific applicational needs best and fits in with the company's existing computing and networking architecture is difficult and requires study and experimentation on the part of all the affected parties. In the remaining chapters of this book, we attempt to guide you through this and other difficult decisions and help you deal with the consequences of your choices.

Part II

Understanding Needs and Requirements

Chapter 7

Evaluating Sales Automation

Evaluating sales automation is a process that begins with understanding the needs and requirements of your organization and then applies the appropriate automation tools to increase the effectiveness of your revenue producers. Increasing effectiveness results in increased productivity and, ultimately, increased profits through lower costs and increased sales.

Where do you start? You start by evaluating where you are now. What automated or manual systems are presently used? Why are they used? Installing an SA system offers a tremendous opportunity to improve the policies, procedures, and methods used by your company for transacting business, both internally and with your customers. For example, discounters Kmart and Walmart have received a lot of publicity in the business press for requiring their suppliers to accept purchase orders and payments electronically as part of long-term projects at both retailers to improve efficiency by creatively applying technology to their business operations.

Sales automation systems are part of a broad category of systems called performance enhancement systems. Performance enhancement systems are designed to help people perform at higher levels by providing easily accessed information that has been created or collected by themselves or others and that can be used to enhance decision-making capability.

When evaluating the needs and requirements of sales

automation systems, you should seek input from functional areas of the company that interface with, provide information to, and receive information from the sales force, as well as from the sales force itself. (Developing a planning and evaluation team is the subject of Chapter 8.)

First Steps

The first step in evaluating sales automation requirements is to conduct a thorough assessment of your company's present systems, procedures, and processes. How does the sales team perform its job? What does the prospect or customer require and expect from your sales resources? What does sales management need to drive the business? What competitive advantage can be attained? What information is available on present systems? How is product, pricing, promotion, and other sales information distributed? How are orders, call reports, competitive information, and customer requirements delivered from the field to corporate executives?

There are a number of other questions to ask as well. What manual systems are presently used? Are they effective? Does information from manual systems ultimately end up on the present information systems? Is the information that is presently available on automated systems of any value to the sales force? How are leads collected and distributed? Who is responsible for lead follow-up? How old are the leads when they arrive in the salesperson's in-box?

Well-defined and effective manual systems can provide the design foundation for automated SA systems. Usually a thorough analysis of needs was undertaken as the company planned forms and information content of its manual systems; if these findings are still valid, you can use them as the basis for screen layouts for the new SA system.

Asking your salespeople and sales management about how they presently use their time is a good starting point for evaluating your needs and requirements. Surveys can reveal how much time salespeople spend with customers selling and how much time they spend in internal meetings, traveling, performing nonselling administrative tasks, performing selling-related administrative tasks, preparing proposals, writing orders, and preparing call reports.

The results of surveys can be eye-opening. One major company thought its salespeople spent 50 percent of their time on customer-related activities. A survey of the sales staff, however, revealed that they were spending only 25 percent of their time in this way; the largest portion of their time went to noncustomer-related activities.

A survey can easily be developed by a small team that includes representatives from each level of the sales team (such as a salesperson, a district manager, and a regional manager). Different surveys may have to be developed for each type of sales resource. The main component of each survey is a time log in which the salesperson records the type of activity and the length of time spent on that activity. The survey should cover a long enough time period to include all the major activities a salesperson performs. For example, if a salesperson has to call on distributors at the beginning and end of a quarter and end-user customers during the middle of the quarter, the survey period should be a quarter. It is important that the survey be conducted from a sample that represents a good cross section of salespeople; many companies survey several districts in different regions of the country.

The results of the survey can be collected and tabulated as the survey progresses. It is important that the participants understand that the results of the survey are going to be used in a positive manner and that their accurate input is important and will play an important role in what capabilities and features are implemented in the new SA system.

Survey results provide a road map of automation potentials. They show how your sales resources are utilizing their time and may identify areas or activities that need improvement. The summary of how time was spent can also be used as a baseline against which you can later measure the effectiveness of the SA project in increasing sales force productivity.

The details of how the salespeople spend their time offer opportunities for automation. If salespeople spend significant amounts of time writing orders by hand from large product lists with multiple discount levels and promotion alternatives, an important SA application might be an automated order entry system. For a sales force that has a short sales cycle and that has to follow up on many leads, the survey may show that leads become stale or are not followed up at all. In this case, a lead tracking and contact management application that controls the flow of leads and offers prospect targeting and follow-up capabilities would be the primary application for an SA system.

The survey can also be used to get salespeople's ideas and opinions on the types of information and productivity tools that would help them perform their jobs better. The salespeople may well be more receptive to the new system if they have "authorship" of key elements. They may also know what type of SA systems your competitors have installed and can ask your customers what types of capabilities or increased service levels would enhance the buyer-seller relationship.

The results of the internal analysis of procedures, policies, and systems, combined with the sales force survey, provide the raw materials necessary to create an initial functional requirements statement. A functional requirements statement is a document that provides an overview of the required capabilities and functions of the system. It describes the nature of your business, the sales environment, the types of customers you sell and service, as well as your sales process and sales cycle; it defines the types of internal systems—the hardware products, operating systems, networking systems, application programs, and communications capabilities—already in place. It also describes your present information flow and how you would like information to flow in the future.

In the process of preparing the functional requirements statement, you should analyze which systems and applications lend themselves to automation. Typically, transaction-oriented activities are ideal candidates for automation. Examples include order entry, call reports, lead tracking, and quotation preparation. Sales, pricing, and order status reports that are distributed on paper can be transmitted and presented electronically to the user on a more timely basis. There should be one point of entry for any new data in the system; once the data are stored electronically, they can be moved from one system to the next without being keyed again.

As a general rule, the larger the sales force, the greater the likelihood that custom modifications will be required. There are several reasons for this, the most significant of which is that companies with large sales forces already have central computer systems in place to manage their day-to-day business operations. A company introducing SA will at some point want to move information between the corporate systems. At the very minimum, the ability to populate the new SA system with customer information that is already available electronically will save significant amounts of sales time when the new system is introduced.

Compatibility does not mean, however, that the chosen SA system has to operate under the same operating environment as the corporate system. Compatibility in the SA environment means data compatibility; the chosen SA system and its operating environment should offer proven ways to move data between systems, and its communications and data transfer utilities should meet industry standards.

The functional requirements should also address the productivity tools that may be needed. These tools may include word processing, spreadsheets, and graphics. While it is important to maintain corporate standards, outfitting your salespeople to match the corporate system may not be the best decision. The most popular products in this category are very powerful and feature-rich. Because of their power, they are complex and difficult to use. The typical salesperson may not require the power of these products. An alternative product that is easier to learn and use may be a better choice. The important features to look for in alternative products is ease of use and file compatibility with your corporate standards.

The functional requirements statement should address the capabilities the system will have in its first version and also those capabilities that will be required in the future. The system should be designed to accommodate change, and the requirements document should address this need. It should also provide a general timetable for a phased implementation of the proposed system.

A general outline for a functional requirements statement follows:

I. Company Background
   A. Company size and industry
   B. Location
   C. Primary sales and marketing objectives
   D. Size and structure of current sales force
   E. Growth strategy
   F. Market structure and distribution channels
   G. Long-term business strategy
   H. Strategies affecting SA system

II. Functional Requirements Summary
   A. Major functional areas—narrative
   B. Major functional areas—schematics
   C. Major functional areas—functions and features—detailed checklist
   D. Long-term requirements

III. Service Requirements
   A. Software design and installation
   B. Hot-line support
   C. Hardware management
   D. Hardware support
   E. Training
   F. Documentation

IV. Key Technical Requirements—Narrative

The key objectives of a functional requirements document are to (1) help your organization understand the scope and requirements of your sales automation system, (2) help outside suppliers understand your organization and the required elements of your system, and (3) provide a benchmark for evaluating alternative vendors and proposals.

The functional requirements statement is your road map to success. A well-done statement helps vendors understand your needs and requirements, whereas a poorly done statement leads to many false starts and costs beyond expectations.

Chapter 8

The Planning and Evaluation Team

Nothing can be more crucial to the success of your sales automation program than selecting the team that plans, selects, and implements it. Choosing the wrong project team can send you down the proverbial primrose path to ruin.

But why a team in the first place? Why not just hand over the responsibility to a competent, knowledgeable unit inside or outside your company and be done with it?

There are two very good reasons for putting together a team: (1) The resulting system is going to be shared by people representing different, widely divergent functional areas of your company, all of whose needs, work modes, fears, and foibles need to taken into account; and (2) most of the users are not professional data processing people and will use the system only if they have a sense that it is to their benefit to do so. Therefore, each user constituency must have its genuine (and sometime idiosyncratic) needs taken into account, and each must feel a sense of "ownership" of the result. The system must be "ours," not "theirs."

Who Should Be Represented on the Team

Figure 8-1 lists some of the departments or functions that might utilize the SA system. The list will vary with your particular business and SA objectives. For example, if field order entry is

Figure 8-1. Functions represented on the SA team.

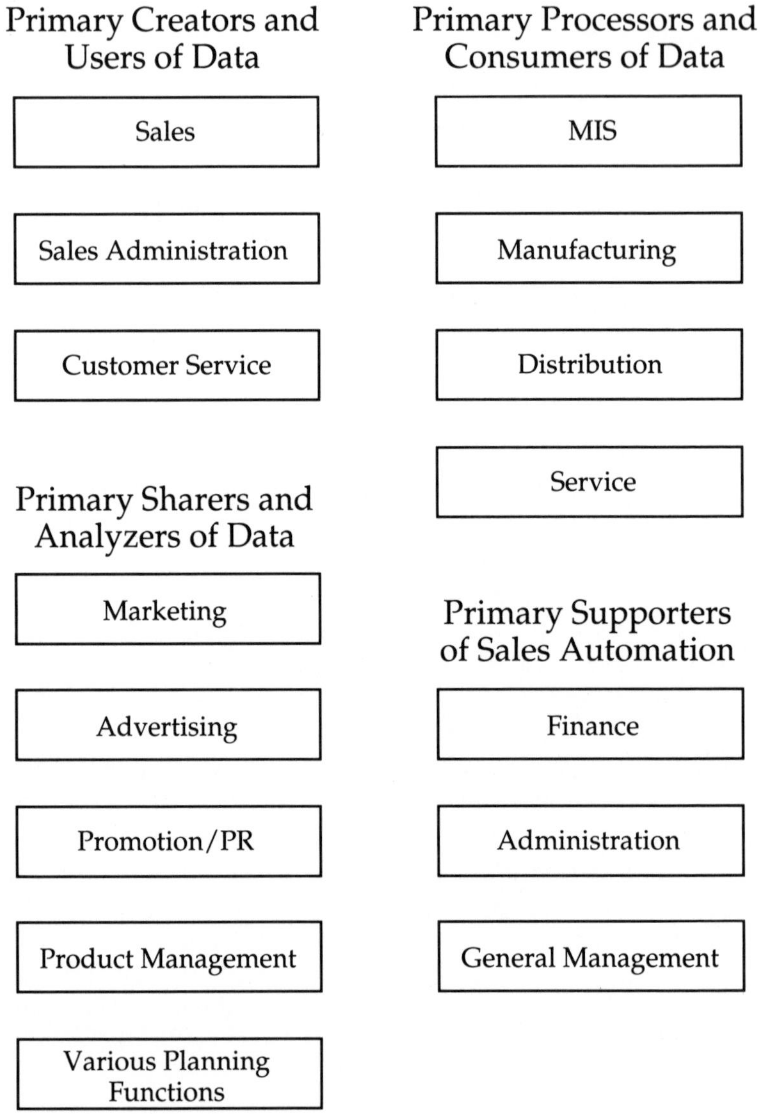

Primary Creators and Users of Data

- Sales
- Sales Administration
- Customer Service

Primary Processors and Consumers of Data

- MIS
- Manufacturing
- Distribution
- Service

Primary Sharers and Analyzers of Data

- Marketing
- Advertising
- Promotion/PR
- Product Management
- Various Planning Functions

Primary Supporters of Sales Automation

- Finance
- Administration
- General Management

not in the nature of your business, then manufacturing and distribution may be completely out of the loop as far as SA is concerned. Certainly not all stakeholders in the company need to be on the committee—that would be unwieldy—but some means of representing their interests must be devised.

Many companies use a two-tier approach, as illustrated in Figure 8-2. In this case, there is a high-level steering committee to which the project leader reports. The steering committee concerns itself with strategic, policy, and fiscal matters, making sure the proper capital and operating funds are made available and spent wisely and that the company as a whole provides the necessary facilitation and support to ensure the project's success. This group meets far less frequently than the project

Figure 8-2. An SA task force—typical two-tier approach.

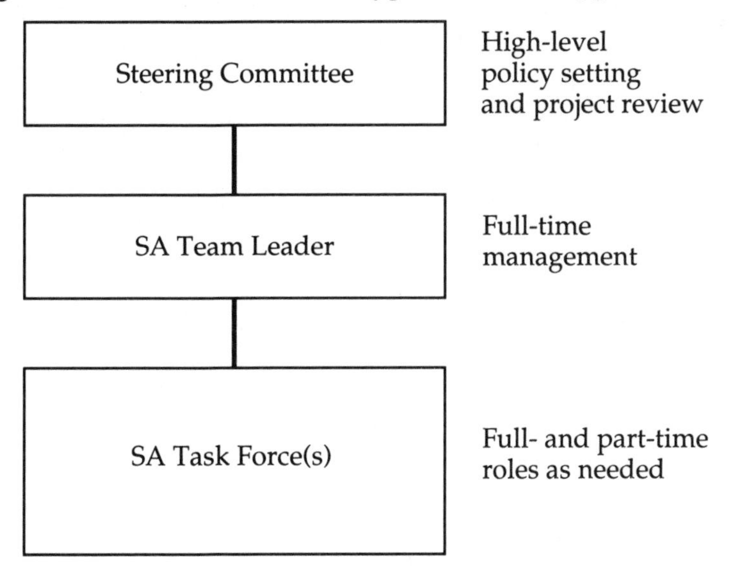

task force and generally receives assessments from the latter as to where the project stands, what serious problems exist, what is being done about them, and what additional help, if any, the team requires.

The team, on the other hand, consists of handpicked representatives of the various constituencies involved and is responsible for planning and implementing the system. In rare cases, particularly with very large systems in very large companies, there may be a third tier of task force members who take on limited assignments to be pursued in great depth within specific areas of the company. An example is a subteam in, for instance, human resources, whose mandate is to study sales force recruitment, orientation, and compensation issues and to make recommendations, without being ensnared in the ongoing design, development, and implementation processes.

All candidates for the team must have at least the following five attributes:

1. They must have deep understanding of the area they represent.
2. They must have an open channel of communication with other stakeholders within their particular domain.
3. They must be particularly good communicators.
4. They must exhibit a cooperative team spirit and a deep personal commitment to the success of the project in its teamwork setting.
5. They must have, or be given, the time it takes to participate and fulfill their responsibilities.

The Project Leader

The most crucial decision of all is who is to lead the SA project and precisely how the leader is going to be empowered to get the job done. The overwhelming vote goes to someone from sales, someone who has the experience of working in the field organization, who has earned its respect and trust, and who genuinely has the best interests of the sales department at heart.

This choice is partly symbolic—a message to sales and the rest of the company about priorities—and it's partly operational in the sense that any deadlocks should always be broken with a bias toward sales. Chances are that sales is paying for this project, and sales has the most to win or lose depending on the outcome.

How technically competent does the leader have to be? The answer is, Not at all. The leader's mission is to organize and lead team members representing the necessary areas of functional and technical competence, not to play autocrat and to dictate a system. In that sense, it might be well to choose a sales department leader who does *not* exhibit any particularly noteworthy computer background but who, like all the other members of the sales department, is going to have to learn it from scratch. If the leader can't understand the system, then what chance will the poor foot soldier in the field have?

The Leader's Role and Responsibilities

As we've said, the leader's primary responsibility is to organize and lead a team in the decision-making process, culminating in the design and implementation of a sales automation program. The leader should help choose the team members from various areas and should listen to their ideas, gain their cooperation, and orchestrate a team atmosphere in completing the assigned tasks.

As an example, the team will need to find out what kind of feedback the marketing department needs from the field regarding, for instance, the results obtained from sales leads generated by advertising, trade shows, and public relations efforts. The leader will not know the answer to this question, nor will the marketing representative(s). Someone will undoubtedly be delegated to go back to the people responsible for these activities, query them for needs and ideas, and then come back with a well-researched and carefully thought out proposal for consideration by the entire team. Should the team member ask for too much data, collection of which would alienate the sales force, the leader could step in and negotiate a compromise.

The leader must structure the team's activities, that is, set up regularly scheduled meetings and determine the agenda; preside at the meetings; keep the discussion moving and reasonably on target; and cause the results to be promulgated to the members and to supporting management (the steering committee, for example). Keeping formal minutes of each meeting is not a bad idea. As a starting point, you might follow a format like that in Figure 8-3, which not only spells out what happened in the meeting but addresses what open action items were resolved and how, which ones remain open, what new issues came up, leading to new action items, who is charged with the responsibility of carrying them out and by when, and where each one stands at the moment. It's not a bad idea to highlight the activities that appear to be in trouble, that are running behind schedule, or that require crucial action or information not currently available. Such emphasis can remind the responsible parties that they should take action or risk upsetting the whole project. It also focuses attention on these critical items at the next meeting; perhaps knowing such attention is forthcoming will encourage the participants to put forth extra effort in the meantime.

A team effort calls for absolute honesty and forthrightness, no matter how much it hurts. If people start hiding, or even shading, project shortcomings, the effort is heading for disaster. The leader, the team, and management must know what difficulties are being encountered. Too much is at risk to sweep anything under the rug. Corrective action is best applied while it can be helpful, not after the SA system has failed.

The leader needs to make it clear that nobody is going to be penalized for telling the truth, no matter how unpalatable it might be. Nobody should be dealt with harshly for making a mistake; that will encourage people not to take any risks or, alternatively, to cover up any adverse results.

Does the Leader Need to Be a Vice-President?

The short answer is, probably not, at least not unless freed from all other responsibilities. We are aware of one situation in which a large company empowered a senior vice-president to head up a sales automation program, which was to entail a six-month pilot program in a small number of field sales offices. Two and one half years later, the pilots were still going on and the results were inconclusive. The problem was that the proper

Figure 8-3. Sample SA task force meeting summary.

1. Date __________________ Place ____________________

2. Attendance

3. Summary of Meeting

4. Action Items Resolved This Period

Description	Due Date	Responsible Party	Resolution

5. New and Carry-Over Items for Next Period

Description	Due Date	Responsible Party	Status*

*Critical item at risk. Explain.

6. Overall Evaluation and Comments

use of the new automation tool required a change in selling, time, and territory management techniques. There were full-time systems analysts assigned to the project from MIS, but who were they to tell (or even coach) senior field sales representatives and managers on how to do their jobs? The senior sales executive in charge of the project had a million and one other things to do besides coddling a few field people in the intimidating intricacies of using computer data to change the work habits of a lifetime. Commanding them to do so didn't work.

As a result, a complete restart had to be undertaken three years into the program. Not only was the restart costly, but it implied enormous opportunity cost in the time lost while competitors were implementing and perfecting their SA systems.

In our view, the leader functions best in a classical matrix management role similar to the familiar "product manager," who is responsible for the success of a product but who has no direct authority over the resources required for producing the product. Sounds impossible to those who haven't tried it, but the product—or in this case, project—leader bases his or her authority on strength of focus and knowledge. No one else in the company spends quite as much time and energy on the SA project as the project leader, who is at every meeting and who talks, eats, and sleeps sales automation day and night, becoming totally identified with the project in the minds of everyone else involved. The project leader becomes the most knowledgeable member of the team, the one person who has an iron in every fire and a finger in every dike. The leader is the one who knows the meeting schedule, the agendas, who and who won't be there next time, what management's latest thoughts are about the program, what the consultants are saying, and what the vendors are doing.

With this visibility and knowledge comes power—the power to persuade. By and large, the project leader simply persuades the task force members to do their parts and meet their commitments. Certainly, each member is subject to public embarrassment at the next meeting if his promised action item hasn't been properly attended to. Furthermore, having established a posture of prestige and omniscience, the project leader is in position to lower the boom on any recalcitrant and irredeemable rascal, should it come to a showdown. This, of course, isn't desirable, and it seldom becomes necessary, but the potential is always there as a deterrent.

Roles and Responsibilities of the Other Members

All team members are knowledgeable communicators who take a very active part in representing their particular area of interest and funnel information between their departments and the team. For example, representatives from the field sales organization play a predominant role in selecting, setting up, supervising, and measuring the results of any kind of field trial, such as a preliminary prototype test or a pilot installation or in field visits to other users' sales departments as part of the vendor selection process.

Additionally, task force members actually do the work—the long, arduous analysis and decision making regarding goal setting, determining overall design parameters, selecting vendors, budgeting, designing the system, and planning and implementing it. In many cases, this amounts to a full-time job for one or several of the task force members, including the leader. Certainly, enough is at stake to warrant such a commitment of resources.

Not everybody needs to work full-time on the project, and not even the full-timers have to do so forever. Continuity is, however, essential. An endlessly revolving door with people in briefly and out again won't contribute to a planned, focused vision with a predictable outcome.

We suggest that the leader develop a staffing plan for the project that includes her best possible estimate of the length and intensity of service that will be required of each participant, subject to revision. That staffing plan is an integral part of the overall project plan and budget. If it's not, completing the rest of it doesn't make any sense—there's no use buying millions of dollars worth of computers and software if there aren't going to be enough willing hands around to make it work.

The steering committee, if there is one apart from the

project team, should probably meet once a month with the leader to review progress, counsel, and take on certain essential management assignments. This group is responsible for setting, or at least endorsing, the overall goals of the program, but it does not meddle with the details, since it lacks both the necessary time and knowledge. It should therefore resign itself to watching the team do its work and making sure it gets the support needed to be successful.

The team, on the other hand, needs to meet frequently, perhaps once a week as an umbrella group, with subcommittees and subtask teams meeting more often. In some cases, members will need to visit the field, vendor shops, or other SA users. Don't forget to allocate some funds for travel to cover the costs of such visits.

Techniques for building consensus in the team are discussed in Chapter 10. Coming together to work toward a common goal is among the most important of the team's responsibilities.

Management Commitment: Don't Leave Home Base Without It

Two characteristics of SA require top management's highest level of support: its high cost and the change it brings in the way people work. If the computer system simply replaces the current pen and pencil with a keyboard or a mouse, it's not worth doing. In addition, people generally resist change; therefore they need encouragement from top management to accept SA. To help facilitate change, management should refrain from demanding that day-to-day performance not be adversely impacted during the transition from the old system to the new one. Left to itself, this isn't the way it is likely to happen. The first time a senior executive picks up the phone and accuses a field manager of missing quota because he's out there "playing computer games," it's all over for SA in that particular domain.

In view of this reaction, one of the most important of the team leader's responsibilities is to maintain top management's enthusiastic support of the program. Without such support, SA absolutely will not succeed.

Chapter 9

Justifying the System

Since the development of the computer, people have found ways to impact their business environment dramatically by applying technology to their business practices. Early uses of the computer were mainly scientific in nature and were funded by the government, which provided ample resources. Businesses, however, do not have the luxury of being able to tax their customers and have to work within budgets, with each functional group fighting for the same limited set of dollars. The functional group with the best plan, the one that meets strategic and return-on-investment goals, usually receives the funding to develop and implement its project.

The pool of budget dollars can be increased two ways: by increasing sales while maintaining profit margins or by increasing profit margins while maintaining sales. There are many ways to accomplish these goals. This chapter presents the benefits of sales automation and describes how those benefits can result in revenue enhancements, cost savings, and cost avoidances. It gives specific examples of direct and indirect cost savings and discusses how they can be identified and quantified. It provides examples of intangible benefits, including marketplace advantage, competitive advantages, and sales force and customer retention. The likely cost elements, including hardware, software, support, and maintenance, are addressed.

The best place to start looking for cost justification opportunities are areas where automation can provide direct tangible benefits to the bottom line. For many applications, these areas can be identified early in the project cycle, at the conceptual stage, before any major costs are incurred. The following examples show how two organizations developed cost justifications to get approval for their projects.

CASE #1

At a major consumer goods company, each salesperson on average was responsible for selling over $10 million in products to his or her accounts, which were military commissaries. The terms and conditions of contract performance and pricing were heavily weighted toward the customer. All prices had to be the lowest available. Pricing mistakes in favor of the seller had to be reimbursed to the government, and pricing mistakes in favor of the government stood as sold.

The average individual order for a single customer location contained over 500 line items. Prior to writing up the order, the sales representative took a physical inventory at the customer location to determine the appropriate order quantities. An order was then calculated by hand, a process that not only was time-consuming but carried the potential for error. The order was then called in by phone to a data entry clerk who either entered the order while on the phone with the sales representative or wrote it on paper for entry at a later time. A typical order took from five to seven hours of the sales representative's time for preparation. There were ten data entry clerks at different distribution locations supporting the sales efforts of thirty sales representatives.

Analysis of the order, billing, and pricing process revealed that, on average, each order contained at least three mistakes that cost the company an average of $1,000 per order. This loss was composed of unrecoverable revenue from prices that were lower than contract or deal pricing and the labor (both sales and clerical) associated with fixing pricing mistakes that favored the seller. Each salesperson wrote an average of 160 orders per year; thus, the total loss to the company for order mistakes was over $4.8 million per year. The graph in Figure 9-1 represents a typical salesperson's time analysis prior to sales automation.

On the basis of this information, the sales department con-

Figure 9-1. Salesperson time analysis before sales automation: company #1.

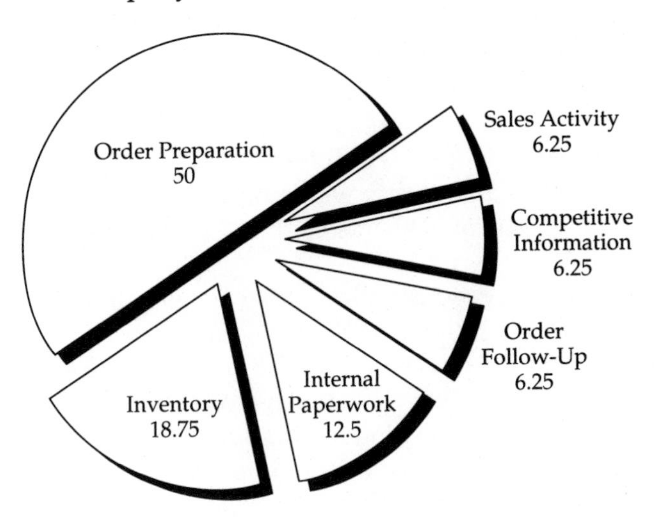

tracted to develop an automated order entry and inventory management system. The system comprised three components: (1) a handheld computer and bar-code wand used to collect inventory and stocking information at the customer location, (2) a laptop computer–based order processing and inventory tracking system, and (3) a microcomputer-based pricing system located at headquarters. The systems were interfaced with the company's mainframe-based order processing and billing systems through electronic data interchange (EDI).

After the system was installed, a salesperson would take a physical inventory of the commissary's store shelves and warehouse to determine its inventory levels, using the handheld computer and bar-code wand. This information was then transferred to the laptop computer and processed by the order processing and inventory management system. The order processing system produced an "ideal order" based on the last four inventory levels at the customer site and merged that order with the latest contract and deal pricing. The resulting order was then reviewed and modified by the salesperson as necessary. The graph in Figure 9-2 represents a salesperson's activities after sales automation.

Installation of the SA system yielded dramatic results. Complete elimination of order mistakes resulted in annual savings of $4.8 million. Reduction in the number of data entry clerks from ten to one resulted in annual savings of $360,000. Six months after the system was installed, sales were 10 percent higher than the year before in an industry with a historical annual growth rate of less than 4 percent. This resulted in $30 million in additional sales.

The company received many other benefits from the system. Because the system tracked the last four order cycles, product movement could be tracked, preventing stockouts or overordering of slow-moving products. Local or regional buying trends could be monitored and new product introduced to the appropriate markets. Past sales information could be referenced and used as a tool to motivate buyers to purchase. The amount of time spent preparing an order dropped from between five and seven hours to less than two. The available time was then used by the salespeople to build product displays, collect competitive information, and perform merchandising activities. The system enhanced the rela-

Figure 9-2. Salesperson time analysis after sales automation: company #1.

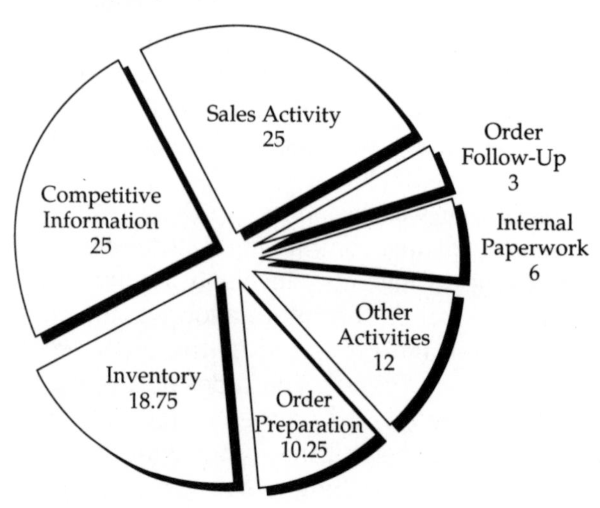

tionship between the buyers and the salespeople. In fact, after the system had been operational for some time and buyers learned to trust the results of the computer-generated order, buyers would give the salespeople priority when scheduling meetings and allocating shelf and end cap space.

CASE #2

A company in the food services industry used a push-and-pull marketing/sales strategy. It used a 170-person sales force to sell its products to distributors, who sold to end-user customers such as restaurants and hospitals, and to headquarters locations for companies like McDonald's or Marriott, which then distributed the product to their local outlets. The company's sales force called on the distributors and headquarters locations to get products into the distribution channel and then called on the end users to get them to buy products and participate in sales programs.

It was a very complex selling environment, with contract and volume pricing for a broad product line. The salespeople had to keep track of costly equipment that was supplied to end users who met specific volume commitments. Large amounts of paper-based information circulated among salespeople, sales offices, and headquarters. This information included call plans, call reports, territory plans, sales history reports, volume-tracking reports, order status reports, booking reports, promotion and deal programs, expense reports, and pricing and contract information.

Salespeople were buried under paper, in many cases receiving information that was no longer timely or that was not in usable form. Despite this, the division showed the most profit as a percentage of sales of any in the company. Sales management needed a way to justify the system before spending a large amount of capital. Since the salespeople and district managers were very unhappy with the way information was disseminated, divisional sales management analyzed the way information was distributed and collected. Sales management found it was using a number of methods and services: regular mail, overnight shipping, facsimile machines, and the telephone. Over a period of a quarter, it analyzed what was sent and by which method and then totaled up the costs. The total was astounding. It was costing over $500,000 per year to distribute information inefficiently to the sales force.

Sales management then explored alternative ways of distributing the information. It found that the vast majority of the information could be sent electronically if the appropriate systems were in place. Analysis of the cost of transmitting the information electronically determined that it would cost $250,000 annually to send the same information it was now costing $500,000 to distribute less effectively.

Management then determined that it would cost $1 million to put systems in place to duplicate the present level of information distribution. This information would be more valuable to the salespeople because it would be received sooner and be presented in a more meaningful way. Management also believed that an electronic sales information system would be easier for the salespeople to use than the paper system. It then looked for ways the system could affect how the company was managed. Analysis of how employees were spending their time (see Figure 9-3) and ways they could change activity levels to have a positive effect on their business was undertaken.

Sales management believed that increasing the amount of

Figure 9-3. Time analysis before sales automation: company #2.

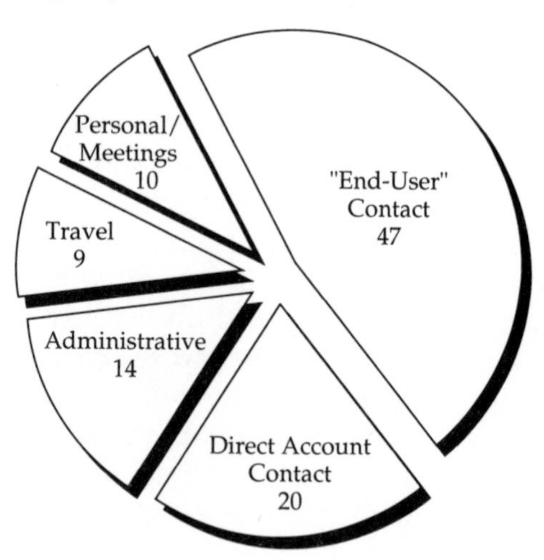

time salespeople spent with end-user customers would have a positive effect on business. This was established as a major goal of the system. While management could not determine what the effect would be before investing in sales automation systems, it established a target of a 15 percent increase in end-user sales activity. It then determined what it would cost to increase end-user sales activity by increasing sales resources through the addition of salespeople. Their average cost per salesperson was $75,000. Sales representatives spent 47 percent of their time calling on end-user accounts. The formula management developed was $75,000 × 47% = $35,250 cost for end-user sales calls per territory; $35,250 × 170 salespeople = $5,992,500 cost for end-user sales calls for the division; $5,992,500 × 15% = $898,875 cost to increase end-user sales by 15 percent by adding 12 salespeople ($898,875/$75,000 = 12).

Management then prepared a pilot project plan using (1) the potential $250,000 annual savings from the electronic distribution of information, and (2) $898,875 annual sales resource cost avoidance. Using the company's two-year return-on-investment model, it prepared a plan that offered a potential return of $2,297,750 for an investment of $1 million. It asked for and received funding of $300,000 to pilot the system in a thirty-salesperson region.

The results of the pilot are presented in Figure 9-4. The key component is the increase of 23.4 percent in end-user sales calls, from 47 percent of salespersons' call activity to 58 percent. Call activity to direct accounts decreased by 10 percent during the same period. There were also other significant benefits, including a 28.5 percent reduction in administrative time from 14 percent to 10 percent and an 11 percent reduction in travel time from 9 percent to 8 percent of sales activity.

The division experienced other benefits that had a direct positive effect on its bottom line. These included (1) increased sales and profits in the pilot region, and (2) a significant decrease in sales force turnover. The system also provided a foundation for additional sales automation applications that have been added as sales management became accustomed to using technology in the business environment. It has since automated its whole sales force and built a complete closed loop sales and marketing system,

Figure 9-4. Time analysis after sales automation: company #2.

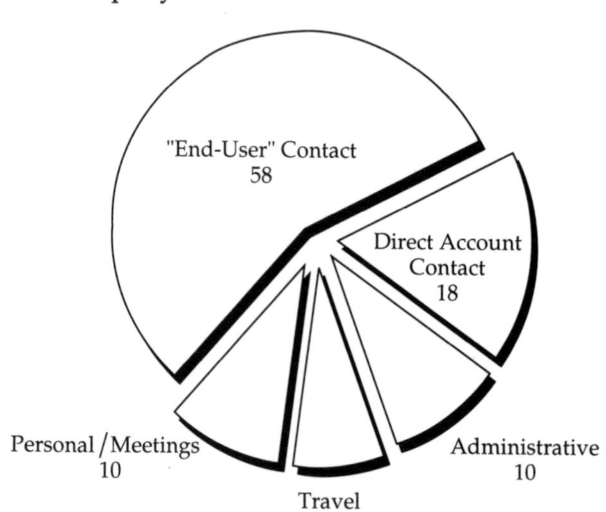

including a telemarketing system, a sales resource deployment system, and a marketing database containing over 150,000 entries; it is close to reaching the goal of being a completely automated division.

These examples show how two organizations developed two different cost justifications to get approval for their projects. Since the methods they used may not apply to your sales environment, the following section describes alternatives for you to consider.

Cost Justification Methods

Sales automation can be used to restructure time and territory management. Many companies have justified SA systems by establishing a goal of increased sales calls, and others have gone further, establishing a goal of more effective sales calls through target marketing—calling on predetermined prospects who meet buyer profiles for their products. Time and territory management sales automation systems focus the salespeople by streamlining their prospecting methods and sales reporting. If salespeople who make an average of twenty sales calls a week can increase that figure by 20 percent, there is a significant likelihood that they will close more business. A simple formula is:

Cost per salesperson/number of sales calls = cost per sales call

For example:

$50,000/800 calls per year = $62.50 per call

A 20 percent increase in sales calls would result in 160 additional sales calls per year (800 × 20% = 160). That would lower the cost per sales call to $52 per call, a $10.50 savings per call and a $10,080 annual savings ($50,000/[800 + 160] = $52). If a salesperson closes business an average of once every five sales calls and an average order is $5,000, you can expect an increase in sales of $160,000 per salesperson ([160/5 = 32] × $5,000 = $160,000).

Focusing salespeople only on those opportunities that offer a high probability of success through target prospecting can have an effect on close ratios. A sales database with appropriate analysis tools can focus sales activity on potential customers who meet specific criteria, leading to higher close ratios. Using the previous example, if salespeople were able to increase close ratios from one in five to one in four and they maintained the same level of call activity (800 calls per year), the result would be an increase in closes from 160 per year (800 calls/5) to 200 per year (800 calls/4). Using an average sale of $5,000 per close, annual sales would increase by $200,000.

Distribution Management Systems

Cost-justifying sales automation systems used in distribution management (e.g., in consumer goods companies) can use inputs from traditional financial reports. For example, a client of one of the authors, a manufacturer of leisure products, did an analysis of lost orders (orders that are booked but later canceled for some reason by the customer). Analysis of the detailed information showed the following: (1) Over $5 million of orders annually fell into this category, (2) of the orders, 50 percent ($2.5 million) were canceled because product was not available for shipment in a reasonable amount of time, (3) the company had sufficient inventories of substitute products at the time the original products were ordered or canceled to provide alternative products to the customers. The company believed that its salespeople, if provided with availability information, could have influenced customers to substitute alternative products 30 percent of the time, either at the time the order was written or before it was canceled. A sales automation system was put in place that provided inventory and order status information to the salespeople. The result was the recovery of $1 million in annual revenue that had been lost prior to the system's installation.

Other Cost Justification Areas

The cost of a sales automation system can sometimes be justified by the creation of a closed loop sales and marketing database. Business spends billions of dollars each year on advertising, trade shows, and direct marketing. The leads that are generated are typically processed and sent to the sales force for follow-up. Usually, at that point they have reached the end of their journey—in a salesperson's garbage can. The reasons for this are many. The prospects may have been poorly qualified to begin with, or perhaps they were not "hot" anymore, or perhaps the salesperson's experience with previous leads had been less than satisfactory.

Distributing leads electronically can shorten the delivery cycle and allow salespeople to follow up on them more quickly. "Hot" leads provide better results than "cold" leads. A company can expect a significant increase in positive responses to leads by shortening the follow-up response time.

Many computer-based lead tracking systems provide analysis features to help determine the effectiveness of alternative media and promotion choices. This is accomplished by capturing the results of the salesperson's lead follow-up. The results of the sales calls are entered into the system by the user and electronically transferred back to the lead tracking database. As the salesperson moves the prospect through the sales cycle, the lead database is continually updated to reflect the outcome of sales activity. The outcomes are measured for number of leads generated by specific advertising and/or marketing activity. Advertisements and media and marketing programs that generate more leads of a higher quality can be targeted for future use, resulting in increased sales and lower costs for qualified lead generation.

One method for measuring cost justification in a closed loop lead tracking and contact management system follows. Prior to installation of a system, target goals are set to increase the number of leads per dollar spent and to increase the quality of the leads generated. The quality of leads is measured by tracking the leads to see which, over time, result in business. If a company spends $1 million a year on advertising to generate 100,000 leads, each lead costs $10 to generate. If 10 percent of the leads result in sales, the cost per sale would be $100. If, after analysis, advertising and promotion vehicles are chosen that generate 50 percent more qualified leads, the cost per lead drops to $6.66 and the cost per sale drops to $66.66. The company can also track the size and profitability of the sales. This analysis can determine which promotion vehicles produce the most revenue and profits per sale.

The examples given earlier in the chapter are real-life techniques used by companies to justify their sales automation projects. As early adopters of SA, they had to determine the techniques they used through logical reasoning and good business judgment. It is important to remember that savings can be derived from areas that are not directly part of the sales function. Administrative and operational savings were realized by one of the earlier examples. Cost justification can come from increased revenue, lower costs, or cost avoidances. As more companies adopt SA systems, latecomers will have to introduce them as a defensive tactic rather than as a strategic measure, making cost justification moot.

Software—The Make-vs.-Buy Alternative

There are presently over 1,000 sales automation software packages. With so many alternatives, why have many companies chosen custom solutions over shrink-wrapped packages? The first point to understand is that the vast majority of SA software products offer capabilities for a limited custom implementation. Their custom capabilities include the naming of a limited number of data fields and the entries to populate those fields. Reports can also be customized to reflect an individual company's requirements. While this limited capability may meet the requirements of some companies, others will find severe shortcomings.

Many of the SA applications offered by vendors today are designed for significant customization. They provide core modules (for example, electronic mail, contact management) and the vendors use software development tools to create custom applications that meet the client's specific requirements. The development tools fall into two categories: (1) low-level programming languages (for example C and COBOL) and (2) high-level fourth-generation languages combined with relational database "engines." High-level languages offer significantly faster development cycles. Many have prototype development systems that create running applications. By using iterative prototyping techniques in conjunction with the client's SA team, the vendors quickly create applications to meet the client's custom requirements.

It has been our experience that the requirement for custom SA applications increases with (1) the size of the sales force, (2) the requirement for movement of data between the sales force and other corporate databases, (3) the complexity of the sales cycle, (4) the complexity of the company's product lines, and (5) the technological investment at the company.

Custom development charges range from $500 to $1,500 per day for application design and development. Development times can range from months for high-level language development to years for low-level language development. The resulting cost can range from the tens of thousands to millions of dollars.

Whether custom or shrink-wrapped applications are chosen depends on the individual company and the requirements that have been determined by the SA team. Companies can expect to pay from $1,000 to $5,000 or more per salesperson for SA software license and application development fees. The company in one of the previous cost justification examples spent $10,000 per salesperson for the software. Responses from eight different SA vendors to a major company's request for proposal for a second-generation SA system for its 2,000 sales representatives produced software cost estimates ranging from $1,000 to $4,000 per sales representative. Including hardware, training, and support costs, the proposals ranged upward to $20 million over the expected three-year project life. However, these automation costs represent less than 5 percent of the company's sales costs. Without the SA system the company could not meet its targets for revenue and profitability.

Sales automation systems typically cost between $7,000 and $15,000 per salesperson to implement and operate over a project's three- to five-year life. These costs include hardware, software, software maintenance, communications, training, service, and support. The cost ranges for each category are typically:

Hardware	$2,000–$7,000 per person
Software	$1,000–$4,000 per person
Central Communications and Application Server	$20,000–$500,000 per server
Training	$500–$2,000 per person
Communications	$500–$2,000 annually
Hardware Service	5%–15% of the cost of hardware annually
Software Maintenance	10%–15% of the cost of software annually
Software Support	$150–$500 per person annually

Closing the sales automation system loop requires an effective communications networking platform. Most SA software vendors include a communications network as part of their solution. The technological alternatives available include microcomputer networks, minicomputers, or mainframes. SA software vendors typically choose one platform for the communication server portion of their solution.

Microcomputer networks offer advantages over minicomputers or mainframes. Microcomputer-to-microcomputer data transmissions are more efficient, resulting in 15 to 30 percent higher data throughput rates. These rates are attained because a computer processor is dedicated to the data transmission at each end of the transmission. This will result in lower communications costs over the life of the project.

Minicomputers are also used as communications servers. Typical servers in this category use the Unix operating system, Digital Equipment Corporation's VMS operating system, or IBM's AS400 with PC support. Minicomputers have historically supported asynchronous dial-up capabilities. Most early SA systems used this technology and it is still viable today.

Mainframes are also used as communication servers by some SA vendors. Most third-party value added networks also use mainframe technology. It is unlikely, however, that mainframes will remain a significant communication server platform in the future.

Value added networks provide an easy way to implement a national or international communications network. They provide local dial-up capabilities in most areas. They can be expensive because most providers charge for connect time, the amount of data transmitted, the amount of data stored, and the processing time. Their rates also increase for high rates of data transmission—for example, 9,600 BPS (bits per second) versus 2,400 BPS.

The least-cost alternative for data transmission is "800" dial-up service. The per-minute rates can be fixed on the basis of expected usage. The charges are typically billed by the minute or less. There are no additional charges beyond these except for the initial installation charges. A problem that can be encountered using this service is "noisy" lines at the remote user's location in remote areas. This problem should be overcome in the future as more local phone companies upgrade their systems with digital transmission capabilities.

Most sales automation systems are connected to the corporate information systems. How this is done must be considered during the early phases of the SA project. There are a wealth of options available today, and your corporate information systems department or outside resources should be used to ensure the success of this SA system function. With this key element in place, the vast resource of corporate systems and data will become available to the SA system.

The communications server can reside in-house or in a third-party location. Many SA vendors offer this service as part of their solution. The basic benefits are lower head count and no requirement for additional information system facilities. The drawbacks are a loss of control over the system and dependence on the third party, who has to answer to your users.

With all SA systems, the users need training and ongoing support. This training and support can be provided by in-house resources, the SA vendor, or another third-party training vendor. The initial training should be focused on key elements of the system that provide value to the user. Training should last from two to three days. Many companies piggyback training on regional or national meetings. Class sizes should range from ten to twelve users with a trainer and two facilitators for each class. Good candidates for facilitators during the national rollout are members of the pilot group.

Ongoing support should be provided through "800" hot lines with staff able to answer questions and resolve technical issues. At the very least, the hot lines should be available during business hours and preferably during the early morning and evening as well. The hot-line staff should be expert users of the SA system and have knowledge of the hardware used.

Implementing sales automation is a major effort but the potential rewards are great. A clearly defined cost justification strategy will ensure project approval and provide the framework for measuring success. The software, hardware, and support alternatives chosen will be determined by need and corporate standards. The result will be a comprehensive system implementation that will increase the productivity and effectiveness of sales resources.

Part III

Planning, Implementation, and Execution

Chapter 10

The Human Factor

In a clerical, administrative, or data processing shop, people are judged and rewarded on the basis of how well they perform prescribed procedures. On the other hand, sales and marketing people are hired to get results, not to follow procedures; most of them avoid procedure, by either nature or accustomation.

The methods for using computers look very much like procedures—computer tasks can be accomplished only in certain highly structured ways—and have the added drawback of looking complicated and technological. Most sales and marketing people dislike technology as well as procedures, and there is often a problem in motivating them to learn and use the system; it simply goes against the grain.

There's another problem. Everybody knows there is a database inside the computer that can, and most certainly will, be accessed by management. This possibility raises the specter of "Big Brother" watching, monitoring every move. The typical sales representative, selected for self-confidence and independent spirit, is unlikely to be happy with an electronic watchbird reporting every time he takes a long lunch or an afternoon off, accomplishes fewer calls on a given day, or fails to meet stated objectives on a given call.

Certainly, most companies value creative self-direction in their sales representatives, provided, however, the reps are able to drive themselves in the right direction. That's what SA is all about: providing the salesperson with a technologically based edge to enable him to do a better job of planning his activities, targeting where it can do the most good, and recording and reporting in such a way that important things don't fall through the cracks and that the overhead is reduced to its irreducible minimum. And SA tries to achieve these improvements in a matter of weeks.

But an SA system simply won't fly, no matter how good it is, if it is perceived as:

- Difficult to use;
- A management tool to whip the sales force into shape; or
- Having no particular benefit for the sales representative who is being turned into a keypunch operator.

Therefore, the whole approach, from conception through design, procurement, implementation, and ongoing support, must emphasize the benefits of the system for *users*—and find ways to convince users that these benefits are real.

You can make sure the system offers benefits for the user by doing a superior job of needs analysis up front, ensuring that the system will perform extremely useful functions for the sales representatives that either are not being performed at all now or are being done in a crude and inadequate way. Along with advantages for the sales representatives comes a similar one for their immediate managers. If the immediate boss thinks little of the system, perceiving no great value in it for either himself or the representatives, then there will be a chilly downdraft blowing on the program in the field, which will eventually kill it. Thus, it's important that the preliminary analysis incorporate advantages for the field sales manager and that those benefits, as well as the ones for the sales force, be made abundantly clear to field management.

You can look at the program as an enormous sandwich consisting of a huge slice of needs analysis on top, an equally large slice of public relations on the bottom, and a bit of carefully prepared meat in the middle. It's the meat in the middle that most people think of as SA, but without the surroundings, nobody will eat it.

The top slice, as stated, has to be chock full of tasty ingredients needed to meet the recommended minimum daily requirement of an undernourished field organization. But the whole package has to look and feel palatable to the participants. Palatability is as much ambiance and presentation as it is actual taste and feel, so the fundamentals of enlisting the field's enthusiastic participation must include these three principles:

1. The sales representatives must know that you have carefully and exhaustively considered their requirements and ideas in the initial conception and design of the system.
2. The field must be kept informed (and if possible enthused) about the development and implementation of the system as it unfolds.
3. The system must be presented to them during orientation and training phases in ways that make it seem beneficial and easy to use, and in no way a threat to them.

The first principle suggests that the opinions of many, if not all, members of the field organization be solicited as part of the needs analysis phase. It need not be done in person; a mailed questionnaire might be perfectly okay. And nobody says that every single wild or wily idea from the field has to be incorporated—just considered, that's all.

The second principle suggests a newsletter, frequent bulletins, appearances at sales meetings, background coverage in house organs, and periodic face-to-face meetings and group orientations for as many of the prospective users as possible. A secondary benefit of this public relations blitz is continued visibility for the system's planners with the top decision makers without whose continued support the program will wither and die.

Many developers have carried this principle to its logical extreme, with a catchy name and logo for the project, a special letterhead, a dedicated house organ, audio and video informational presentations, brochures, and other paraphernalia. In our experience, this hoopla does correlate with success; the more there is of it, the more likely it is that a particular program will get the management support and field reception it deserves.

The third principle, like almost everything else in life, has both a substance and a perception angle to it. The substance is the real effort to discipline management *not* to bias the system toward surveillance, control, and information gathering. Management must keep repeating, "This is for the field, not us. This is going to make their jobs easier to do, make them more money, and enhance their life and work styles. And we're going to get some useful by-product information out of it, as well." The appearance aspect has to do with how the system is presented to the user community. Data One, for example, which has been involved with many so-called rollouts to the field of laptop computer–based SA systems, often takes on the responsibility of receiving and testing machines, loading up the initial complement of software, and transshipping them to representatives just prior to initial "hands-on" training. In that initial software load is a set of interesting computer games with easy-to-understand instructions. The result is that many representatives arrive at their assigned training sites as full-blown computer hackers, almost as accomplished as their nine-year-old children.

The Training

To be effective, training in sales automation has to be interesting and professional, and it most assuredly should not be a total immersion shock treatment. Many, many companies make the mistake of attempting to cover too much of the system at one sitting. Users become restless, especially those peripatetic field sales representatives; they should not be required to sit in class or at keyboards for days at a time.

Another reason for breaking the training into manageable units is that there is a certain satisfaction in having just mastered a sector of the system—"Look, Ma, I can log in a sales call!"—that is lost if there is another round of exposure to the unfamiliar, such as, "You ain't seen nothing yet. Here's how to format your own custom reports from the system using our handy-dandy report generator, which looks simple to us career data processing specialists who used to do the same thing the hard way by rubbing two sticks together." It may look simple to the people who designed or selected it, but it won't look that way to first-time users on their first exposure.

You get the idea. The system has to be taught to the field in small, easily digestible, and rewarding increments, after which reps need time to practice and assimilate what they've learned. Accountants and sales managers alike will immediately rise up in indignation with the outcry that this means multiple trainings, more time out of the field, more travel and lodging costs, and delayed implementation of the total system. Yes. But which is preferable: delay and extra cost, or failure? The former must be built into the plan right from the start in order to avoid the near certainty of the latter.

We go into more of the details of this gradual approach to implementation and training in Chapter 12, but be sensitive to the fact that exposure to too many totally unfamiliar new ideas and techniques at once leads to psychic overload, which generates discouragement and hostility that may be very difficult to overcome later. We are reminded of one major company that brought 600 previously uninitiated representatives and managers to the home office for five days of intensive training on the new, perfectly wonderful sales automation system. Every single one of them got on an airplane Friday night vowing never, never to touch that monstrosity again, and sure enough, they didn't. There was nothing wrong with the system—just with how it was thrown at them over a single torturous week of schooling.

Dealing With "Computerphobia"

Some old-timers among representatives and managers would sooner step into a pit of rattlesnakes than touch a computer keyboard. Fortunately, their numbers are diminishing as young, computer-literate people enter the work force, as experienced people are recruited from companies where they have already been exposed to automation, and as many of the resisters simply succumb. The goal of any SA orientation and training program is to break down any residual resistance and bring everyone up to a high level of proficiency in using the powerful new tool.

Still, a few of the "students" are going to make this very difficult, so let's take a moment to give these hard cases special attention. There are two schools of thought in dealing with this problem. One advocates taking the directive approach, which says, "This is the way we now do things. Get with the program or polish your resume." Only you know whether this is the right approach in your company with your people.

An alternative, however, is to tolerate resistance by allowing the laggards to continue to use written and telephoned responses and assigning someone else, a secretary or sales administrator, to update and retrieve computer records. Actually, in some companies this isn't a bad way of dealing with the system permanently, especially if representatives spend a lot of time driving and can be in contact via cellular telephone with a computer operator wearing a headset who gets them the information they need and captures from them the data the system needs. Costly, yes, but the resulting improvement in effectiveness in the marketplace might more than justify it.

There are certainly ways of building in incentives for the field to adapt to the system quickly. The obvious one is to make it so attractive and productive that everyone will want to use it. Another is to build in convenience functions or, conversely, to make doing the corresponding functions the old way inconvenient. For example, one division president determined to get his sales department on board with automation. His first step was to introduce electronic mail to his staff. The sales vice-president happened to be a computer-averse young lady, but she found herself out of the loop when it came to recent pronouncements, policy and price changes, and directives from the head office. To stay informed, she conquered her reluctance and began using the Email system to good effect. The next step was to do exactly the same thing with the sales force. In order to keep up to date, sales representatives found it highly desirable to master the keyboard and get into the Email network. Next came an on-line order entry system that cut days and even weeks off the time it took to get an account set up and sales commissions credited.

Then came the clincher. The president ruled that because of the cost and incompatibilities of the old paper-based system, it had to be discontinued altogether. That meant that no sales representatives could enter an order or be paid sales commission without first tapping the order into a keyboard. Needless to say, even the staunchest resisters came around quickly for computer lessons.

Tools in the Educational Kit Bag

Clearly, the front line in converting your staff to the use of an automated system is training, probably formal classroom-style, whether at the home office, regional or other cluster locations, or individual branches. If this training is done well, the job of remediation—handling the slow or reluctant learners—will be minimized, but it will still be there.

Videotapes can be used to impart and reinforce skills. A somewhat similar but more intense and more expensive approach is computer-based training (CBT), which uses a specially developed training program with which the user interacts at the keyboard and that is specifically designed to teach uses of a particular application. The advantage of this approach is that it can be distributed widely and cheaply, wherever a floppy diskette can go, and each learner can proceed at her own pace, in private.

There are some drawbacks to CBT, however. First, the standard, simple, packaged SA applications programs on the market today are considered so easy to use by their authors that no CBT, apart from the program itself, has been developed. If you wish to develop one from scratch, which you would have to do for your own custom SA program, go ahead—but be ready for a five-figure price tag. Further, once you've made the investment, be prepared to see the package become obsolete as changes and improvements are made to the subject application. That's a given, and it will be both hard and costly to keep up to date.

If the number of students to be trained and their geographic dispersion justify CBT, then it can be a big help in bringing people up the learning curve. It may be especially advantageous for people who need to learn in private to avoid embarrassment over their fumbling and mistakes.

The most potent tool for teaching SA, however, is patient, one-on-one instruction. By definition, this type of learning is self-paced and, if the teacher is a diplomat, unembarrassing and nonthreatening. It is clearly very expensive, but it may be the only way to bring the really tough, sensitive cases along, the kind to be found typically among older, top-performing sales representatives and managers.

Skill vs. Behavior

One of the stumbling blocks constantly encountered in providing automation support to sales organizations is not just overcoming computer reluctance and imparting specific keyboard skills but seeing to it that the system is used to advantage. This, in the final analysis, is the real challenge, and the toughest.

In the pharmaceutical industry, for instance, representatives tend to call on doctors who will see them without a struggle, who are friendly, and who accept samples of the product. These doctors may not be the most frequent prescribers of the particular kind of drug the representative is promoting. The high prescribers may be, and often are, extremely busy, already wedded to the competition, and very difficult to get in to see for even a minute or two.

A properly designed SA system containing good marketplace data classifies the population of doctors for the territory representative and singles out high prescribers and other points of significant influence. The system includes everything the representative needs to orchestrate a planned, coordinated attack on these high-potential accounts—where they are in the sales cycle, what has been accomplished to date, what to cover next, and connections with other company resources such as brochures, seminars, or specialists willing to conduct clinical trials with the target physician or group.

All that can be in the system, but will it actually affect the representative's behavior? Will the representative stop making the old familiar rounds and adopt a more strategic, planned approach? The answer is much more likely to be yes if:

- The training deals with how to accomplish the potential enhancements to personal and territory management, not in the abstract but in real situations.
- There are "ringers" in the group who take to the new methods like a duck to water and set the example for everyone else.
- Most important, the immediate supervisors—branch, district, regional, and country managers—want it to happen and are willing to coach representatives carefully and continuously to make sure it does happen.

A properly planned and executed pilot program in the right atmosphere, with measured and indisputably positive results, brings along resistant reps and managers because it demonstrates what's in it for them, namely, better performance. Nonetheless, people tend to slip back into old habits, so eternal vigilance is required to keep stimulating and inspiring the field to make full use of the system. Troubleshooting field visits, remedial training, and continued dissemination of propaganda about the power of the system and the success of leading-edge users among sales peers can motivate the sales department and help it achieve the predicted results by which the system was justified. This includes keeping the system growing and changing with the times, as well as providing ongoing training on new features and techniques. It's likely to be an endless job, but it's also simply part of *the* job, just as routine procedures are the responsibility now of representatives and their managers. In other words, mastery and use of the SA system should be viewed not as a frill but as integral to "the way we do things around here."

This will not happen if the representatives don't want it to happen. They can and will defeat any system they feel is not devised in their best interests, by either ignoring it, lying to it, complaining endlessly about it, or a combination thereof. They will find (or create) errors in the data that can be magnified out of all proportion. They may, if the pressure gets too intense, invent phantom sales calls, follow-ups, and demonstrations. If the system goes down, the hardware fails, or some other glitch arises—which most certainly will happen on rare occasions—they can either take it in stride or write an anonymous letter to the chairman of the board threatening class action litigation for loss of livelihood.

The Help Desk

You are going to need hot-line support at least during working hours and perhaps far beyond, since field people often work strange hours. If the representatives feel supported, have some place to go with questions and difficulties, and get a quick, positive response, they are much more likely to develop positive feelings for the system than if such help is not available. The help desk personnel need to view the field reps as their internal "customers," who, like all customers, need to be always and everywhere satisfied.

Significance of the Human Angle

If we have succeeded in frightening you a bit about the sensitivity of your SA system to the vagaries of people's attitudes, prejudices, and predilections, then we've done you a service. Handling the human factor is without doubt the most vulnerable aspect of every sales automation project. It deserves your utmost effort and attention and, like so much else about SA, probably needs to be experimented with until the right pattern emerges. Don't forget, the original stated purpose of the pilot program was to learn. If the pilot fails, that's no tragedy. Get up, dust off, make alterations, and go at it again . . . and again, if need be.

Chapter 11
Planning and Procurement

Choosing the right suppliers and hardware and software products from the thousands of potential alternatives may seem difficult to you. It can be. This chapter presents a process you can use to whittle down the thousands of choices to a manageable few—how to determine what services your project will require, how to analyze application software and hardware to find the right characteristics for your sales team, and how to utilize resources to make the decision process easier.

In the preceding chapters we have discussed the importance of sales leading the charge to automation. Your project team has been defined; your financial managers have blessed the logic behind your project cost justification. Now it is time to evaluate the application software, hardware, and service alternatives available to you.

Designing the SA System

Your first step is to determine the characteristics and qualities you will require from your suppliers and their products. Large organizations have different needs from small organizations. Joe's Computer Store may be able to support the needs of a local manufacturer's sales representative but would be hard pressed to support the needs of a national sales force of 500 people.

Needs vary across industries and, in many cases, across companies within the same industry. The sales force in a company that sells consumer goods primarily manages the distribution process, making sure the product is available at retail stores when a potential customer is there. Capital goods and many service companies have different needs; their sales forces primarily manage the sales cycle, moving the potential buyer through the sales process from suspect to customer. The length of time required to close may vary from a single sales call to several years.

Sales and Marketing Management magazine's recent listing of sales and marketing software comprised over 500 vendors and 1,000 software products. These offerings operate on a multitude of hardware and operating system platforms. Obviously, the potential for confusion is enormous.

First let's define some basic requirements of sales automation software systems. (Later we look at the types of suppliers and resources that are available to help evaluate and implement these systems.)

- In the coming years, information will become a company's most valuable asset. Information itself is useless unless it can be meaningfully analyzed, presented, and shared among salespeople, sales management, marketing, corporate management, customer service, and, in many cases, the customers. The larger the organization, the greater the requirement for sharing information. *The sales automation solution you choose should have the ability to present information in meaningful ways to you and your user community.*

- Each year companies invest from 1 to 5 percent or more of their revenues in information processing systems, software, and resources. For some companies, this investment represents billions of dollars. Leveraging this valuable asset is a key goal of sales automation. *The sales automation solution you choose should have the ability to share information with these previously installed systems.*

- People in general, and salespeople in particular, are resistant to change. However, they do welcome change when it has a positive impact on their ability to perform. *The sales automation solution you choose should be easy to use and provide value to your salespeople.*

• Over the past decade the vendor/customer partnership became a reality, and today's futurists and business leaders are declaring this partnership the way of the future as well. *The sales automation solution you choose should provide value to, and enhance your relationship with, your customers.*

• In the battlefield of business, results are measured by profits. Delivering technology to your salespeople without financial justification can be a mistake. *The sales automation solution you choose should increase sales and profits, cut costs, or avoid future costs.*

• The business environment is constantly changing. New products, competitors, markets, and technologies become available every year; old products, competitors, markets, and technologies become obsolete and disappear. *The sales automation solution you choose should be dynamic and easily modified as your needs and requirements change.*

In summary, your sales automation solution should present meaningful information; share information with previously installed corporate systems; be easy to use; provide value to your salespeople and customers; increase profits; and have the capability to be easily modified. This may seem like a lot to ask of an SA system, but it isn't. Let's look more specifically at sales automation system features in light of some of the criteria just defined.

• *It should present meaningful information.* Most companies provide their salespeople and managers with a wide variety of reports that may or may not be of value to them. Many reports may require further analysis, cross-referencing, or summarizing to be of value to the user. Some may never be touched. One of the major advantages of installing an SA system is that it forces managers to evaluate their present reporting and information distribution systems and to determine their real needs and requirements.

Through this evaluation process they determine what information and application systems are of greatest value to the sales team, whether it be the timely distribution of leads, order status, and pricing information or a sales history by customer.

• *It should share information.* Salespeople are required to interact with customers, peers, management, and subordinates every day, passing along information about products, accounts, goals, needs, and requirements. A computer-based sales system should enhance the movement of information by shortening the time it takes for collection and distribution.

A simple example is an automated electronic order entry system for a consumer goods company. Remember the example in Chapter 9. Before automation, the salesperson would meet with the buyer and determine purchase requirements for the hundreds of products the buyer carried. The salesperson was responsible for knowing all the different products and the promotions or deals available to the customer on that day. He carried the pricing and promotion information in a large binder. The salesperson would write up the order by hand, calculate it, and send it by mail to the home office where it would arrive several days later. The order was then entered by a data entry clerk and an order confirmation printed and sent to the salesperson by mail. This whole process required a week to ten days.

Automation changes this process dramatically. The salesperson now uses a notebook computer–based electronic order-entry system. Prior to the sales call, she receives the latest pricing and order status information via modem. The order is prepared on the notebook computer at the customer's location. The appropriate deals and promotions are applied automatically by the system (they can also be adjusted by the salesperson). The salesperson then sends the order electronically to the home office and receives the order confirmation and the latest pricing information the next day. The whole process is completed in less than twenty-four hours.

• *It should be easy to use.* Sales automation software should be easy for your salespeople to use. Today there are many "user interfaces" and operating system environments available;

you should look for one with an "intuitive user interface"—one where the user with little or no training can recognize and understand on her own how the application functions. As an example, we use the electronic order entry system discussed earlier.

The example screen in Figure 11-1 depicts an actual application. When the salesperson wants to write an order, she picks "Enter Orders." The next screen (Figure 11-2) then asks the user to provide a customer number or to press the "?" key if she would like a list of customers. When she presses the "?" key, a list of customers appears from which she can make a selection (Figure 11-3). She is then asked for confirmation of her selection by pressing a Y for yes or N for no (Figure 11-4). She is then presented with instructions asking for the purchase order number, order date, requested ship-by date and arrive-by date, and any special instructions (Figure 11-5). After con-

Figure 11-1. Electronic order entry system—screen 1.

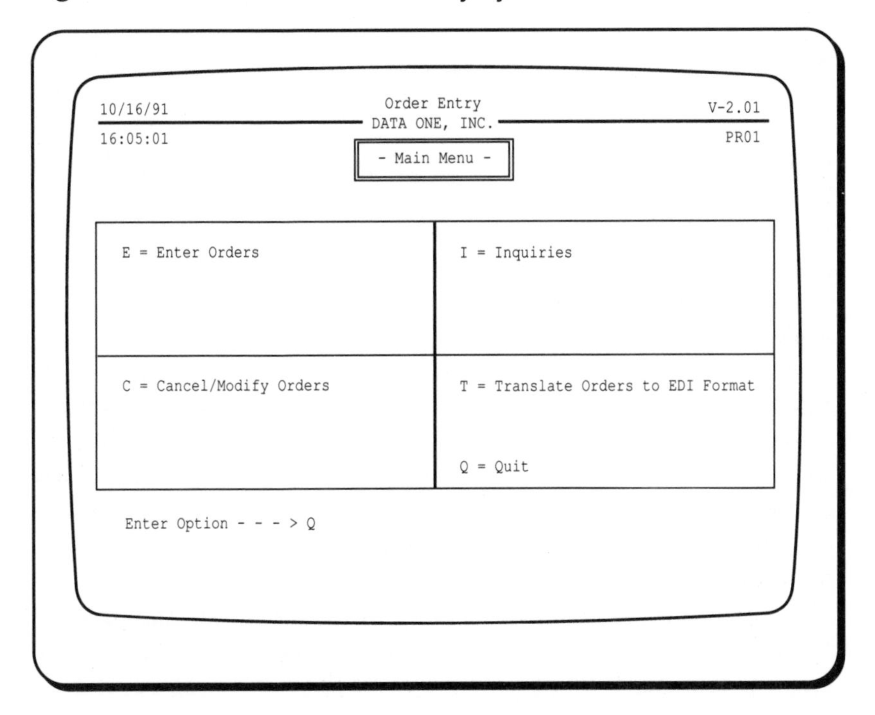

Figure 11-2. Electronic order entry system—screen 2.

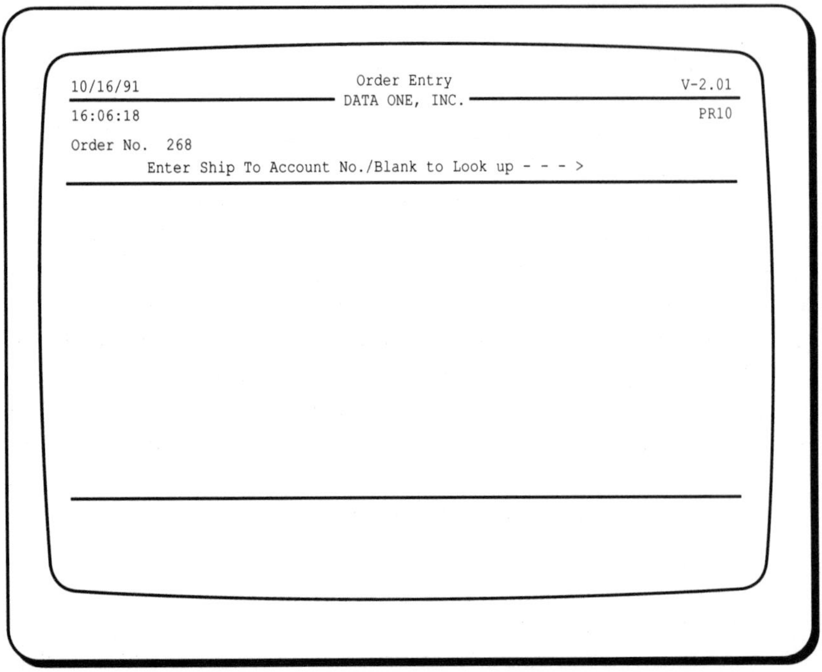

```
10/16/91                    Order Entry                    V-2.01
                          DATA ONE, INC.
16:06:18                                                   PR10

Order No.  268
        Enter Ship To Account No./Blank to Look up - - - >
```

firming this information, the user is presented with a list of products from which to choose (Figure 11-6). She selects the product; the list of brands is presented and the user is prompted to enter the order quantity (Figure 11-7). The system allows the user to enter only valid order quantities. This process continues until the product selection is complete.

The user is then presented with the promotions and deals that are available (Figure 11-8). The user selects the appropriate choices, and the order is automatically totaled (Figure 11-9). The user can then review the order or save it. If the user chooses to edit the order, she can change it. After final changes are made, the order is saved. The user can then send it to headquarters for processing.

The order entry application is an example of a character-based application using menu lists to guide the user. Today there is another type of user interface that uses "icons" to lead

Figure 11-3. Electronic order entry system—screen 3.

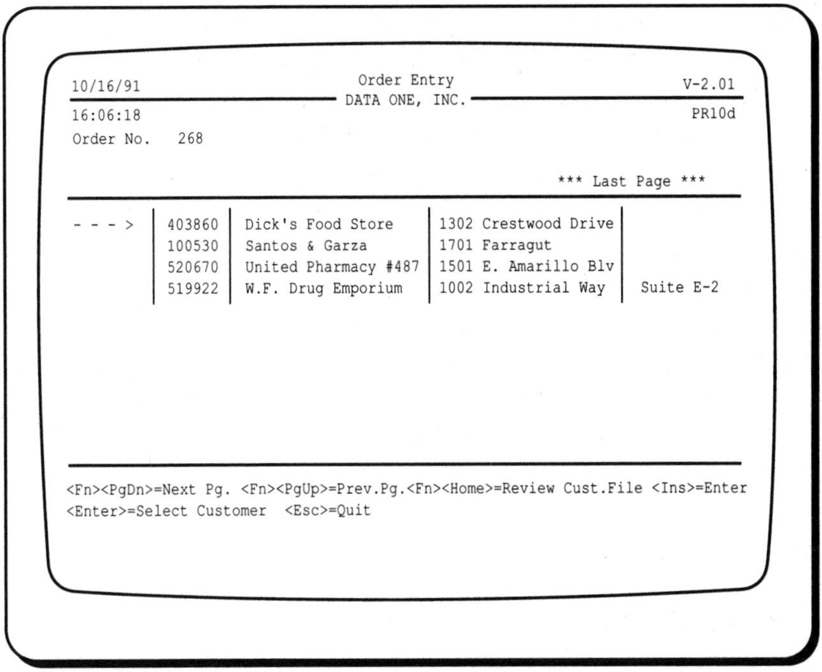

10/16/91 Order Entry V-2.01
DATA ONE, INC.
16:06:18 PR10d
Order No. 268

*** Last Page ***

- - - >	403860	Dick's Food Store	1302 Crestwood Drive	
	100530	Santos & Garza	1701 Farragut	
	520670	United Pharmacy #487	1501 E. Amarillo Blv	
	519922	W.F. Drug Emporium	1002 Industrial Way	Suite E-2

<Fn><PgDn>=Next Pg. <Fn><PgUp>=Prev.Pg.<Fn><Home>=Review Cust.File <Ins>=Enter
<Enter>=Select Customer <Esc>=Quit

the user through the application. Icons are pictures or images that represent a function. An example is a picture of a file cabinet, representing the "file" or "save" function (Figure 11-10). The user selects the function by placing the cursor on the file cabinet and pressing a key that presents her with a list of options. This type of user interface is called a "graphical user interface," or GUI.

Whichever user interface is chosen, the application should include the following "ease of use" characteristics: (1) Commands are executed by a single keystroke, (2) the user should recognize the information presented and understand how to act on it, (3) help screens should be available for the specific screen or function being worked with (this type of help screen is called "context sensitive"), (4) the application should prevent the user from making mistakes and should provide an easy way to recover from mistakes that do occur, and (5) if the user

Figure 11-4. Electronic order entry system—screen 4.

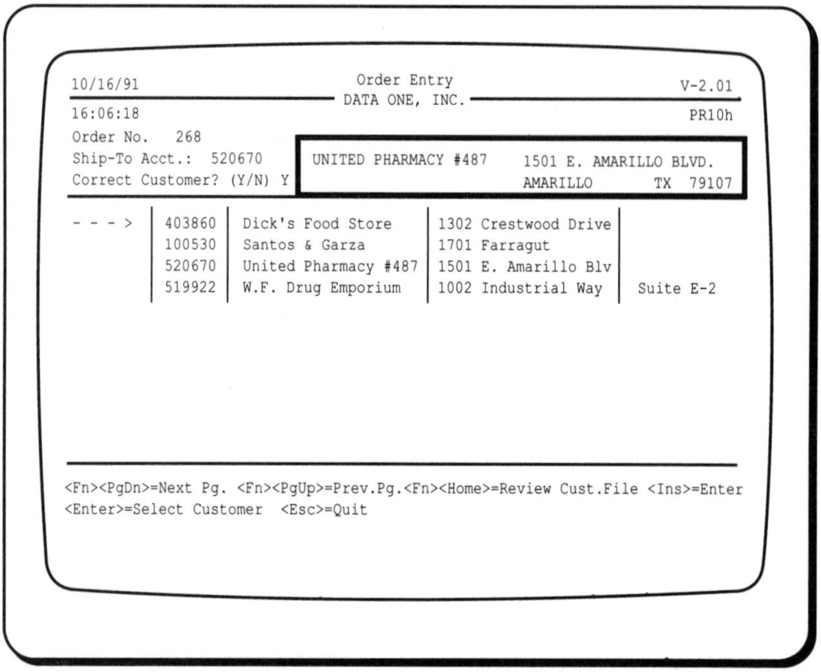

```
10/16/91                        Order Entry                        V-2.01
                              DATA ONE, INC.
16:06:18                                                            PR10h
Order No.   268
Ship-To Acct.:  520670     UNITED PHARMACY #487     1501 E. AMARILLO BLVD.
Correct Customer? (Y/N) Y                           AMARILLO        TX  79107

- - - >  403860  Dick's Food Store      1302 Crestwood Drive
         100530  Santos & Garza         1701 Farragut
         520670  United Pharmacy #487   1501 E. Amarillo Blv
         519922  W.F. Drug Emporium     1002 Industrial Way    Suite E-2

<Fn><PgDn>=Next Pg. <Fn><PgUp>=Prev.Pg.<Fn><Home>=Review Cust.File <Ins>=Enter
<Enter>=Select Customer  <Esc>=Quit
```

is required to enter known information, such as a customer number, he should be given lists of alternatives to choose from.

Whatever the look and feel of the interface, it should be common to all the main applications the sales rep is expected to use, so that the same keys or icons always perform the same or similar functions; "F-1" should always mean "help" or "F-10" always mean "continue," for example. The color, format, and placement of messages and instructions should be the same from application to application; differences in these characteristics increase learning time, create confusion, and risk resistance.

SA's Value to the Sales Department and to Customers

In addition to simplifying the sales representative's job, a good SA system provides benefits for customers, who receive valid

Figure 11-5. Electronic order entry system—screen 5.

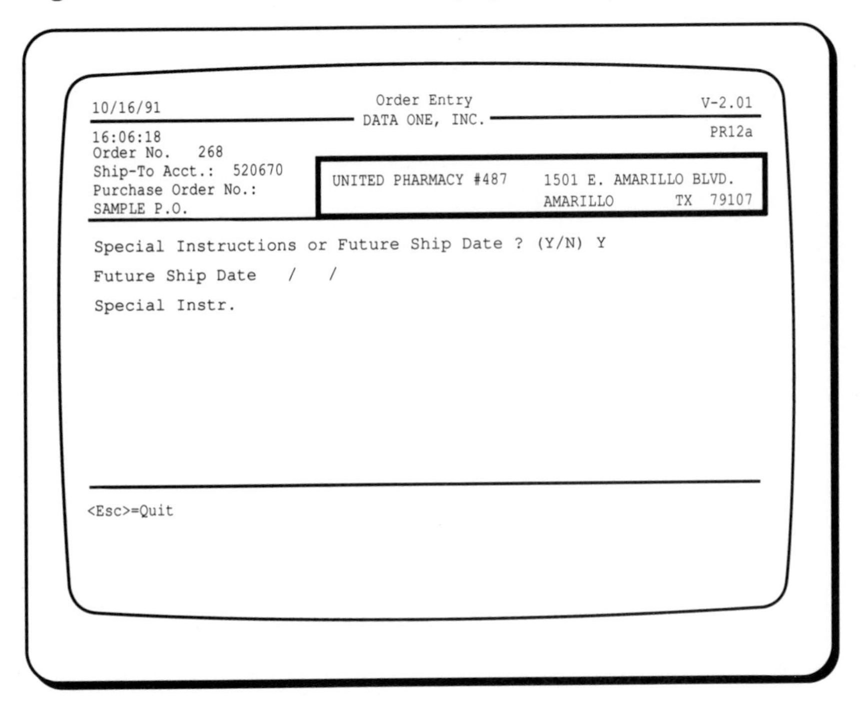

orders sooner, preventing stockouts and lost sales, and no longer have to waste time following up on order mistakes. Customers also receive appropriate deals and promotions, enhancing their profitability.

While providing value to your salespeople and customers can be easy, sometimes it is more difficult to determine specific SA applications that might benefit your overall sales organization. Sales automation applications should: (1) decrease the time it takes to collect and report information; (2) shorten the time it takes to prepare, distribute, and analyze information; (3) enhance communications between salespeople, management, and customers; (4) promote reliable follow-through; (5) decrease errors; (6) make it easier for salespeople to do a better, more professional, and more productive job of serving their markets.

Sales automation projects are evaluated using the same

Figure 11-6. Electronic order entry system—screen 6.

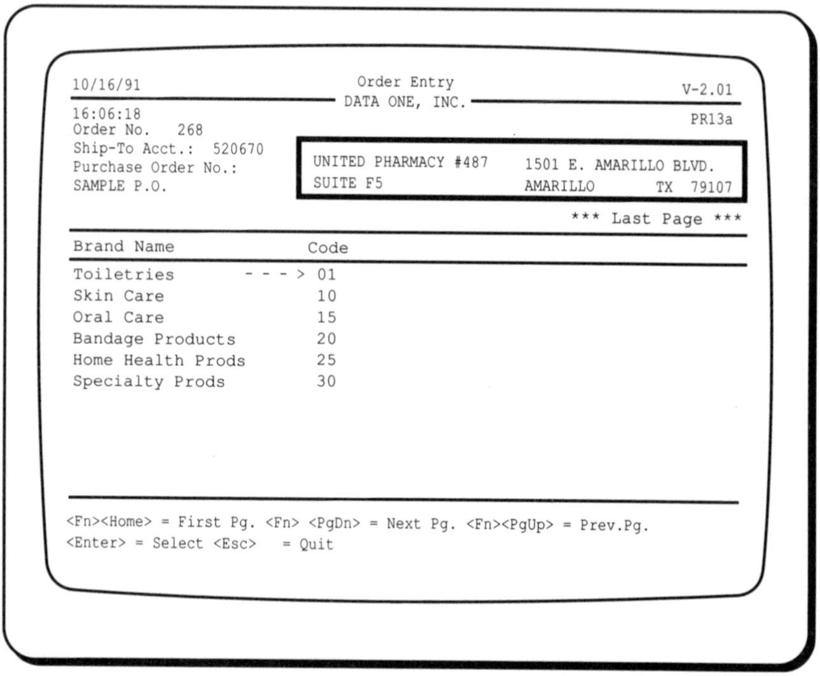

```
10/16/91                      Order Entry                      V-2.01
                            DATA ONE, INC.
16:06:18                                                        PR13a
Order No.    268
Ship-To Acct.:  520670
Purchase Order No.:      UNITED PHARMACY #487     1501 E. AMARILLO BLVD.
SAMPLE P.O.              SUITE F5                 AMARILLO       TX  79107

                                                  *** Last Page ***
Brand Name                Code
Toiletries         - - - > 01
Skin Care                  10
Oral Care                  15
Bandage Products           20
Home Health Prods          25
Specialty Prods            30

<Fn><Home> = First Pg. <Fn> <PgDn> = Next Pg. <Fn><PgUp> = Prev.Pg.
<Enter> = Select <Esc>   = Quit
```

investment and strategic criteria that senior management uses to assess any capital project—the likelihood of the project's providing strategic benefits and a high return on investment. The initial applications you choose to implement for your sales team should surpass your company's investment goals. This approach will ensure senior management support and also increase the likelihood of funding for new and enhanced applications and equipment in the future.

Choosing Your Hardware

Sales automation systems are developed using many different techniques. However you go about it, the systems you choose should be adaptable enough to meet future requirements. Whether you install an off-the-shelf system or have one custom

Figure 11-7. Electronic order entry system—screen 7.

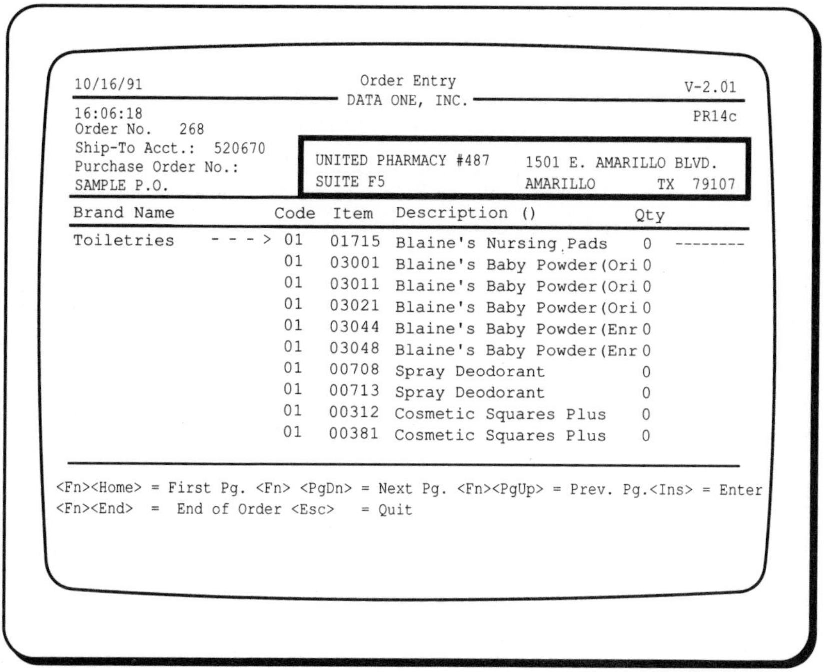

```
10/16/91                     Order Entry                      V-2.01
                            DATA ONE, INC.
16:06:18                                                      PR14c
Order No.    268
Ship-To Acct.:  520670
Purchase Order No.:      UNITED PHARMACY #487    1501 E. AMARILLO BLVD.
SAMPLE P.O.              SUITE F5                AMARILLO       TX  79107
Brand Name          Code  Item   Description ()            Qty
Toiletries    - - - > 01  01715  Blaine's Nursing Pads      0   --------
                      01  03001  Blaine's Baby Powder(Ori 0
                      01  03011  Blaine's Baby Powder(Ori 0
                      01  03021  Blaine's Baby Powder(Ori 0
                      01  03044  Blaine's Baby Powder(Enr 0
                      01  03048  Blaine's Baby Powder(Enr 0
                      01  00708  Spray Deodorant            0
                      01  00713  Spray Deodorant            0
                      01  00312  Cosmetic Squares Plus      0
                      01  00381  Cosmetic Squares Plus      0

<Fn><Home> = First Pg. <Fn> <PgDn> = Next Pg. <Fn><PgUp> = Prev. Pg.<Ins> = Enter
<Fn><End>  =  End of Order <Esc>   = Quit
```

designed and developed, you need to consider future growth and requirements in your selection process.

Users sometimes find themselves overwhelmed by new systems and technology. An implementation plan that provides for the introduction of new applications over time can be more successful than one that gives users all the system's capabilities at once, and products that allow "application modules" to be added as the user community becomes proficient with each application can be more successful than those that give them all the capabilities at once. Complex applications can cause user frustration and lead to low acceptance levels.

Hardware Characteristics

In recent years there has been a significant amount of new portable computer hardware technology delivered to the mar-

Figure 11-8. Electronic order entry system—screen 8.

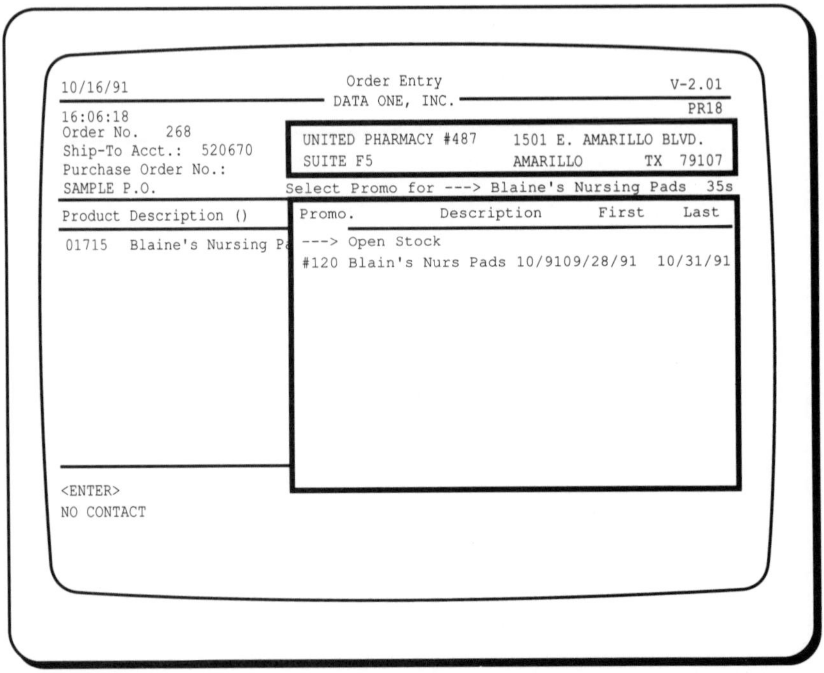

```
10/16/91                        Order Entry                          V-2.01
                               DATA ONE, INC.
16:06:18                                                               PR18
Order No.   268              UNITED PHARMACY #487     1501 E. AMARILLO BLVD.
Ship-To Acct.:  520670       SUITE F5                 AMARILLO     TX  79107
Purchase Order No.:
SAMPLE P.O.                Select Promo for ---> Blaine's Nursing Pads  35s
Product Description ()       Promo.          Description        First     Last
01715   Blaine's Nursing P   ---> Open Stock
                             #120 Blain's Nurs Pads 10/9109/28/91   10/31/91

<ENTER>
NO CONTACT
```

ketplace. Products that used to have marketplace life cycles of two to three years now have marketplace life cycles of less than twelve months; manufacturers are using shortened new-product development as a competitive weapon against their adversaries in the marketplace. Rapidly changing technologies are making it more difficult for users to decide when, and in some cases if, they should deploy technology; managers worry about making the wrong decision or about being second-guessed by their superiors.

All these factors can lead to decision paralysis. By not making a decision today, managers believe they open the way to better decisions tomorrow. This is a fallacy. We live in a dynamic environment in which the business climate changes daily. Good managers make the best possible decision based upon the information and alternatives available today, taking into consideration potential needs and requirements in the

Figure 11-9. Electronic order entry system—screen 9.

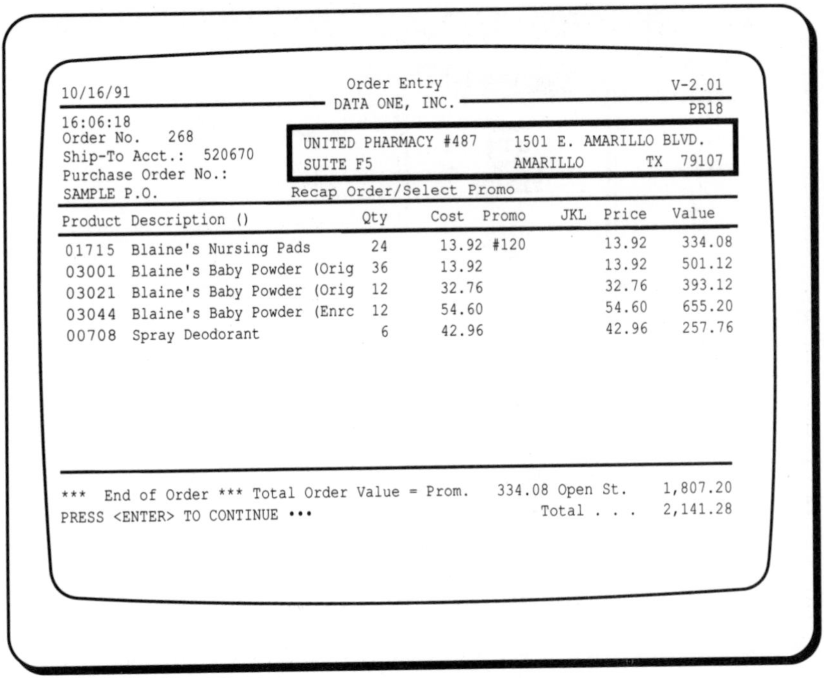

```
10/16/91                         Order Entry                          V-2.01
                              DATA ONE, INC.                            PR18
16:06:18
Order No.    268              UNITED PHARMACY #487     1501 E. AMARILLO BLVD.
Ship-To Acct.:  520670        SUITE F5                 AMARILLO       TX  79107
Purchase Order No.:
SAMPLE P.O.                   Recap Order/Select Promo
Product Description ()              Qty     Cost  Promo    JKL  Price    Value
01715 Blaine's Nursing Pads          24    13.92 #120          13.92   334.08
03001 Blaine's Baby Powder (Orig     36    13.92               13.92   501.12
03021 Blaine's Baby Powder (Orig     12    32.76               32.76   393.12
03044 Blaine's Baby Powder (Enrc     12    54.60               54.60   655.20
00708 Spray Deodorant                 6    42.96               42.96   257.76

*** End of Order *** Total Order Value = Prom.    334.08 Open St.    1,807.20
PRESS <ENTER> TO CONTINUE •••                            Total . . .  2,141.28
```

future. While products become obsolete in the marketplace, they do not necessarily become functionally obsolete.

The hardware platform you choose should meet several criteria:

- It should be able to support your initial applications and those you plan to add over the useful life of the asset (most companies use a three-year depreciation schedule for assets of this type).
- The product should offer an upgrade path. As your users become accustomed to the technology and its capabilities, they will come up with new and better ways to use it. An upgrade path, perhaps including changing the central processing unit or replacing the equipment with completely new systems, should also include the ability to add additional memory or mass storage as required.

Figure 11-10. Icon-driven application.

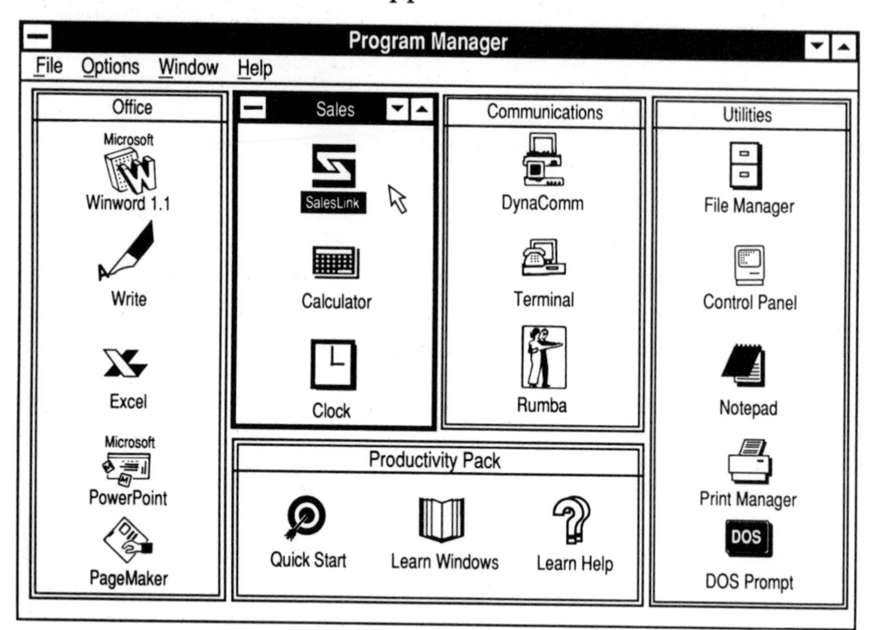

• The hardware manufacturer should offer a family of products, since in many cases different equipment is required by different levels of users within the same sales force. Usually products within a family have similar characteristics (for example, keyboard layouts), which can reduce support and training requirements.

• The manufacturer should have staying power. Since products now become obsolete quickly, only those manufacturers with significant resources will be able to continue to develop new products and support old products as well.

• Products should be readily available. Do not plan your deployment around a manufacturer's scheduled first shipment of a product, because initial delivery dates always slip. Portable computers are very complex, a blending of multiple technologies at the leading edge of development. Typical expenses for conducting training sessions range from $500 to $2,000 per user, and cancellation charges for hotels, airfare, and facilities can vary from 10 to 100 percent. So, when you commit to introduction and training schedules, you must be sure the product will be there.

- Products (especially new products) should be ordered from hardware manufacturers who have shown a consistent ability to deliver high-quality, reliable products. Ask your suppliers to provide data on the past history of their products, and talk to other users about their experiences with suppliers.
- Products need not carry the lowest price. Paying a little more now may prevent sleepless nights later.

Using these general criteria provides a solid foundation for making your hardware selection. A six- to eight-figure capital investment should provide value to your company throughout its useful life. Adhering to the above criteria can help ensure that this will be the case.

Available Resources for Learning About SA

In this chapter we have looked at the basic requirements of sales automation and, more specifically, at the broad features required of SA application software and hardware. Your initial analysis has determined your specific application requirements, which can be matched against available SA applications products, potential supplier capabilities, and other resources necessary to ensure the project's success. Having done this, you are ready to investigate the outside resources available to help you develop a successful project plan. These resources include users, user groups, consultants, software and hardware vendors, value added resellers, newsletters, and magazines and other publications.

- *Users and user groups.* Users can provide you with first-hand accounts of their experiences with SA. It may be difficult to get users in your industry to speak with you directly, but there are many forums where users speak publicly about their experiences. You can contact users at industry trade groups or by networking with peers in the industry. Potential suppliers can also be a source for user contacts.

• *Consultants.* Sales automation consultants can be a very good resource. However, since sales automation is relatively new and there is no formal SA trade association, they can be difficult to find. The Appendix includes a listing of known SA consulting groups. As with any management consultant, your selection should be based on your needs and requirements.

• *Software vendors.* Much can be learned about SA through software suppliers. After all, vendors developed their applications software to meet the needs of customers. A significant amount of relevant information is available from their product and marketing people; some SA software vendors even have consultants on staff or can supply names of consultants.

• *Hardware vendors.* Manufacturers of the computer hardware used in SA can be a valuable source of information. Many have sales and marketing consultants who know how their technology can be applied by customers. Since many vendors offer similar products, their recommendations can be followed regardless of whose product you end up with. Some vendors can help you identify potential SA software solutions.

• *Value added resellers (VARs).* VARs are a unique breed in the computer industry. In addition to selling products and services, they act as consultants. They are specialists in their application area and typically provide client solutions on a "turnkey" basis, including SA software, hardware, training, and support services. In many cases they can offer solutions from a variety of software and hardware vendors, integrating these systems into a complete solution, or can develop a custom solution utilizing powerful development tools.

• *Newsletters.* There are several newsletters on SA (see the Appendix) available. They typically profile users, review industry conferences, and address issues relating to SA.

• *Magazines.* There are several magazines that address SA on a regular basis (see the Appendix). They review hardware and software products, profile users, compile product lists, and publish relevant articles on SA. Computer industry publications profile SA on occasion, and there are several databases available on CD ROM disks that provide easy access to specific topics.

SA Suppliers

In the previous section we presented the resources available to help you learn about SA and the potential it may offer your organization. During the discovery phase you should not only learn from these resources but also qualify those that may be potential suppliers during the later phases of the project. The suppliers you choose to work with as you implement your SA system can make or break your project. The demands put on suppliers typically increase with the size and scope of a project. We now discuss these broad requirements in detail as they pertain to the different phases and aspects of an SA project.

Types of Software Suppliers

Packaged SA software products typically are designed to meet the generic requirements of sales forces. The companies that provide these products should provide telephone support for their products. Whether the supplier offers the support free or charges for it is not the important issue; what is important is the quality and availability of that support. The support should be available when the user needs it, typically beyond business hours, and the support personnel should be responsive and know the product. The supplier should have an installed base and show a history of improving and enhancing its product, offering an upgrade program as new versions of the product become available. The product documentation supplied should be easy to use and understand.

Sales software developers should have a deep understanding of the sales process. They should be able to identify and understand your requirements and how their product can address your needs. They should have a business sense and a willingness to investigate how your sales force operates. If possible, they should have an understanding of your industry and the types of non-SA systems utilized in your industry.

Custom SA developers need the same characteristics as SA developers, and some others. People usually choose a custom alternative because they have requirements beyond those available in standard SA products. Therefore the custom developer you choose should have a deep understanding of your internal data processing systems. The developer should use development tools with prototyping capabilities, have a history of delivering systems on time and within budget, insist that your users and MIS personnel be on the application design/development project team, and participate in regular meetings to go over the project's status. Once the project's scope is defined and specified in detail, the developer should be willing to enter into a contract at a fixed price.

Finally, *system integrators* should have the same characteristics as custom SA developers, with added mastery of the hardware, networking, and training aspects of implementing a successful SA project, and should be willing to undertake responsibility for it.

Some form of source code licensing should be available from SA software developers, custom SA developers, and system integrators when applicable. There are several types of source code licensing. The minimum requirement is to have the source code placed in escrow and available should the supplier go out of business or be unable to support the product in the future. The maximum protection (and the least likely to be offered) is complete ownership and title to the product. A significant premium is usually required for this type of license.

Hardware Supplier Characteristics

Hardware manufacturers should offer a family of products with an upgrade path. The manufacturer should show a history of building reliable products and delivering new products on or very near their initial announced delivery date. They should also be large enough and profitable enough to support new product research and development and ongoing support for the products they sell.

Hardware resellers should understand the scope and implications of deploying large numbers of systems on a broad basis. They should offer software and hardware support programs that meet the needs of geographically dispersed user communities. These programs should include turnkey deployment services and twenty-four-hour replacement of faulty equipment (replacements should be set up exactly the same as the equipment the user had previously). The reseller should also offer repair services for the equipment it sells. It is a false assumption to think that a reseller with many locations nationwide can necessarily provide better support than a reseller with one location. Sometimes it is quite the opposite. SA support programs with central control historically work better than those that do not offer central control.

Value added resellers (VARs) should offer the same capabilities as hardware resellers. They should also be able to offer custom support programs to fit unique requirements.

Other Issues in Choosing a Supplier

There are other resources that you will require for a successful SA project. These include training resources, which may be available from suppliers, from dedicated training companies, or internally within your company. In addition, computer-based training (CBT), in which custom modules can be developed to meet your application requirements and referenced by the users after initial training has taken place, is used by many companies. Video training may be a useful adjunct. Many SA users find a combination of classroom, computer-based, and video training to be ideal.

As with any vendor/customer relationship, you should expect honesty and integrity. Beware of the supplier who never says no. Get commitments in writing. Check references, tour their facilities, and meet their management. Remember, you are developing a long-term relationship that will have a major effect on you and your company's future.

When to Commit Your Resources and Money

At what point do you start to expend resources and money? The time to commit money and resources comes when you have identified the applications that can have a positive effect on your business and the suppliers who can provide them. At this time a comprehensive project plan and cost justification identifying the known hard cost savings and the potential soft cost savings, describing the applications and their potential effect on your sales force and business, and identifying the internal and external resources required to implement the project should have been performed. The next chapter provides a methodology for developing a winning implementation plan.

Chapter 12
Implementation

One company implemented a comprehensive SA system over several years that includes a telemarketing system, a corporate marketing and customer history database, and a territory management system for the sales representatives and district managers. All the systems are connected and form a closed loop sales and marketing database; the users and corporate management are connected through an electronic mail system.

The project director, a former sales manager, is not enthralled by technology; he only hunts and pecks at the keyboard. He did have a little vision and had learned through his years in the field that in many cases there is a better, easier way to do things. The project director learned through investigation what could be done with technology, rather than how the technology works, and hired the appropriate technical resources to implement the system step by step, with each phase building on the last.

Today his division has a state-of-the-art SA system and is the envy of his competitors and company peers. What he *did* use was a methodology. He identified business problems and methodically solved those problems by developing technology-based application solutions. He and his team then prototyped, piloted, and implemented these systems with their sales force. The sales force was trained as each new application was deployed, and it continues to receive ongoing support.

Designing, developing, and installing a successful sales automation system takes careful planning and execution. The process is not magic. Buying a bunch of laptop computers and packaged software products and handing them over to your salespeople will not necessarily result in increased productivity and enhanced sales and profits; more than likely, it will create confusion among the sales force and adverse reactions from senior management. The expected project results will be delayed for several years as the project team picks up the pieces and convinces management, and the sales force, that the idea was correct but the implementation was handled poorly. Meanwhile, the team members' credibility will have vanished, and possibly their positions.

Technology itself does not increase productivity. If it did, every sales force in the world would have purchased laptop computers long ago, and there would be no need for us to write this book. Only proper application and implementation of the technology increases productivity.

The SA system development methodology we describe will result in a winning implementation plan. The major phases include: application selection, prototyping, piloting, final deployment, and ongoing support.

How to Implement a Winning SA System

Application Selection

Any successful SA system must begin with selecting applications. Several criteria are used to determine application selected:

1. Will the application provide value to users? Will it make their job easier to perform? Will it shorten the time it takes to perform regular reporting or other mundane tasks? Will it help users make more effective use of their time?
2. Will the application provide value to customers? Will it enhance the customer relationship? Provide them with information on a more timely basis? Reduce response time? Reduce order cycles? Prevent pricing and billing errors? Increase customer service?

3. Can the application be cost-justified? Will the application save money? Increase revenues? Decrease costs? Can these cost savings be determined prior to implementation? Can a valid case be made for probable cost savings?
4. Can the application be developed and installed in a reasonable amount of time? Will it take months or years? Is the effort worth the result? Will the environment change?
5. Will the application work with or leverage previously installed systems? Can installed corporate information systems and databases be used to enhance the system? Will the new applications be compatible or share data with the installed systems?

Meeting these criteria is critical. Successful implementations of sales automation systems must meet at least the first four.

These criteria are important because, without support of the user community, the system will typically fail. Systems that provide value to the user community enjoy a very high degree of success; those that don't, gather dust.

The scorecard of business is profits. Applications that can be justified through hard cost savings and revenue enhancements, or through valid assumptions of potential savings and revenue enhancements, will receive management approval and also provide salespeople with increased opportunities for income, commissions, and bonuses with less effort.

The initial applications should be chosen to meet management's expectations of a return on its investment and users' expectations of a valuable work tool, but many companies have tried to bite off more than they could chew with their initial applications, with disastrous results. Technology and a competitive environment may make an application with a long delivery period obsolete before it is even installed. It is much easier and less risky to choose a smaller number of simpler functions that can then be used as building blocks for more complex applications in the future.

Applications that leverage and utilize previously installed

systems can offer great benefits to a company. Two simple examples are an electronic order entry system for a consumer goods company that uses the electronic data interchange (EDI) capability of the company's mainframe system, and a call reporting and contact management system that ties in to a company's telemarketing and lead generation system. The sharing of information between these systems can result in more timely distribution of data between different corporate functions, lower costs for implementation, and additional utility and value to the company from the original systems.

It is the job of the profit finders—the planning and evaluation team—to determine which applications will provide the most benefit to the company. Using the criteria we have outlined, they determine a set of applications that will have a positive effect on the sales team, customer relationships, and the bottom line.

Developing a Prototype

Although the list of potentially profitable applications may include as many as eight to ten different areas, as the project team moves into the prototype phase it will have to shorten that list to two or three. At least one of these applications should be a strategic sales application, and the other should be a generic application, such as electronic mail. Electronic mail systems are a very cost-effective way to communicate, and the application by itself may provide the cost justification for the SA system.

The prototype phase is a period of designing and testing, of change and evaluation. The project team designs the layouts of the display screens (or evaluates off-the-shelf products) and determines what information has to be presented, modified, changed, collected, and reported. It decides where the information will come from and where it will have to go. The project team internally tests the selected applications to see whether they are easy to use, if users can intuitively understand what they need to know, and whether the content is appropriate. The technical issues associated with the applications are determined, including database requirements and layouts, communication platform, sales system host, mainframe interfaces, and user hardware requirements. Costs for developing (or purchasing) the prototype system are determined.

The project team starts to develop a functional specification document for the SA system at this time. This document addresses the goals of the system, user requirements, and how the system will work. It defines the database requirements, screen layouts, and report layouts, and generally provides an overview of the proposed system. Estimated costs for the pilot phase and final implementation are determined, and measurement criteria to determine the effectiveness of the system are developed (more on this in Chapter 13).

The team also develops an initial implementation plan that includes training requirements, training logistics, support programs, a deployment schedule, and the costs of these functions.

The next step is to develop a working SA application prototype for testing. The prototype is then presented to actual users for their impressions and feedback. If necessary, modifications are made to the system. Initial field testing with several users can take place at this time. The communication platform, hardware links, and data transmission vehicles are tested for reliability and performance, and the screens are evaluated for content, uniformity, and ease of use. Problem areas are modified and context-sensitive help developed to make the system easier to use.

Initial training requirements and course content for the pilot phase are determined, including hardware training ("care and feeding") and sample training examples representing practical application of the system in the salesperson's job. The training should show the user how to use the system to solve customer problems, develop customer presentations, use time more effectively, increase the sales volume, and other appropriate uses.

The training program should be focused and interesting and should help the users recognize the value of the applications and understand how the system will help them perform at a higher level. It is highly recommended that, if possible, the project team members from the sales department act as facilitators or instructors. The training classes should include from ten to twelve trainees, an instructor, and two facilitators and should last no more than two to three days to maintain maximum interest.

The Pilot Phase

Measurement criteria and surveys developed by the project team are filled out by the user group and members of other related functional areas during the pilot phase. Criteria might include: time measurements (how much time is spent selling, in meetings, researching and fulfilling customer requests, performing administrative tasks, traveling, etc.); accuracy and timeliness of orders; quality and timeliness of reporting; the impact of the system on other functional areas, including marketing, customer support, and operations; the impact of the system on sales volumes and profitability; increases in customer contacts and sales calls and in the quality of those calls.

The surveys should be filled out by the pilot users and a representative group of other users and the information compared and analyzed at the end of the pilot. The results typically point to a variety of hard and soft cost savings and can be used to justify the full-scale rollout of the SA system to the field.

Appropriate support programs are also tested during the pilot phase. These programs should include next-day replacement of a faulty system with an identically configured system, leaving the user out of commission for a maximum of twenty-four hours. A telephone support hot line should be in place to answer application and hardware questions, and the support personnel should be knowledgeable about the application and hardware. Users should receive an immediate response or, at a minimum, a call back within an hour.

During the pilot phase, the reliability of the hardware chosen and the supplier's support capabilities are tested. After the pilot, their programs and capabilities should be reviewed and modified if necessary.

The Deployment Phase and Ongoing Support Services

The final implementation plan should reflect the results of the pilot and incorporate any necessary changes. Additional applications can be added, if required. The hardware should be reevaluated and, if necessary, changed to take advantage of new technologies. A comprehensive rollout and training schedule should be determined and approved by management. For larger sales forces, the rollout should take place on a district-by-district (or regional) basis. User training attendee lists should be developed and provided to the equipment supplier for equipment assignment and management.

The equipment order should be placed forty-five to ninety days prior to the training sessions (this is extremely important for extensive rollouts). The supplier should provide turnkey support programs, including turnkey deployment services, hardware support, and software support. Turnkey deployment services provide: assembly, testing, and burn-in of the system; software loading and configuration of the system; consistent, identical configuration of all laptop computers that are part of the field sales system; deployment of ready-to-use systems to field sales personnel regardless of location; and tracking of users and assigned machine serial numbers. Hardware support programs should include guaranteed delivery of an identically configured substitute laptop system anywhere it is needed within twenty-four hours and maintenance and repair of the equipment and its return to inventory. Service agreements typically are at a fixed price and include all parts and labor required to repair and return the machine within a designated time period (e.g., five working days). Software support programs should include dedicated "800" telephone hot lines and up to twenty-four-hour coverage, if needed. Support for off-the-shelf products, third-party commercial software packages, special-purpose vertical market application packages, and proprietary software systems such as custom-designed and written application programs for specific requirements should also be included.

All of the service programs should include management reports with the following information: date, user, products, serial numbers, type of incident, problem, problem resolution, resolution date, and recommended preventive training and maintenance.

Installing an SA system requires significant resources and careful planning. It also requires planning for the future. The business environment and technologies change daily, so the selected applications should provide for modification and integration of new applications. The hardware, if capitalized, should be depreciated over a short time, typically three years. This provides for the implementation of new technology in a timely manner without a large write-off for obsolete equipment. Leasing an SA system with new technology upgrade options is another way to protect equipment investment and take advantage of new technologies as they become available.

One thing you can be sure of: What you begin with will not be what you end up with one, two, or five years later. The way you sell, the way the SA system is used to support that selling effort, the specific function of the software, and even the hardware itself are likely to undergo significant evolution throughout the development and implementation of your sales automation program. That means that growth potential has to be built into every aspect from the beginning so that needed adjustments and enhancements can be incorporated easily and smoothly into the program, the training, and the ongoing support facilities.

Chapter 13

Measuring the Effectiveness of the Implementation

In this chapter we present ways to measure the success or failure of your SA system. One Fortune 50 company continually reevaluates its SA projects. Many of its applications have had borderline cost justifications, and senior management frequently questions the value and payback of the projects. However, if management took the systems away from the sales force, it would have a major revolt on its hands, experience a significant increase in sales force turnover, and provide a lower level of service to customers. Results, then, depend on the viewer's perspective.

A sales automation project's success is determined by how well the project performs compared to the goals set at the start of the project. Measuring success can be easy or difficult, depending on the project goals. Measuring the results of projects that automate manual tasks, such as an automated order entry system, is usually easier than doing the same for projects such as a call reporting and territory management system, designed to help make the salesperson more effective.

Setting reasonable target goals helps create a favorable decision-making environment. The expectations of management and the user community should be set at levels that are attainable; a well-designed and well-implemented system typically exceeds expectations. Two issues should be taken into account when selecting applications and developing the corresponding measurement criteria:

1. Does the application provide value to the salesperson? Can that value be measured? In time savings? In productivity? Can those savings be translated to dollars?
2. Does the application provide value to your customers? Can that value be measured? Can it be measured in dollars?

Measurement criteria fall into two categories: quantitative and qualitative. An example of quantitative measures is decreases in the amount of time spent in entering orders. You can reduce the results of quantitative measurements to numbers and ultimately place a dollar value on those measurements for cost justification purposes. The qualitative measurements are more elusive, yet they can be significant factors in the success of a project, from the perspective of both users and customers.

How do you calculate the direct tangible benefits? Let's first determine how the potential applications can positively impact the sales force, your business practices, and your customer relationships. You also have to look beyond the sales function, since sales automation can have a significant effect on other areas of the company, including administration, finance, marketing, purchasing, engineering, distribution, and manufacturing.

Will SA add new capabilities? Allow the organization to perform at new levels of efficiency? Over time companies can develop business practices that do not meet their current needs. These can be as simple as reports that are sent to the field and never read or as complex as outdated marketing and sales programs that do not reflect current market conditions.

Take, for example, a company that had a commission compensation plan that provided a fixed commission rate on gross sales regardless of the profitability of different product lines or individual products. This policy provided no way of motivating the sales force to emphasize higher margin products. Salespeople also had no idea what was in inventory to sell and therefore took orders for products that could not be delivered. After the SA system was installed, the commission plan was changed to motivate the salespeople to sell higher-margin products and to sell products that were in stock. This change resulted in lower inventory levels, increased order fill ratios, higher profits, and increased compensation to the salespeople—a win-win situation for the company, the salespeople, and customers.

Prior to deploying the pilot, the company should conduct surveys to determine where it is now. These surveys help determine how salespeople are spending their time. What reports does the sales force prepare? How are these reports used by management, and what is their value in managing the business? What reports are prepared by headquarters (such as sales history and order reports) for the sales force in the field? How are they used and why?

These surveys can be developed internally and the results analyzed using a simple spreadsheet program. There are also outside organizations that specialize in analyzing sales force effectiveness. These organizations develop an appropriate survey and then provide a comprehensive report detailing the results. Using outside consultants can offer many benefits; they have experience with many different companies, in many industries, and may be able to identify areas to survey and analyze that are not obvious. They can also provide fresh ideas and unbiased recommendations.

The surveys can also be used to collect ideas from the sales force. Given the opportunity, your salespeople will provide some of the best ideas on how to use the SA system to perform their function. Ask them what tools they would like to have. Ask them what the competition is doing. Ask them to survey their customers about applications or information that would enhance the client/customer relationship. Measure the effectiveness of lead generation and advertising programs. How many leads make it from an inquiry to a close? Measure the close ratios of your sales force. How many opportunities does each salesperson manage over a period of time, and how many of those opportunities result in sales? What were the sizes of those sales? Determine the average period of time it takes to close an opportunity from first contact to booking an order.

Establish a control group. Measure the pilot group and control group before automation and after. Groups that are part of a study typically improve their performance, and it is very possible that you will see performance increases even in the control group.

Perform follow-up surveys with your customers. Ask them if service has improved. Do salespeople respond in a more timely fashion? Are responses to requests better? Has the quality of the relationship improved? Have deliveries improved? Have back orders decreased? Ask them how you can further improve service to them. Are you responding better than the competition? How and why? Incorporate viable suggestions into the system.

The surveys can be developed and implemented as computer-based systems or as paper systems. There are programs, originally developed for the computer-based training marketplace, available for developing testing and assessment programs. These programs can be used to develop customer surveys and tests very rapidly. The results can be reviewed on an individual or combined basis.

Changes in expense categories, increased sales calls, decrease in order mistakes, shorter order cycles, increased inventory turns, increased profit margins, lower staffing requirements, and lower communication costs are just some of the specific criteria that can be evaluated as part of the assessment of the effectiveness of the SA system. Other factors are lower sales force turnover, more reliable and timely information, shorter closing cycles, increased customer satisfaction, more reliable forecasts, more effective target marketing, and improved ability to provide more information and to direct sales activities based on that information.

Fundamentally, what we're suggesting is this:

1. Pick an array of measurable parameters about your sales force and its marketplace—items such as percentage of time spent in front of customers, revenue per call, revenue per rep, time to fill an order, fill rate, cost per

lead, closes per thousand leads, customer attitudes, and ratings. Include everything that's germane.

2. Measure them all *before* sales automation begins, thereby establishing the "baseline."
3. Measure them again and again as the program enters the pilot stage, early rollout, full rollout, and thereafter.
4. Then look at the changes and trends. Project the tangible results and estimate the value of the intangibles. Then and only then will you have any grounds for determining whether your SA program is, or will be, a success. And, if not, you'll have strong indicators as to where you're falling down and clues as to what to do about it.

Chapter 14

The Future of Sales Automation

We have covered a lot of ground in this book. We have presented a process for understanding and implementing sales automation, introduced techniques for the discovery of potential applications, examined alternatives, and learned how other companies addressed their needs and requirements. We have determined ways to cost-justify sales automation systems and presented techniques to measure a project's success or failure.

It is now time to try to predict the future. There is one thing we are sure of: There will be change, and those companies that manage change effectively will be the leaders in the coming century.

There are some significant trends that will have a dramatic effect on how business is conducted in the future. Looking at both world history and the information systems industry in recent years leads us to believe that change, already breakneck, will take place at an even faster pace in years to come. The ideological and trade barriers of the past have fallen, and there have been dramatic changes in the geopolitical environment. New markets and opportunities have opened up, creating something close to a true world economy, uninhibited by borders and artificial trade barriers.

Companies that understand change and build systems that help them understand or at least detect it at the earliest possible moment will benefit from this changing world economy. One such company recently implemented a system that took these issues into account. Although the first phase of the system was developed for and funded by the domestic operation, the international division participated in the design and development of the system. The company understood it is competing in a world economy and that its customer relationships are not bound by borders or oceans.

This company had the advantage of entering its second generation of sales automation. Having learned from the limitations of its first system, it selected a software architecture and development system with extraordinary flexibility (after evaluating thirty SA vendors). Using the resources of its SA system supplier, it developed the design specification for the system with a heavy emphasis on global corporate requirements. Phase one of the system was deployed with international capabilities, even though there were no international users. Over the course of the next three quarters, international users were added to the system to form global marketing and sales teams for multinational customers.

Information systems technology has moved rapidly forward, advancing faster than many people expected. The portable computing industry started in the late seventies with portable "dumb" terminals used to access mainframe systems over telephone lines using acoustic couplers. These terminals transmitted information at a rate of 300 bits per second, which represents about 40 characters per second. Today a user can carry a notebook computer weighing far less than the 1970s portable terminal. This new notebook computer is more powerful than the mainframe the 1970s user was accessing. Information can be transmitted between the portable computer and today's mainframes at rates of over 30,000 characters per second.

One important lesson should be learned from this rapidly changing technological environment. If it is not here today, it will probably be here tomorrow. An example of this: In fall 1989 the fastest notebook computer modem transmitted data at 2,400 bits per second, whereas in fall 1991 that speed had increased to 36,000 bits per second—a 1,500 percent increase in performance. When developing a long-term sales automation plan, do not fall into the trap of limiting yourself to what can be done with today's technology; develop strategies that will take advantage of tomorrow's technology and beyond.

In the near future you can expect to have a set of computing tools that work very closely together. A palmtop computer you carry in your pocket will have wireless data transmission capabilities, with the ability to tie into your notebook and host computers anytime, anywhere. It will have voice recognition for data input and inquiry. When you get back to the home office, you will attach it to your notebook computer for high-speed data transfer of the information you collected on your sales calls. The system will automatically transfer the information to the appropriate people within your organization without your help or interaction. The user interface for all the systems you use will be the same, so you won't have to go through training every time you adopt a new application.

These advances are the result of a strong drive for standardization among users and suppliers of technology. Ten years ago the prevailing standards were driven by the manufacturers who developed them. Today they are driven more and more by the users of technology. Open systems and the integration of systems across disparate technologies are the forces behind computing in the 1990s. From the user perspective, you will not have to be concerned about the complexities of the technology but only about how to utilize it to accomplish your market mission.

Historically, advances in software technology have trailed the meteoric pace of hardware and communications technology. This lag can be attributed to several factors—multiple hardware and operating system platforms diffusing software resources; the performance constraints of the hardware and operating system software; a lack of industrywide software programming and interfacing standards; and the requirement for compatibility with older software technology and systems. It has been only recently that a number of standards have been accepted by the market, industry suppliers, and international standards organizations. These forces have created an environment of relative cooperation that will allow software developers to design and deliver systems more powerful and easier to use than ever before. When combined with the latest hardware and communications technologies, they will permit significant productivity advances.

The notable standards that have emerged over the past few years fall into several categories: those defined by the market, those defined by international standards organizations, and those defined by vendor alliances. Some marketplace standards include Microsoft's MS-DOS and Windows, which has sold over 10 million copies since its introduction; Novell Netware, which has over 70 percent of the microcomputer networking marketplace; and the Unix operating system, which is marketed by every major computer supplier in the world. Whether these products are still dominant in the year 2000 is not the important issue. The fact that the marketplace has defined them as a standard is significant. It will help save you from locking yourself into technological blind alleys.

International standards organizations have developed standards for electronic mail, communications, and electronic data interchange (EDI). These standards allow information to pass between different vendors' products and therefore provide a framework within which software developers can design products that work with other vendors' products. Vendor alliances have developed standards for how systems should interact with one another, how applications should appear on the screen, and how hardware products physically connect with one another.

During the 1980s, significant advances were made in artificial intelligence (AI) software technologies. Neuro-network technology, based on the architecture of the human brain, will help salespeople in the future work with greater "intelligence" and therefore more effectively than ever before. Salespeople working in complex sales environments will use AI software systems to help determine the most qualified prospects, the most effective sales methods to use with those prospects, and the most effective ways to solve customer problems. Product-matching systems will help salespeople deliver the best solutions to their customers' needs.

Pad or tablet computers, initially developed in the late 1980s, will play a significant role in many sales forces in the 1990s. New products from Momenta, GO, Microsoft, GRiD,

NCR, DFM, IBM, NEC, Toshiba, and others were introduced or announced in the early 1990s. These devices fall into two categories: those that recognize handwriting using a stylus (a penlike device) and those that use touch-screen technology. Conceptually, they work the same way. The user fills out a form by tapping the screen with a pen or touching it with a finger to select predetermined answers. Nonstandard responses are entered by using the pen to "write" on the screen or initiating a simulated keyboard and selecting the letters or numbers by "pressing" the keys with the pen or a finger.

Several classes of pad and tablet computers are being developed. These have been defined as follows by Portia Isaacson of Dream Machine, Inc., a consulting organization dedicated to the emerging pen and tablet marketplace: general purpose tablets; convertible pen computers; minitablet pen computers; megatablet pen computers; multimodal megatablets; and special purpose, data entry, and data collection tablets.

General purpose tablets are designed to replace pads of paper. General purpose tablets will primarily be used to replace paper-based forms. General purpose applications such as a telephone directory, calendar, appointment schedule, note pad, and calculator function will be available. These products will be very light, with the ultimate goal of attaining the size and weight of a pad of paper.

Convertible pen computers will offer the same capabilities as general purpose tablets but will be optimized to operate either with a pen or keyboard. Traditional applications would function as they do today. Present designs include special hinges, which allow the screen to be flipped around to the bottom of the system to create a padlike configuration.

Minitablets will be designed to fit in your pocket; they will be the size of a daytimer. This application category is currently addressed by the Hewlett-Packard 95LX and Sharp Wizard handheld personal organizers, which use keyboards for data entry. Over time these products will be as powerful as today's notebook computers.

Megatablets will have large displays or writing surfaces, ranging in size from traditional drawing paper to large wall boards.

Multimodal megatablets will offer the capabilities of pad, notebook, and desktop computers. These systems will have desk stations that the pad plugs into to create a fully functional microcomputer. Their capabilities will rival those of today's standard desktop computers. Multimodal tablets will be available in all classes of pen computers. In the future users will require only one computer to perform the functions they do today as well as all the new applications available in the pen computing environment.

Data entry tablets will be very lightweight; they will be designed to perform specific applications. Handheld computers are currently addressing this application area.

Pen and tablet computers will become a major hardware platform for future SA applications. The convertible and multimodal products will dominate because they offer the greatest flexibility. The number of vendors and products available will increase rapidly over the next several years, and the same price/performance curve that the portable computer market experienced will prevail in the tablet market.

Wireless communication technologies have finally reached an advanced enough technical and infrastructure stage to be viable alternatives to traditional land-line communication technologies. Cellular communication in particular is very attractive because it offers both voice and data capabilities. The first successful uses of cellular data communications took place in the mid-1980s, but its popularity has been limited by the amount, size, cost, and limited capabilities of the equipment and the size of the cellular network. Recent advances in handheld cellular phones and modem technology, coupled with the expanded cellular network, make cellular communications potentially a powerful sales automation tool. Salespeople will be able to send or receive data anytime, anywhere, providing higher levels of service to their clients and customers.

Radio frequency technologies will also offer real-time links to corporate host computer systems. Based on the same technologies as today's paging systems, they go one step further by providing both send and receive capabilities. The first commercially available network, ARDIS, was jointly developed by IBM and Motorola for use by IBM's service organization and became available to the public in 1991. It is a very effective data communications vehicle for applications that require only short-duration data transmission.

The cost of these wireless technologies will continue to decrease rapidly as usage increases. By the mid 1990s wireless communications products and their usage fees will drop by 50 to 75 percent. During this same period the transmission quality of the wireless networks will improve and coverage areas will increase. The enhanced quality and lower costs will make the technologies more viable and useful to many companies.

The technology that will have the most dramatic effect on sales automation in the 1990s is in the software arena. "Object orientation," a software programming technique first developed by researchers at Xerox's Palo Alto Research Center in the 1970s, will have a great impact on the software products and application systems of the future. It is based on the concept of breaking down software programs into reusable components, or objects, that are usable by other programs. Objects are defined similarly for different tasks, such as printing, and used by all the other programs in a system. This is significantly different from earlier software, in which each program had its own printing component. In a sales automation system, objects are defined for sales tools such as account plans, call reports, or order forms. How the different objects interact with one another is defined in each object. In object-oriented systems, software "objects" relate to standard office tools such as folders for saving account information or call reports and file drawers and cabinets for storing lots of folders.

There are several major benefits to object-oriented systems. They are easier for users to understand and use. They are easier to program once an object-oriented foundation has been established. They are easier to maintain and upgrade as needs and requirements change. Because of these benefits, users of object-oriented systems have more powerful application programs and learn these programs faster than they would programs developed under traditional methods. As the business environment changes, these programs are more easily modified and upgraded. In the long run, companies adopting object-oriented sales automation systems enjoy lower costs of ownership and a faster payback on their investment.

Object-oriented systems based on graphical user interfaces (GUIs) will dominate the future of software development. They are being promoted by all major parties in industry, including suppliers, developers, manufacturers, and customers.

Multimedia is another emerging trend in SA. Multimedia is the blending of several technologies, including voice, sound, video, still pictures, monochrome and color graphics, and traditional computer applications. The first notebook computers with multimedia capabilities built-in were the Apple Computer Corporation's Powerbooks. These products include inputs and outputs for voice, video, and graphics. Multimedia applications include interactive sales training, visual product demonstrations, order entry systems with pictures, and video-captured product demonstrations. Voice response capabilities will displace the keyboard, mouse, and stylus as the computer's data input and output mechanism. Multimedia technologies will develop rapidly as the required technologies advance and decrease in cost.

One thing we can be sure about the future—it is going to be exciting. Information technology has finally caught up to the fast-paced world of sales and marketing professionals. Pocket phones and computers and wireless voice and data communication are here to stay. No sales professional will venture out into the territory without them.

Appendix: Sales Automation Resources

Consulting Organizations

Business Counselors, Inc.
115–17 Hilltop Terrace
Kinnelon, NJ 07405
(201) 838-6532

Coopers & Lybrand
Management Consulting Services
80 Park Plaza
Newark, NJ 07102
(201) 621-1297

Cross Communications Company
1881 9th Street
Boulder, CO 80302-5151
(303) 444-7799

Data One
Princeton Corporate Plaza
7 Deerpark Drive, Suite E
Monmouth Junction, NJ 08852
(800) 274-7863

P.O. Box 870
4530 River Road
Moline, IL 61265
(800) 328-2663

Many of the references in this Appendix are provided courtesy of *Portable Technology Update*.

The Perera Group
33 Sleeper Street
Dockside Place at Boston Wharf
Suite 207
Boston, MA 02210-1207
(617) 391-3965

Conferences, Trade Shows, and Seminars

Fall

ABCD Breakaway
Conference and exhibition for vendors and ABCD-member resellers.
ABCD: The Microcomputer Industry Association
1515 E. Woodfield Road
Shaumburg, IL 60173
(800) 333-9532

Blenheim Online
London Docklands Arena, London.
Blenheim House
Ash Hill Drive
Pinner, Middlesex, HA5 2AE, UK
44-1-868-4466

Calgary Business Computer Show
Calgary Round-up Center, Calgary, Alberta.
IND Trade and Consumer Shows, Inc.
20 Butterick Road, Toronto, Ontario M8W 3Z8
(416) 252-7791

Compu
International fair for information and related equipment.
Quito, Ecuador.
Ecuasistem Ecuatoriana De Sistemas Mecanizados
Inglaterra 1373 Y Avenue
Amazonas, Quito, Ecuador
593-2-450-807-244-2277

Computer
International exchange of computers, telecommunication and office automation.
Convention Center, Central Plaza,
Bangkok, Thailand.
Thai Trade Fairs Co. Ltd.
300/31 Rachadapisek Road
Bangkok 10310, Thailand
66-2-277-7041 or 277-9434

Computer and Electronics Show
Hartford Civic Center, Hartford, Connecticut.
Daniels Productions, Inc.
1155 New Britain Avenue
West Hartford, CT 06110
(203) 233-9611

Computer Graphics
Wembley Conference Center, London.
Blenheim Online
Blenheim House
Ash Hill Drive
Pinner, Middlesex HA5 2AE, UK
44-1-868-4466

Computer Thai
International exhibit of computers, office equipment, stationery, furniture
Bangkok, Thailand.
Thailand Exhibit and Management Co. Ltd.
4FL, 87 Nailert Building
Sukhumvit 5
Bangkok 10110, Thailand

Computing
Showgrounds, Wellington, New Zealand.
Wellington Show Association, Inc.
P.O. Box 7105,
Wellington, New Zealand
64-4-896199

COMTEC
Computer systems and technology exhibition.
Hall 3/5, World Trade Center.
Singapore ITP Services (Private) Ltd.
994 Bendemeer Road, #04-03
Singapore 1233
65-291-3238

Edmonton Business Computer Show
Convention Center, Edmonton, Alberta, Canada.
IND Trade and Consumer Shows, Inc.
20 Butterick Road
Toronto, Ontario M8W 3Z8
(416) 252-7791

EXPO AFI
Automation in financial institutions.
Hong Kong, China.
Management Resources International
Hang Seng Bank Building,
200 Hennessy Road, 7th floor
Hong Kong
852-5-891-3168

Halifax Business Computer Show
Halifax Metro Center, Halifax, Nova Scotia, Canada.
IND Trade and Consumer Shows, Inc.
20 Butterick Road,
Toronto, Ontario M8W 378
(416) 252-7791

INFO
Jacob K. Javits Center, New York City.
Cahners Exposition Group
P.O. Box 3833, 999 Summer Street
Stamford, CT 06805
(203) 964-0000

Infotex
National Exhibit Center, Canberra, Australia.
TIG Australia, Inc.
Level 9
8 West Street
North Sydney, NSW 2060, Australia
61-2-959-5555

Interop
4th Interoperability Conference and Exhibition.
San Jose Convention and Cultural Center, San Jose, California.
Advanced Computing Environments
480 San Antonio Road, Suite 100
Mountain View, CA
(415) 941-3399

Laptop
An annual trade show for portable office computer products and services.
The Penta Hotel, Seventh Avenue and 33rd Street, New York City.
Laptop Expositions, a division of Data Systems Computer Centre
35 Fordem Road, Springfield, NJ 07801
(201) 467-2300

MacWorld Expo
Darling Harbour, Sydney, Australia.
TIG Australia, Inc.
Level 9
8 West Street
North Sydney, NSW 2060, Australia
61-2-959-5556

NETWORLD Dallas
119 seminars and 210 exhibits.
The Infomart, Dallas, Texas.
385 Sylvan Avenue
Englewood Cliffs, NJ 07632
(201) 569-6536

NOPA (National Office Products Association)
Exhibition and conference for office products and computer resellers.
McCormick Place, Chicago, Illinois.
National Office Products Association
301 N. Fairfax Street
Alexandria, VA 22314
(800) 542-6672

Northeast Computer Fair
Hynes Convention Center, Boston, Massachusetts.
Interface Group, Inc.
300 First Avenue
Needham, MA 02194
(617) 449-6600

Ottawa Business and Government Computer Show
Civic Center, Ottawa, Ontario.
IND Trade and Consumer Shows, Inc.
20 Butterick Road
Toronto, Ontario M8W 3Z8
(416) 252-7791

Portable Computing
Exhibits and in-depth tutorials.
Marriott Marquis, New York City.
IDG
20 Speen Street, P.O. Box 9171
Framingham, MA 01701
(617) 769-8950

Power Selling
National Conference and Exposition
Leading conference dedicated to sales automation.
633 Third Avenue
New York, NY 10017
(212) 984-2421

Research and Technology Show
Use of computers in society.
Trieste, Italy.
Autonomo Fiera Di Trieste
Piazzale De Gasperi-1,34139
Trieste, Italy
39-40-393961

Rochester Computer and Business Show
Rochester Riverside Convention Center, Rochester, New York.
Southex Exhibits
1450 Don Mills Road
Don Mills, Ontario M3B 2X7
(416) 442-2077

SACIA'S Business Expo
Connecticut's largest and most successful business-to-business trade show.
Southwestern Area Commerce and Industry Association.
One Landmark Square
Stamford, CT 06901
(203) 359-3220

SCIB
Canadian computer/office technology show.
Palais des Congres, Montreal, PQ, Canada.
IND Trade and Consumer Shows, Inc.
20 Butterick Road
Toronto, Ontario M8W 3Z8

Supercomputing World
Civic Center, San Francisco, California.
MG Expo Group
1050 Commonwealth Avenue
Boston, MA 02215
(800) 223-7126

Systems, Computers and Communications Users
Congress and International Trade Fair, Munich, Germany.
Munchener Messe-Und Ausstellungsgesellschaft MBH
P.O. Box 121009
8000 Munich 12, Germany
49-89-51070

Winter

Baltimore Computer Conference and Exposition
For business and government professionals.
Baltimore Convention Center, Baltimore, Maryland.
National Trade Productions, Inc.
313 S. Patrick Street
Alexandria, VA 22314
(703) 836-4436

PC European Forum
Porte DeVersailles, Paris, France.
PC Expo
385 Sylvan Avenue
Englewood Cliffs, NJ 07424
(201) 569-6536

Sales & Marketing Exposition and Conference
Dedicated sales and marketing automation conference.
Flagg Management
P.O. Box 4440
New York, NY 10163
(212) 286-0333

Singapore Informatics
World Trade Center, Halls 3, 4, 5, Singapore.
Singapore Technofairs Corp. PTE Ltd.
11 N. Bridge Road, #16-01
Eninsula Plaza
Singapore 0617
65-337-6265

TBT Conference and Exhibition
The largest telemarketing conference of its kind.
One Technology Plaza
Norwalk, CT 06854
(203) 852-6800

Spring

Hanover Fair-CEBIT
World center for office, international telecommunications technology.
Messegelande Exhibit Hall, Hanover, Germany.
Deutsche Messe-Und Ausstellungs-AG
Messegelande
3000 Hanover 82, Germany
49-0511-891

Infotechasia
Asian Computer Communications and Information Systems
World Trade Center, Singapore.
Singapore Exhibit Services PTE Ltd.
11 Dhoby Ghaut
#15-09 Cathay Building
Singapore 0922
65-229-5651

Telenet
International trade fair for telecommunications and computer networks.
Kortrijk, Belgium.
CV De Hallen-Kortrijk
Doorniksesteenweg 216
8500 Kortrijk, Belgium
32-5621-5551

Spring/Fall

COMDEX
Computer Dealers Exposition—more than 1,500 exhibits and 50 seminars.
Las Vegas Convention Center, Las Vegas, Nevada.
Spring show in Chicago, Illinois.
Interface Group, Inc.
200 First Avenue
Needham, MA 02194
(617) 449-6600

PC Expo
Chicago, Illinois, and New York City.
H.A. Bruno, Inc.
385 Sylvan Avenue, Englewood, Cliffs, NJ 07632
(201) 569-8542

Sales Automation Day
Sales & Marketing Executives of Greater New York
13 E. 37th Street, 8th floor
New York, NY 10016
(212) 683-9755

Industry Groups

Sales & Marketing Executives of Greater New York
13 E. 37th Street, 8th floor
New York, NY 10016
(212) 683-9755

Sales Automation Association
1105 Washington
Dearborn, MI 48124
(313) 278-5655

Portable Computing Product Suppliers and Manufacturers

Access/Supplies/Upgrades

Adtron
745 N. Gilbert Road
#124 BX361
Gilbert, AZ 85234
(602) 961-7511

Advanced Electronic Support Products, Inc.
1801 NE 144th Street
North Miami, FL 33181
(800) 446-2377
(305) 944-7710

Aluminum Case Company
3333 W. 48th Place
Chicago, IL 60632
(312) 247-4611

American Cryptronics Inc.
1580 Corporate Drive, Suite 123
Costa Mesa, CA 92626
(714) 540-1174

Amherst International Corp.
540 N. Commercial Street
Manchester, NH 03101
(800) 547-5600
(603) 644-3555

Cables To Go
28 W. Nottingham
Dayton, OH 45420
(800) 826-7904
(513) 275-0886

CenTech
1375 West Street, 8040 South
West Jordan, UT 84088
(801) 255-3999

Cherry Corporation
3600 Sunset Avenue
Waukegan, IL 60087
(312) 662-9200
(Peripherals also)

Chicago Case Company
4446 S. Ashland Avenue
Chicago, IL 60609
(312) 927-1600

Chips and Technologies Inc.
3050 Zanker Road
San Jose, CA 95134
(408) 434-0600
(OEM sales only)

Cirrus Logic Inc.
1463 Centre Point Drive
Milpitas, CA 95035
(408) 945-8305
(OEM sales only)

CT & M Ltd.
80 Burns Place
Goleta, CA 93117
(805) 683-1148

CWW Inc.
3 University Place, P.O. Box 185
Great Neck, NY 11022
(212) 267-1941

Digital Systems
7959 178th Place NE
Redmond, WA 98052
(206) 881-7544

Diversified Technology
112 E. State Street
Ridgeland, MS 39158
(800) 443-2667
(601) 856-4121

Drive Phone Inc.
37 Springvalley Avenue
Paramus, NJ 07652
(201) 843-6400
(Communications also)

Electronic Specialists
171 S. Main Street
P.O. Box 389
Natick, MA 01760
(800) 225-4876
(508) 655-1532

Gemini Incorporated
103 Mensing Way
Cannon Falls, MN 55009
(507) 263-3957

Innovative Manufacturing Corp.
3704 NW 82nd Street
Miami, FL 33147
(800) 950-2286
(305) 836-1035

Input Systems
15600 Palmetto Lake Drive
Miami, FL 33157
(305) 252-1550

Intel Corporation
2625 Walsh Avenue
Santa Clara, CA 95052
(408) 765-4280

ISIS International
7100 N. Broadway, Suite 6L
Denver, CO 80221
(303) 650-1492

Kalmar Designs
3303 Merrick Road
Wantagh, NY 11793
(516) 221-8400

KAO Info Systems
10300 SW Nimbus Avenue
Portland, OR 97223
(503) 620-1888

Kelly Micro Systems
39 Musick
Irvine, CA 92618
(800) 350-3900
(714) 859-3900

Madison Line
228 Harrison Street
Oakland, CA 94607
(415) 465-3760

Micron Technology
2805 E. Columbia Road
Boise, ID 83706
(800) Micron-1
(208) 386-3900

Midern Computers Inc.
18005 Cortney Court
City of Industry, CA 91748
(818) 964-8682

NS International Inc.
4 Hills Park Lane
Smithtown, NY 11787
(516) 366-0700

Oak Technology Inc.
139 Kifer Court
Sunnyvale, CA 94086
(408) 737-0888
(OEM sales only)

P.A.C.E.
180 S. 600 West
Logan, UT 84321
(800) 359-6670
(801) 753-1067

Printworx
3322 S. Memorial Parkway
Huntsville, AL 35801
(800) 777-9679
(205) 880-3626

Rick's RamStar Inc.
P.O. Box 759
Sardis, GA 30456
(800) 327-2303
(305) 233-1991

Sopris Softworks
P.O. Box 916
Glenwood Springs, CO 81602
(800) 334-6046
(303) 945-0366

Source One Systems
9234 FM 1960 West
Houston, TX 77070
(713) 469-7000

Sportcase Inc.
610 13th Avenue South
Hopkins, MN
(612) 933-4545

SRW Computer Company
18385 Bandilier Circle
Fountain Valley, CA 92708
(714) 963-5500

Statpower Technologies Corp.
7012 Lockheed Highway
Burnaby, British Columbia V5A 1W2
(604) 420-1585

Stone Bridge Luggage Inc.
232 Washington Place
Wayne, PA 19807
(215) 647-8534

Strong Group
105 Maplewood Avenue
Gloucester, MA 01930
(800) 852-8437
(508) 281-3300

Targus
6190 Valley View
Buena Park, CA 90620
(714) 523-5429

TVMP Inc.
P.O. Box 771869
Houston, TX 77215
(800) 762-3361
(713) 266-9779

Unlimited Systems
9225 Chesapeake Drive, Suite 6
San Diego, CA 92123
(619) 277-3300

West Coast Telcom
P.O. Box 230456
Portland, OR 97223
(503) 620-1888

Yamaha Systems Technology
3051 N. First Street
San Jose, CA 95134
(408) 433-5260
(OEM sales only)

Zirco
10900 W. 44th Avenue
Wheat Ridge, CO 80033
(303) 421-2013

Communications

Bluelynx
63 Maple Street, P.O. Box 335
Friendsville, MD 21531
(301) 746-5888

Coker Electronics
1430 Lexington Avenue
San Mateo, CA 94402
(415) 573-5515

Digital Products Inc.
108 Water Street
Watertown, MA 02172
(800) 243-2333
(617) 924-1680
(Peripherals also)

D-Link Systems Inc.
3303 Harbor Boulevard, E8
Costa Mesa, CA 92626
(714) 549-7942

GVC/Chenel Corp.
99 Demarest Road
Sparta, NJ 07871
(800) 243-6312
(201) 666-1443

Hayes Microcomputer Products
705 Westeck Drive
Norcross, GA 30092
(404) 449-8791

Holmes Microsystems
2620 S. 900 West
Salt Lake City, UT 84119
(800) 443-3034
(801) 975-9929

Information Machines
20219 Chapter Drive
Woodland Hills, CA 91364
(818) 884-5779

Lightspeed Technology
14250 NW Science Park Drive
Portland, OR 97229
(503) 626-2291

Medbar Enterprises Inc.
71–08 51st Avenue
Woodside, NY 11377
(718) 355-0404

Megahertz Corporation
4505 South Wasatch Boulevard
Salt Lake City, UT 84124
(800) LAPTOPS
(801) 272-6000

Microcom
500 River Ridge Drive
Norwood, MA 02062
(617) 551-1957

Migent Inc.
865 Tahoe Boulevard
Incline Village, NV 89450
(702) 832-3700

O'Neill Communications
100 Thanet Circle
Princeton, NJ 08540
(201) 696-4744

Product R&D Corporation
1194 Pacific Street, Suite 201
San Luis Obispo, CA 93401
(800) 234-5584
(805) 546-9713
(Access/supplies/upgrades also)

Prometheus Products Inc.
7225 South West Bonita Road
Tigard, OR 97223
(503) 624-0571

Pure Data
1740 South 1-35, Suite 240
Carrolton, TX 75006
(214) 242-2040

Quadram/Asher
One Quad Way
Norcross, GA 30093
(404) 923-6666

Quay Computer Corporation
216 Matheson Boulevard East
Mississauga, Ontario L4Z 1X1
(416) 890-1956

Rose Electronics
P.O. Box 742571
Houston, TX 77274-2571
(713) 933-7673
(Peripherals also)

Simple Net Systems Inc.
545 W. Lambert Road, Suite A
Brea, CA 92626
(714) 529-8850

Softklone
336 Office Plaza Drive
Tallahassee, FL 32301
(904) 878-8564

Software Link
3577 Parkway Lane
Norcross, GA 30092
(404) 448-5465

Spectrum Cellular
800 North Tower, 2700 Stemmons
Dallas, TX 75207
(214) 630-9825

Sunhill Inc.
1000 Andover Park East
Seattle, WA 98188
(800) 544-1361
(206) 575-4131
(Adaptors/batteries also)

3X USA
One Executive Drive
Fort Lee, NJ 07024
(800) 327-9712
(201) 592-6874

Touchbase Systems Inc.
160 Laurel Avenue
Northport, NY 11768
(516) 261-0423

U.S. Robotics
8100 N. McCormick Boulevard
Skokie, IL 60076
(312) 982-5150

Western Digital
2445 McCabe Way
Irvine, CA 92714
(800) 847-6181
(714) 863-0121

Xecom
374 Turquois Drive
Milpitas, CA 95035
(408) 945-6640

Xircom
22231 Mulhulland Highway, #114
Woodland Hills, CA 91364
(818) 884-8755

Computers

Agilis Corp.
1101 San Antonio Road
Mountain View, CA 94043
(415) 962-9400

Altima Systems Inc.
1390 Willow Pass Road, Suite 1050
Concord, CA 94520
(800) 356-9990
(415) 356-5600

Amstrad Inc.
1915 Westbridge Drive
Irvine, TX 75038
(214) 518-0668

Apple Computer Corporation
20525 Mariani Avenue
Cupertino, CA 95014
(800) 538-9696
(408) 996-1010

Atari Corporation
1196 Borregas Avenue
Sunnyvale, CA 94088
(408) 745-2000

Bi-Link Computer Inc.
11606 E. Washington Boulevard
Whittier Park, CA 90606
(213) 692-5345

Bi-Tech Enterprises Inc.
10 Carlough Road
Bohemia, NY 11716
(516) 567-8155

Bondwell Industrial Company
47485 Seabridge Drive
Fremont, CA 94538
(415) 490-4300

Broadax Systems Inc.
4440 Telstar Avenue, Suite 4
El Monte, CA 91731
(800) 872-4547
(818) 442-0020

Bull AG
200 Smith Street
Waltham, MA 02154
(617) 895-6929

Cambridge North America
424 Cumberland Avenue
Portland, ME 04101
(207) 761-3700

Casio Inc.
570 Mount Pleasant Avenue
Dover, NJ 07801
(201) 361-5400

Chaplet Systems USA Inc.
252 North Wolfe Road
Sunnyvale, CA 94086
(408) 732-7950

Chicony/Digicom Technology
307 W. Central Street
Natick, MA 01760
(800) 344-4211
(508) 820-1102

Club American Technologies
3401 W. Warren Avenue
Fremont, CA 94539
(415) 490-2201

Colby Systems
2991 Alexis Drive
Palo Alto, CA 94304
(415) 941-9090

Commax Technologies Inc.
721 Charcot Avenue
San Jose, CA 95131
(408) 435-5000

Compaq Computer Corporation
2055 FM 149
Houston, TX 77070
(713) 370-0670

CTXT Systems Inc.
9205 Alabama Avenue
Chatsworth, CA 91311
(818) 341-4227

Custom Design Technology Inc.
780 Montague Expressway
San Jose, CA 95131
(408) 432-8698

Data Entry Systems
701 Pratt Avenue, Suite 101
Huntsville, AL 35801
(205) 539-2483
(Pen computers)

Data General Corporation
4400 Computer Drive
Westboro, MA 01580
(800) DATA-GEN
(508) 366-8911

Datavue Corporation
One Meca Way
Norcross, GA 30093
(404) 564-5555

Dauphin Technology
1125 E. Saint Charles Road
Lombard, IL 60148
(800) 782-7922
(312) 627-4004

Dell Computer Corporation
9505 Arboretum
Austin, TX 78759
(800) 426-5150
(512) 343-3450

Delta Computer Corporation
300 N. Continental Boulevard, #200
El Segundo, CA 90245
(213) 322-4222

DFM Research and Development
1776 22nd Street
West Des Moines, IA 50265
(515) 225-6744

DFM Systems, Inc.
1101 King Street, Suite 601
Alexandria, VA 22314
(215) 259-0486
(Pen computers)

Dolch
2029 O'Toole Avenue
San Jose, CA 95131
(800) 538-7506
(408) 435-1881

Doradus Corporation
6095 East River
Minneapolis, MN 55432
(800) 538-3008
(612) 572-1000
(Communications also)

Dynabook Technologies
1751 Fox Drive
San Jose, CA 95131
(415) 847-0660

Dynamac Computer Products
555 17th Street, Suite 1850
Denver, CO 80202
(303) 296-0606

Dynatron Associates Inc.
5880 W. Las Positas Boulevard, #49
Pleasanton, CA 94566
(415) 734-0560

Epson America Inc.
2780 Lomita Boulevard
Torrance, CA 90505
(800) 922-8911
(213) 539-9140

Fortek Inc.
240 James Street
Bensenville, IL 60106
(312) 595-2540

Fortis Information Systems
6070 Rickenbacker Road
Commerce, CA 90040
(213) 727-1227

GRiD Systems Corp.
47211 Lakeview Boulevard, P.O. Box 5003
Fremont, CA 94537
(800) 222-GRiD
(415) 656-4700
(Pen computers also)

Hewlett-Packard
19310 Pruneridge Avenue
Cupertino, CA 95014
(800) 752-0900

Hitachi Office Automation Systems
6 Pearl Court
Allendale, NJ 07401
(201) 825-8000

Husky Computers Inc.
1133 4th Street
Sarasota, FL 34236
(813) 365-5180

Hyundai Electronics America
166 Baypointe Parkway
San Jose, CA 95134
(408) 473-9200

IBM
155 Chestnut Ridge Road
Montvale, NJ 07645
(201) 622-4471

Inforite Corporation
1670 S. Amphlett Boulevard, #201
San Mateo, CA 94402
(415) 571-8766
(Pen computers also)

Intelligence Technology Corp.
16526 Westgrove
Dallas, TX 75248
(214) 250-4277

International Systems Marketing
943-A Russell Avenue
Gaithersburg, MD 20879
(301) 670-1813

Itron Inc.
4505 S. Wasatch Boulevard
Salt Lake City, UT 84124
(801) 272-6000

Kaypro
533 Stevens Avenue
Solana Beach, CA 92075
(619) 259-4789

Laser Computer
550 E. Main Street
Lake Zurich, IL 60047
(312) 540-8086

Leading Edge Hardware Products
225 Turnpike Street
Canton, MA 02021
(800) 872-5323
(617) 828-8150

Linus Technologies
11130 Sunrise Valley Drive
Reston, VA 22091
(703) 476-1500

LXE-Electromagnetic Science Inc.
303 Research Drive, Suite 225
Norcross, GA 30092
(404) 447-4224

Matrix Digital Products
1181 N. Keystone
Burbank, CA 91504
(800) 227-5723

Maxtron
1825-A Durfee Avenue
South El Monte, CA 91733
(818) 350-5705

Melard Technologies Inc.
5 Odell Plaza
Yonkers, NY 10701
(914) 376-0100

Micro Direct
2010 Revere Beach Park
Everett, MA 02149
(800) 872-4286
(617) 387-2200

Micro Express
2114 S. Grand Avenue
Santa Ana, CA 92705
(714) 662-1973

Micro Palm Computers
13773-500 Icot Boulevard
Clearwater, FL 34620
(813) 553-0128

Micro Slate
9625 Ignace Street, Suite D
Brossard, Quebec J4Y 2P3
(514) 444-3680
(Pen computers also)

Mission Cyrus Corporation
18303 Eighth Avenue South
Seattle, WA 98148
(604) 432-7727

Mitsuba Corporation
650 W. Terrace Drive
San Dimas, CA 91773
(800) 648-7822
(714) 592-2866

Mitsubishi Electronics
991 Knox Street
Torrance, CA 90502
(800) 556-1234
(213) 217-5732
(Peripherals also)

Momenta Corporation
295 N. Bernardo Avenue
Mountain View, CA 94043
(415) 969-3876
(Pen computers also)

National Micro Systems Inc.
2833 Peterson Place
Norcross, GA 30071
(404) 446-0520

NCR Corporation
1700 South Patterson Boulevard
Dayton, OH 45479
(513) 445-5000
(Pen computers also)

NEC Home Electronics
1255 Michael Drive
Wood Dale, IL 60191
(312) 860-9500
(Peripherals also)

NEC Information Systems Inc.
1414 Massachusetts Avenue
Boxborough, MA 01719
(508) 264-8000
(Peripherals and pen computers also)

Ogivar Technologies
7200 Trans Canada Highway
Quebec H4T 1A3
(800) 361-3694
(514) 737-3340

Packard Bell
9425 Canoga Avenue
Chatsworth, CA 91311
(818) 773-4400

Paravant Computer Systems
305 E. Drive West
Melbourne, FL 32904
(407) 727-3672

PI Systems Corporation
10220 SW Greenburg Road, Suite 310
Portland, OR 97223
(503) 293-9585
(Pen computers)

Poqet Computer Corporation
5200 Patrick Henry Drive
Santa Clara, CA 95054
(408) 982-9500
(Pen computers also)

Radix Corporation
4855 Wiley Post Way
Salt Lake City, UT 84116
(800) 367-9256
(801) 537-1717
(Peripherals also)

Samsung Information Systems
3655 N. First Street
San Jose, CA 95134
(800) 624-8999
(408) 434-5482
(Pen computers also)

Sanyo Business Systems Corp.
51 Joseph Street
Moonache, NJ 07074
(800) 524-0046
(201) 440-9300

Scenario Incorporated
260 Franklin Street, 5th floor
Boston, MA 02110
(617) 625-1818

Semi-Tech Microelectronics
131 McNabb
Markham, Canada L3R 5V7
(416) 475-2670

Sharp Electronics
Sharp Plaza
Mahwah, NJ 07430-2135
(201) 529-8965

Spread Information Sciences
85-36 Grand Avenue
Elmhurst, NY 11373
(718) 397-1300
(OEM sales only)

Tandy Corporation
1700 One Tandy Way
Fort Worth, TX 76102
(817) 878-4969

Tatung Company of America
2850 El Presidio Street
Long Beach, CA 90810
(800) 827-2850
(213) 637-2105

TekPort Computer Center
1156 E. Ridgewood Avenue
Ridgewood, NJ 07450
(201) 670-0777
(Peripherals also)

Telxon Corporation
3330 W. Market Street
Akron, OH 44313
(800) 537-5488
(216) 867-3700
(Peripherals also)

Texas Instruments
P.O. Box 202230
Austin, TX 78720
(800) 423-4589
(512) 250-6679

Toshiba America
9740 Irvine Boulevard
Irvine, CA 92718
(800) 423-4589
(714) 583-3000

Trans PC Systems
11849 East Firestone Boulevard
Norwalk, CA 90650
(213) 868-6930

TUSK Inc.
1310 Gateway Road
Lake Park, FL 33403
(407) 881-9050
(Pen computers)

UCM Inc.
13918 Equitable Road
Cerritos, CA 90701
(213) 404-5611

U.S. Micro Engineering
2810 Wilderness Place
Boulder, CO 80301

Veridata
11901 Goldring Road, #A & B
Arcadia, CA 91006
(818) 303-0613

Wallaby Systems Inc.
2540 Frontier Avenue, #109
Boulder, CO 80301
(303) 444-4606

Xec Products
13575 58th Street North, Suite 123
Clearwater, FL 34620
(813) 538-4190

Yamaha Corp. of America
6600 Orangethorpe Avenue
Buena Park, CA 90620
(714) 522-9963

Zenith Data Systems
1000 Milwaukee Avenue
Glenview, IL 60025
(312) 699-4839

Peripherals

Alps Electric Company Inc.—OEM
3553 N. First Street
San Jose, CA 95134
(408) 432-6000
(OEM sales only)

Apollo Audio Visual
60 Trade Zone Drive
Ronkonkoma, NY 11779
(800) 777-3750
(516) 467-8033

Areal Technology
580 College Avenue
Palo Alto, CA 94306
(408) 954-0360

Aristotle Industries Inc.
3226 Beta Avenue
Burnaby, British Columbia V5G 4K4
(800) 663-2237
(604) 294-1113

Avatar Corp.
65 South Street
Hopkinton, MA 01748
(800) 289-2526
(508) 435-3000
(Access/supplies/upgrades also)

Axonix Corp.
2257 S. 1100 East, Suite 2C
Salt Lake City, UT 84106
(800) 832-3200
(801) 466-9797
(Access/supplies/upgrades also)

Bay Technical Associates Inc.
200 N. Second Street
Bay St. Louis, MO 39520
(800) 523-2702
(601) 467-8231

Buhl Industries Inc.
14-01 Maple Avenue
Fairlawn, NJ 07410
(201) 423-2800

California Access
780 Montague Expressway, #403
San Jose, CA 95131
(408) 435-1445

Chinon America Inc.
660 Maple Avenue
Torrance, CA 90503
(213) 533-0274

Chisholm
910 Campisi Way
Campbell, CA 95008
(800) 888-4210
(408) 559-1111

Comnet
110 U.S. South
North Brunswick, NJ 08902
(201) 821-6767

Compuquest Inc.
801 Morse Avenue
Schaumburg, IL 60193
(312) 529-2552

Computer Accessories Corp.
6610 Nancy Ridge Drive
San Diego, CA 92121
(800) 582-2580
(619) 457-5500

Connect Computer
9855 W. 78th Street, Suite 270
Eden Prairie, MN 55344
(612) 944-0181

Conner Peripherals
3018 Zanker Road
San Jose, CA 95134-2128
(408) 433-3340
(OEM sales only)

Dukane Corporation
2900 Dukane Drive
St. Charles, IL 60174
(800) 634-2800
(312) 584-2300

Eastman Kodak Company
343 State Street
Rochester, NY 14650
(716) 724-3169
(716) 724-3000

ECA C & C Products
38 Route 46 East
Lodi, NJ 07644
(800) 442-6872
(201) 478-0302

Eiki International
27882 Camino Capistrano
Lagunia Niguel, CA 92677
(714) 592-2511

Elmo Manufacturing
70 New Hyde Park Road
New Hyde Park, NY 11040
(516) 775-3200

Equinox Systems Inc.
14260 SW 119th Avenue
Miami, FL 33186
(800) DATA-PBX
(305) 255-3500

GCC Technologies
580 Winter Street
Waltham, MA 02154
(617) 890-0880

Giltronix, Inc.
1430 O'Brien Drive, Building D
Menlo Park, CA 94025
(800) 521-1330

In Focus Systems Inc.
7649 SW Mohawk Street
Tualatin, OR 97206
(800) 327-7231
(503) 692-4968

Informer Computer Terminals
12781 Pala Drive
Garden Grove, CA 92641
(714) 891-1112

Intec Research Company
550 Cypress Avenue
Sunnyvale, CA 94086
(408) 732-3076

Interpreter Inc.
11455 W. 48th Avenue
Wheat Ridge, CO 80033
(303) 431-8991

Irvin Magnetic Systems
2101 Commonwealth Boulevard
Ann Arbor, MI 48705
(800) 431-1879
(313) 324-3333

Key Tronic Corporation
B 4424 Sullivan Road
Spokane, WA 99216
(509) 928-8000

Kres Engineering
P.O. Box 1268
La Canada, CA 91011
(818) 957-1268

Logitech Inc.
6505 Kaiser Drive
Fremont, CA 94555
(800) 231-7717
(415) 795-8500

Manzana Microsystems Inc.
7334 Hollister Avenue, Suite B
Goleta, CA 93117
(805) 968-1387

Megapower Electronics
12 Winthrop Place
Staten Island, NY 10314
(718) 273-9560

Micronet Computer Systems
13525½ Alondara Boulevard
Santa Fe Springs, CA 90670
(213) 921-0068

MicroTouch Systems Inc.
10 State Street
Woburn, MA 01801
(617) 935-0080

Mountain Computer Inc.
240 Hacienda Avenue
Campbell, CA 95008
(800) 458-0300
(408) 379-4300

nView Corporation
11835 Canon Boulevard, Suite C101
Newport News, VA 23606
(804) 873-1354

Pace Mark Technologies Inc.
3932 N. Kilpatrick Avenue
Chicago, IL 60641
(312) 202-9700

Panasonic
One Panasonic Way
Secaucus, NJ 07094
(201) 348-7183

Phoenix Technologies
846 University Avenue
Norwood, MA 02062
(617) 551-4000
(OEM sales only)

Practical Peripherals
31245 La Baya Drive
Westlake Village, CA 91362
(800) 442-4774
(818) 706-0333
(Peripherals also)

PraireTek Corporation
1830 Lefthand Circle
Longmont, CO 80501
(800) 825-2511
(303) 772-4011
(OEM sales only)

Procom Technology Inc.
200 McCormick
Costa Mesa, CA 92626
(714) 549-9449

Protec Microsystems Inc.
33274 Saint Martin Boulevard West, #101
Lavalc, Quebec H7T 1A1
(514) 682-6461

Quasitronics Inc.
211 Vandale Drive
Houston, PA 15342
(800) 245-4192
(412) 745-2663

Random Corporation
581 Northland Boulevard
Cincinnati, OH 45420
(513) 825-0880

RCI Manufacturing
2418 Warrington Drive
Grand Prairie, TX 75052
(214) 641-8795

Reflection Technology
240 Bear Hill Road
Waltham, MA 02154
(617) 890-5905
(OEM sales only)

Reliable Communications Inc.
20111 Stevens Creek Boulevard
Cupertino, CA 95014
(800) 222-0042
(408) 996-0230

Ricoh Corporation
155 Passaic Avenue
Fairfield, NJ 07006
(800) 225-1899
(201) 882-2000

Systems Peripherals
9747 Business Park Avenue
San Diego, CA 92313
(800) 345-0824
(619) 693-8611

Tallgrass Technologies
11100 W. 82nd Street
Overland Park, KS 66214
(800) 825-4727
(913) 492-6002

Telex Communication Inc.
9600 Aldrich Avenue South
Minneapolis, MN 55420
(612) 887-8531

Tesco International Inc.
2907 State Road & 590, #10
Clearwater, FL 34619
(813) 796-0300

Touchstone Technology Inc.
955 Buffalo Road
Rochester, NY 14625
(800) 828-6968
(716) 235-8358

Valitek
100 University Drive
Amherst, MA 01002
(413) 586-7408

Videx Inc.
1105 Northeast Circle Boulevard
Corvallis, OR 97330
(503) 758-0521

Visualon
3044 Payne Avenue
Cleveland, OH 44114
(216) 566-0506

Weltec Digital Inc.
17981 Sky Park Circle
Irvine, CA 92174
(800) 333-5155
(714) 250-1959

Western Telematic
5 Sterling
Irving, CA 92718
(714) 586-9950
(Access/supplies/upgrades also)

Services

Compuserve
5000 Arlington Century Boulevard
Columbus, OH 43220
(800) 848-8199
(614) 457-8600

MCI International
2 International Drive
Rye Brook, NY 10573
(800) 444-6245

Western Union Corporation
1 Lake Street
Upper Saddle River, NJ 07458
(800) 527-5184
(201) 818-5000

Software

Above Software
3 Hutton Centre, Suite 950
Santa Ana, CA 92707
(714) 545-1181

Amica
1800 Busse Highway
Des Plaines, IL 60016-6727
(800) 888-8455
(312) 635-5700

Applied Creative Technology
8333 Douglas Avenue
Dallas, TX 75225
(800) 433-5373
(214) 739-4200
(Peripherals also)

Borland
1800 Green Hills Road
Scotts Valley, CA 95066
(408) 438-1869

Business Works
5505 Morehouse Drive, #150
San Diego, CA 92121
(619) 455-6094

CMS Enhancements
1372 Valencia Avenue
Tustin, CA 92680
(714) 259-9555

Contact Software International
9208 W. Royal Lane
Irvine, TX 75063
(800) 627-3958
(214) 929-4749

Crosstalk Communications
1000 Holcomb Woods Parkway
Roswell, GA 30076
(404) 998-3998

Dayflo Software
8013 Sky Park Circle East
Irvine, CA 92714
(800) 367-5369
(714) 474-1364

Delta Technology
1621 Westgate Road
Eau Claire, WI 54703
(800) 242-6368
(715) 832-7575

Enable Software Inc.
Executive Park
Ballston Lake, NY 12019
(518) 887-8600

Fair Tide Technologies Inc.
18 Ray Avenue
Burlington, MA 01803
(617) 229-6409

First Phase Inc.
PO Box 4504
Greensboro, NC 27404
(919) 855-8858

Form Maker Software
57 S. Shillinger Road
Mobile, AL 33608
(800) 888-8423
(205) 633-3676

GetC Software Inc.
Box 8110-182, 263 H. Street
Blaine, WA 98230-8110
(800) 663-8066

Gibson Research Corporation
22991 La Cadena
Laguna Hills, CA 92653
(714) 830-2200

Key Systems Inc.
512 Executive Parkway
Louisville, KY 40207
(502) 897-3332

Laptop Connections Inc.
100 Granger Boulevard, Suite 106
Marlboro, MA 01752
(508) 480-8377
(508) 485-9521

Lifetree Software Inc.
33 New Montgomery, Suite 1260
San Francisco, CA 94105
(800) 543-3873
(415) 541-7850

Marcar Personal Computing
1107 Hazeltine Boulevard
Chaska, MN 55318
(800) 635-8020
(612) 448-8895

Microcom Software Division
55 Federal Road
Danbury, CT 06810
(800) 847-3529
(203) 798-3800

Microlytics Inc.
1 Tobey Village Office Park
Pittsford, NY 14534
(800) 828-6293
(716) 248-9150

Modatech Systems Inc.
910-1090 W. Georgia Street
Vancouver, British Columbia V6E 3V7
(604) 662-7272

Mosaic
192 Massachusetts Avenue
Cambridge, MA 02140
(617) 862-7148

NetLine
2155 N. 200 West, Suite 90
Provo, UT 84604
(801) 373-6000
(Peripherals also)

Office Solutions
2802 Coho Street
Madison, WI 53713
(415) 335-2035

PC-SIG
1030 D. East Duane Avenue
Sunnyvale, CA 94086
(800) 245-6717
(800) 222-2996

Portfolio Systems Inc.
156 Flushing Avenue
Brooklyn, NY 11205
(800) SAY-DYNO
(718) 935-9501

Prime Solutions
1940 Garnet Avenue
San Diego, CA 92109

Richmond Software Inc.
6400 Roberts Street, Suite 420
Burnaby, British Columbia V5G 4C9
(604) 299-2121

Rite Software
4144 N. Central Expressway, #530
Dallas, TX 75204
(214) 823-2978

Rupp Corporation
P.O. Box Drawer J
New York, NY 10021
(212) 517-7775

SaleMaker Software
P.O. Box 531650
Grand Prairie, TX 75053
(800) 433-5355
(214) 264-2626

Scherrer Resources Inc. (SRI)
8100 Cherokee Street
Philadelphia, PA 19118
(800) 950-0190
(215) 242-8751

Skl Soft Publishing Corp.
1644 Massachusetts Avenue
Lexington, MA 02173
(617) 863-1876

Software Publishing Corp.
1901 Landings Drive, P.O. Box 7210
Mountain View, CA 94039
(415) 335-2080

TEC Technological Evolution
603 Begonia
Corona del Mar, CA 82625
(714) 723-4426

Teknosys
3923 Coconut Palm Drive, #111
Tampa, FL 33619
(813) 620-3494

Traveling Software
18702 North Creek Parkway
Bothell, WA 98011
(800) 343-8080
(206) 483-8080
(Peripherals also)

White Crane Systems
6400 Atlantic Boulevard
Norcross, GA 30071
(800) 344-6783
(404) 446-0660

Word Perfect Corporation
1555 N. Technology Way
Orem, VT 84057
(801) 225-5000

Publications

Inbound/Outbound Magazine
The Telecom Library, Inc.
12 W. 21st Street
New York, NY 10010
(800) 999-0345

Mobile Office Magazine
A Subsidiary of CurtCo, Inc.
21800 Oxnard Street, Suite 250
Woodland Hills, CA 91367
(818) 593-6100

The 1990/91 Guide to Sales & Marketing Automation
Information Systems Marketing
2950 Van Ness Street NW, Suite 110
Washington, DC 20008
(202) 363-8996

PC Laptop Computers Magazine
L.F.P., Inc.
9171 Wilshire Boulevard, Suite 300
Beverly Hills, CA 90210
(310) 858-7155

Portable Office
Business Computer Publishing, Inc.
An IDG Company
80 Elm Street
Peterborough, NH 03458
(603) 924-0100

Sales & Marketing Management Magazine
Annual Sales Automation Software Directory
Bill Communications, Inc.
633 Third Avenue
New York, NY 10017
(212) 986-4800

Telemarketing
A Technology Marketing Publication
One Technology Plaza
Norwalk, CT 06854
(203) 852-6800

TeleProfessional Magazine
209 W. 5th Street, Suite N
Waterloo, Iowa 50701-5420
(319) 235-4473

Glossary

application. A specific program or task, such as sorting employee records, to which a computer solution can be applied.

application program. A computer program designed to meet specific user needs, such as a program that controls inventory or monitors a manufacturing process.

autodial. A capability of application programs to automatically dial a phone number in order to initiate data communications over telephone lines.

bit. Short for binary digit. It can have only two possible values, 0 or 1. It is the smallest unit of data recognized by the computer. All data (letters, numerals, symbols) handled by a computer are digitized—that is, expressed entirely as a combination of bits.

BPS. **B**its **P**er **S**econd. Used to describe the data transmission speed of a modem.

byte. The number of bits used to represent a character.

central processing unit. *See* **CPU.**

communication protocols. The sequencing rules for requests and responses by which network-addressable units in a communication network coordinate and control data transfer and other operations.

communications. The transmission and reception of data.

communication servers. Systems that provide an interface between remote computers and LANs, minicomputers, and mainframes.

configuration. The assortment of equipment (disks, diskettes, terminals, printers, and so on) in a particular system.

CPU. Central Processing Unit. The electronic components in a computer that control the transfer of data and perform arithmetic and logic calculations.

data. Facts, numbers, letters, and symbols stored in a computer. The basic elements of information used, created, or otherwise processed by an application program. Some examples of data are employee names, weekly deductions from salary, projected sales, or fuel consumption.

database. A large collection of organized data that are required to perform a task. Typical examples are personnel files or stock quotations.

desktop computers. A personal computer designed to fit on a desk. Consists of a CPU, monitor, and keyboard.

distributed data processing. A computing approach in which an organization uses computers in more than one location, rather than one large computer in a single location.

dot matrix printer. A printer that forms characters from a two-dimensional array of dots. More dots in a given space produce characters that are more legible.

download. To electronically transfer data from a central computer system to a remote computer system.

electronic data interchange (EDI). The electronic exchange of data between computers. Many industries have defined data format standards for EDI.

electronic file cabinet. A storage unit that stores data much as a regular file cabinet does, with some distinct advantages: A great deal of information can be stored in a small area, accessed and changed quickly, organized more efficiently, and stored more securely.

electronic mail. A feature that allows short memos or messages to be sent to another computer.

Email. *See* **electronic mail.**

file servers. Systems that provide an interface between compatible peripheral devices on a LAN.

floppy disk. A flexible, flat, circular plate permanently housed in a black paper envelope with magnetic coating; it stores data and software. Standard sizes are 5¼ inches and eight inches in diameter.

gateway server. A system that connects the nodes and networks of different architectures by performing protocol translations. Gateways are used for connections between dissimilar LANs, devices on the same LAN that understand different higher-level protocols, and LANs and long-haul networks of different architectures.

handheld computer. A personal computer designed to be operated while being held in the hand. Handheld computers are usually used for very specific applications. They typically weigh between one and three pounds.

keyboard. The set of keys on a terminal that allows alphanumeric characters or symbols to be transmitted when keys are depressed. It inputs text and instructions to the computer.

LAN. *See* local area network.

laptop computer. A class of portable computer usually weighing between eight and fifteen pounds.

large-scale integration (LSI). Refers to high numbers of electronic components that are built on a chip; ranges from about 3,000 to 100,000 transistors on a chip.

letter quality printer. The printer used to produce final copies of documents. It produces type comparable in quality to that of a typewriter.

local area network. A LAN is most often described as a privately owned network that offers reliable high-speed communications channels optimized for connecting information processing equipment in a limited geographic area—namely, an office, a building, a complex of buildings, or a campus.

mainframe system. A computer that is physically large and provides the capability to perform applications requiring large amounts of data (for example, a mainframe could handle a large-scale payroll system). Such computers are much more expensive than microcomputers or minicomputers.

memory. (1) The main high-speed storage area in a computer where instructions for a program being run are temporarily kept. (2) A device in which data can be stored and from which it can later be retrieved. The computer keeps the data and programs it is working on in memory.

menu. A displayed list of options from which the user selects an action to be performed by typing a letter or by positioning the cursor.

menu-driven. A computer system that primarily uses menus for its user interface rather than a command language.

microcomputer. A computer that is physically very small—it can fit on or under a desk—and which is based on large-scale integration (LSI) circuitry. It is usually the least expensive of the computer types.

microprocessor. A single-chip central processing unit incorporating LSI technology.

minicomputer. A type of computer whose physical size is usually smaller than a mainframe. In general, its performance exceeds that of a microcomputer. Since minicomputers are more modular than mainframes, they can be configured to provide better price/performance systems.

modems. Devices needed to convert digital data signals to analog signals, then modulate them for transmission. Modems are necessary to communicate between remote computers.

multitasking. The execution of several tasks "at the same time" without having to complete one before starting another. Although computers can perform only one task at a time, the speed at which a computer operates is so fast that it appears as though several tasks are being performed simultaneously.

network. A group of computers that are connected to each other by communications lines to share information and resources.

notebook computer. A class of portable computer usually weighing between five and seven pounds, with dimensions similar to a standard notebook.

on-line. Pertaining to a system where data, directly under the control of the computer, is introduced into the CPU immediately.

operating system (OS) software. A collection of computer programs that controls the overall operation of a computer and performs such tasks as assigning places in memory to programs and data, processing interrupts, scheduling jobs, and controlling the overall input/output of the system.

pad computer. A personal computer designed to simulate a notepad. The user enters and edits data using an electronic stylus or pen device. Pad computers usually weigh between two and five pounds.

PC. *See* **personal computer.**

pen computer. *See* **pad computer.**

peripheral. A device that is external to the CPU and main memory (for example, a printer, modem, or terminal) but is connected to it by appropriate electrical connections.

personal computer (PC). A category of computer designed to be used by a single person. Classes of PCs include desktop, portable, laptop, notebook, sub-notebook, pad, and handheld.

processor. The functional part of the computer system that reads, interprets, and executes instructions.

program. Complete sequences of instructions and routines needed to solve a problem or to execute directions in a computer.

record. A collection of related data items.

remote. Not hard-wired; communicating via switches and lines, such as telephone lines. Usually refers to peripheral devices (for example, a printer or video terminals) that are located at a site away from the CPU.

software. The tasks or programs that make the computer perform a particular function.

source code. The program instructions written in computer language that make up an application.

system. A combination of software and hardware that performs specific processing operations.

timesharing. Providing service to many users by working on each one's task part of the time.

WAN. *See* **wide area network.**

wide area network (WAN). A widely disbursed computer network typically connected by land- or satellite-based communication networks.

Index